At the TABLE *of* GOD'S WORD:

The collected homilies of Deacon Joe Kupin

Delivered at Saint Paul Church, 2006-2014

Published by:
Clear Faith Publishing
22 Lafayette Rd
Princeton, NJ 08540
www.clearfaithpublishing.com

ISBN 978-1-940414-24-9

First Printing April, 2014

Cover & Interior Design by Doug Cordes
www.behance.net/DougCordes

Cover Art: Painting of 1st century deacon and martyr, St. Stephen. By: Bro. Mickey McGrath. For more on Bro. Mickey go to: www.bromickeymcgrath.com

DEDICATION

Our faith teaches us that Jesus is present in four different ways in the celebration of the Mass. First and foremost he is present in the Eucharist which we share. The consecrated bread and wine are the body and blood of Jesus, given for our life. The other three modes of Jesus' presence in the Mass are less often contemplated, but are equally real. Jesus is truly present in the person of the priest celebrant who speaks the words of consecration. The priest is doing more than recounting a story for us, he is acting as Jesus at the last supper. The third mode of Jesus' presence is in the gathered community. Jesus' promise to be present wherever two or three are gathered in his name is more than just a pious wish. The fourth and final mode of Jesus' presence in the Mass occurs in the proclamation of Scripture in the liturgy of the word. When we receive the word of God with an open heart, we are receiving the true Word of God, that is Jesus himself.

The homilies in this volume are in humble service of this fourth mode of Jesus' presence. The goal has been to bridge the gap of many centuries that separate the writing of Scripture from its proclamation in our liturgy. When it comes to the important parts of life, the people of Bible times were not so different from ourselves. Their struggles are our struggles and their joys are our joys. For this reason, their witness is valuable in our lives.

I have had many excellent teachers in the art of homiletics. There were those from whom I received formal instruction or whose books I read, and there have also been many occasions in which I sat in the pew while masters of the art engaged the congregation in a profound scriptural experience. However, the best instructor I have had is the people of Saint Paul parish. The Church speaks with much respect of the "sensus fidelum", the hard-won knowledge of God that comes to the faithful as they struggle to follow in the footsteps of Jesus. The people of Saint Paul parish have been generous in sharing this understanding with me, both in the stories of their lives, and in the gentle criticism of what worked or did not work in my latest homily. Of special value has been their pointing out of questions or sticking points that they wished could be addressed.

Therefore, it is to the people of Saint Paul parish, a true community of faith, that the homilies in this collection are dedicated.

DEACON JOE KUPIN
Holy Week 2014

TABLE OF CONTENTS

323   PART B: HOMILIES DELIVERED IN SPANISH

Part A: HOMILIES *in* ENGLISH

It is impossible to express the depth of my gratitude to my content editor, sensitivity reviewer and copy editor, who also happens to be my wife and my constant encouragement, Jane

5th Sunday of Easter, May 14, 2006:
YOU HAVE TO PLUG IT IN.

(Acts 9:26-31; 1 Jn 3: 18-24; Jn 15: 1-8)

About a month ago, our old refrigerator conked out, and we had to get a new one. As I was reading the owner's guide to learn how to adjust the temperature, I happened upon the "troubleshooting" page. Maybe you've seen one of those. They usually come in three columns: first is the problem, then comes what might have caused the problem, and finally what you can do to fix it. Well, the very first problem listed on this page was "Refrigerator does not work". Ok, I can see how that would be a problem. The listed cause was "refrigerator is not properly plugged in" and the suggestion for what to do about this was "plug it in." My first thought on reading all this was: "Who do they write these books for?" Surely everyone knows you need to plug in a refrigerator before it will work!

I think, though, that Jesus' words today about vines and branches were probably just as obvious to his listeners as that stuff about the refrigerator is to us. Of course a branch needs to be connected to the rest of the plant, if it is to produce any fruit! Otherwise, it's just a piece of firewood. It is interesting though, that what is so painfully obvious about refrigerators and grape vines, is not so obvious when it comes to something more abstract, like our faith. But today Jesus reminds us that if we want our faith to work for us, it also needs to be plugged in.

And we do depend on our faith when we are doing difficult things. Today on Mother's day, I think of all the tremendous things that our mothers do: they take care of us when we are sick, they are patient and loving. It cannot be easy to keep that up 24 hours a day, and faith can help with this great work. I remember what it was like when I was called on to be the primary care giver for our children. About four in the afternoon, my patience would really begin to wear thin. I'd be watching the clock waiting for Mr. Rogers to come on. When we are in that sort of a position, we can go to our faith to get the patience we need to get through the rest of the day. We might pray "I can't do this alone God, please help me."

Of course, patience is not the only virtue we can get from the storehouse of our faith in this way. We might need courage to confront a bully, or wisdom to make a life decision, or any number of other virtues and helps.

Sometimes when we go to our faith for help, we receive what we need to keep going, and that is a wonderful experience. But other times, we seem to get nothing. We open the door to our faith in prayer, but the little light does not go on. It seems dead and completely lifeless. When that happens to us, as it likely will at some point to all of us, the first question we should ask is "Is it plugged in?" Is our faith really plugged into the power of God's love?

There are many different ways for us to plug into God's love. I would like to share three of these which have been particularly important in my life.

The first is the Eucharist. That is a great source of strength for us all. But I find that for me to get the best out of it, I have to be the one to make the connection. I need to sing the songs and listen actively to the readings, asking "What is God trying to say to me today in this reading?" and I need to offer my heart on the altar with the gifts of sacrifice. When I do those things, my faith really gets plugged into the power of God's love.

A second thing we can do to plug in is spiritual reading. I have found that pretty much anything written by C. S. Lewis or Henri Nouwen will help me refresh my spirit. I keep a few of their books by the bed, and when I'm feeling down, I just open one and read, and I feel refreshed. Here too, in order for this to work for us, we need to make the connection. We need to find a writer who speaks to our lives. Once our

Parish library gets into its new location, I would suggest each Sunday going and taking out a book. Read a bit and if you like it, keep going. If not, bring it back and try a different one next week. Through this effort, surely we will all find writers that can connect with our lives.

The final way to plug into God's love that I want to mention this morning, is connecting with this wonderful community. Sitting in these pews are many people full of the power of God's love and willing to share. I can hardly explain to you how important that has been for me as I prepared for the diaconate. Sometimes I would have a hundred pages of some dull textbook to read, or a 15-page paper to write before next Tuesday, and I would be dreading it. But then, I would come to Church and someone would greet me warmly, and ask how my studies were going, and talk about how nice it would be when I was ordained. Sometimes, such conversations made it possible for me to go on. Just in case I never thanked all of you for that help, I do it now: "Thank you from the bottom of my heart"

We can all tap into this source of power from God, but again, we need to make the connection to allow it to happen for us. We cannot be content to come to church each Sunday and rub shoulders with strangers. We need to get to know one another. One way to do this is to join a church ministry. For example, Loves and Fishes is coming up soon. There is no better way to get to know good people. Also, we might introduce ourselves to people whom we see around often " Hi, I see you here every week, but I don't know your name. I'm Joe" If we can't think of anything else to talk about, we can always talk about the homily: "Nice homily, but what was all that stuff about refrigerators? Did you get any of that?"

As we continue our liturgy this morning, let us think and pray about the many different ways our faith gets plugged into the power of God's love. I have shared three that are important to me, but there are many more. It is important for us to keep our faith plugged in, in as many different ways as possible, so that it can be of aid to us in times of need. For between us and God, we can overcome any obstacle and do any good thing that God wishes us to do.

WE ARE ONE BODY IN CHRIST

(Ex 24: 3-8; Heb 9: 11-15; Mk 14: 12-16, 22-26)

Two weeks ago, I had the privilege of distributing communion at the Princeton Medical Center, and I'd like to tell you about one visit that made a particular impression on me. I introduced myself to the person on my list, and asked him if he would like to receive communion, and then we began to say the Lord's Prayer together. But then about half way through our prayer, his eyelids began to droop, and soon he fell asleep, with a little smile on his face. When I finished the prayer, I called his name gently to see how deeply he was sleeping, but he didn't respond in any way, so, I gave him a blessing and turned to leave.

But then as I was leaving the room, the other patient in the room caught my eye, and I said "hello" as I passed. He said, "Please pardon me for saying this, but what you just did over there was really strange to me—completely outside my experience. You are a stranger to him, and you come in and pray for two minutes, and then you leave." He was obviously struggling for some way to understand this brief interaction, and didn't quite know what question he wanted to ask me. Well, we ended up talking for a while, and I heard a bit of his life story, and then I left. But later it seemed to me that I didn't really address the question he was struggling with when we began our conversation.

So, I put it to you. How would you have explained to this polite English gentleman, that although my exchange with the man who fell asleep must have seemed strange when it was viewed from the outside, when it is seen from the inside, it was a perfectly ordinary and natural sort of thing.

Here are two things that I wish I had said, or said more clearly, to him.

The first thing to understand about the Eucharist is that there is a power to the rite of communion that does not depend on the personal relationship of the people who are sharing it. Ultimately, it is something that God does, not something that a minister does. As we began our prayer together, that man was entering into something very familiar to him, something with a history that went back to a time long ago when he was all dressed up in his best clothes, with his hair all slicked back, and he shared in communion for the very first time. And, even more importantly, this ritual put that man into contact with the very first celebration of the Eucharist, which we heard described in today's gospel, when the Apostles themselves were all dressed up in their best clothes, with their hair slicked back, and they shared in the very first communion ever. We make a real contact with that event every time we gather for Eucharist.

Now, if that man could slip so quickly into the peace of that eternal moment, that it sent him into a deep and peaceful sleep, so that he didn't even need to receive communion physically, well, that's wonderful as far as I'm concerned. It must be what God wanted for him in that moment.

—of course if any of you should begin to go to sleep on me now, that would be a completely different matter, and I would begin to worry. So please don't do that—

The second important thing to understand is that even though I had never met the man who fell asleep, it isn't quite right to call us strangers. It is true that I didn't know any of the details the world considers important, like what that man was in the hospital for, or his prognosis, and he didn't know anything particular about my struggles and my joys in life, but all of those details are much less important than what we did share.

What it is that we all share in Eucharist was described very well by Pope Benedict in a wonderful reflection that he delivered at the Twentieth World Youth Day last summer. If you can get to the Vatican website on the internet, you should really check it out. It is very profound. The pope said that the transformation of bread and wine into the body and blood of Jesus is only one of the transformations that Jesus initiated on that holy night. The first transformation he accomplished was the transformation of his death from a senseless act of cruelty into a beautiful act of love. He did this through his acceptance of his death for our sake. It is this loving act of Jesus that provided the context for the transformation of the bread and wine into his body and blood. And it is also the context for another transformation that came upon the Apostles, and all of us who follow after them.

By sharing in the Eucharist, we are all transformed into the unity which is the body of Christ, and it is that unity that I shared with that man in the bed. That is what allowed me to greet him as a brother, even though we had never met. As the Pope reminds us, this final transformation is an ongoing thing, which will eventually transform the whole world into the Kingdom of God.

So as we continue our Mass this morning, maybe we could all focus on the power of the Eucharist and its ability to transform us. Let's listen carefully to the beautiful words of the Eucharistic prayer which Monsignor Nolan will pray on our behalf in just a few moments, and ask God to transform us through this experience. Let's give ourselves over to the power of the Eucharist.

Then, when we go home, we can struggle a bit with the words, as all the great theologians have done. How are we to describe what is happening here this morning? And struggle too with the reality of it. How will we allow this Eucharist to transform us more fully into the body of Christ. What will we do differently this week, because we have been here this morning?

15th Sunday in Ordinary Time, Jul. 16, 2006:

HERE I AM, LORD, SEND ME

(Amos 7: 12-15; Eph 1: 3-4; Mk 6: 7-13)

For a while now in our Sunday liturgy, we have been having readings from St. Paul's second letter to the Corinthians. St. Paul had some issues with those people, and that makes certain parts of that letter a tough read. Today, however, we begin St. Paul's letter to the Ephesians. This is a very different sort of letter. In it, St. Paul seems to take a step back from everyday problems to consider the larger questions of our faith, and even though this letter was written from prison, it is very joyful, as today's selection shows.

The hymn of praise we hear today comes from the first chapter of the letter. It is apparently based on an ancient Hebrew prayer form called a "hodayot" or "hymn of thanksgiving" in which the writer praises God for the many things he has done for him. The clue for this is the opening formula "Blessed be God". This is like saying "How wonderful God is!"

Although St. Paul gives us a prayer in this ancient Hebrew mode, he has updated it to fit the Christian message. The beginning is dedicated to God the Father, the middle to God the Son, and the conclusion to the Holy Spirit. In fact, one would have to look far and wide in Scripture to find a better or more succinct statement of the Good News of Jesus than the verses we hear today. All the joy of the Good News is laid out for us, right here.

Because these verses are so compact, though, it might be a bit hard to appreciate all of it in one sitting. It just goes by too fast for that. It would be a good spiritual exercise for this week to take the whole first chapter of Ephesians and read through it slowly, just a few verses per day and really think about what it's saying.

Here are just a few of the treasures we will find if we do this. Speaking of God the Father, St. Paul says, "In love he destined us for adoption to himself." I don't know if you are an adoptive parent, or if you know any, but I know a number of them, and every one that I know experienced tremendous joy when they finally brought their adopted child home, sometimes after years of effort and planning, and who knows how many forms filled out in triplicate, trips taken and fees paid. Just stop for a moment and think about God expending that kind of effort on our behalf, and experiencing that kind of anticipation and joy when we became his adopted sons and daughters through Baptism, just as he had been hoping it would happen all along. What a powerful idea!

Here's another gem. St. Paul says that we were chosen in Jesus, so that we might exist for the praise of God's glory. What a thought-provoking way to state the goal of our life. We exist for the praise of God's glory. Kind of makes us sound like beautiful rosebushes, or those precious and elegant Faberge Easter eggs. Of course, when we come to liturgy we certainly praise God's glory and that is very good, but there is a lot more to our existence than that. We are also to be the praise of God's glory in our everyday lives. We do this when we try to live by the virtues of faith, hope and love. When we do that, our whole existence is wrapped up in the glory of God. Wow!

Just one more gem: Speaking of the Holy Spirit, St. Paul says that the coming of the Holy Spirit is the first installment on our inheritance. As God's children we get an inheritance. That's an interesting idea. All the treasures of God our Father will someday come to us. Just recently I was looking through a dresser drawer and I happened on a silver dollar that my grandfather gave me when I was little. I can still remember how massive it felt in my many hand. So different from the nickels and pennies I thought of as money. I felt special and blessed when he gave that to me.

The Holy Spirit also gives us wonderful gifts. Scripture talks about the twelve fruits of the Holy Spirit. The first of these are love, joy, peace. Then come patience, kindness, generosity, faithfulness gentleness, moderation, modesty, continence and chastity. Each of these is a little piece of heaven right in the here and now. When we encounter one of these, we feel closer to God, just the way holding that silver dollar made me feel closer to my grandfather.

This is all really powerful stuff, and I encourage you to live with this chapter for a while and get used to hearing all of the us's and we's that St. Paul uses as including each of us.

This is such powerful stuff that I think it explains something that has sometimes bothered me about today's gospel. Did you ever wonder where the Apostles got the confidence to go out on mission as we hear them do today? After all, they were not trained preachers and healers and exorcists. They were fishermen and tax collectors. And yet, they found the courage to go where Jesus sent them. They walked into some village full of strangers and went up to sick people and laid their hands on them and said "In the name of Jesus, be healed!" in perfect confidence that that is exactly what would happen. Where did that confidence come from?

I think that at least a part of the answer is that their confidence came from a real grounding in the joy of the Good News, as it is presented in today's epistle. They truly felt like God's adopted children, living in glory, and in possession of a true spiritual inheritance. They were probably eager to get out and give it a try, just as Jesus said they should.

I think that something similar could be true for us too. When we really get the message of the first chapter of Ephesians, we are not going to be able to just set the Bible down and say "That's all very nice, but what's for lunch?" We will want to act on this vision of ourselves. Perhaps we will feel sent down to Trenton to work at Martin House building houses or working with inner city youth. Or perhaps we will feel we should join the group from St. Paul's that goes to visit people in the hospital and the area nursing homes. Or maybe we will be sent to do something else wonderful that we can't even conceive of today. That could easily happen.

The prophet Isaiah tells the story of a dream he once had, in which he was transported to God's throne room, and he saw God sitting there worried over the sad state of the world and muttering to himself "but whom shall I send?" And Isaiah, in a rush of love for God and compassion for his fellow man, said "Here I am Lord, send me!" That is the way we will feel when we get the fire of the Good News into our veins. We will say "Here I am Lord, send me."

20th Sunday in Ordinary Time, Aug. 20, 2006:

A NEW LIFE OF JOY AND HOPE

(Prob 9:1-6; Eph 5:15-20; Jn 6: 51-58)

For a number of weeks now, we have been taking our Gospel readings from the sixth chapter of John's gospel, in which the evangelist lays out for us his deep and rich understanding of the Eucharist. A very important part of his vision is the connection between the Eucharist and everlasting life. This theme was very evident in last week's gospel, and it is present again today. For example, today Jesus says "Whoever eats this bread will live forever." And a bit later he restates the same idea in slightly different words: "Whoever eats my flesh and drinks my blood has eternal life, and I will raise him up on the last day."

Notice that in this second statement of Jesus, everlasting life is not just a fact about the end of time, it is something that we have with us right now. The eternal life that Jesus brings to us in Eucharist is something that we can experience today. Let's explore this idea together, not by focusing so much on the quantity of this life (the fact that it will last forever) but rather on its qualities. What is it like, this new and durable life that we receive in Eucharist?

One wonderful quality of this life that Jesus brings to us is its great joy. As you may recall, Friday a week ago was the first day of this really nice spell of weather we've been having. On that day, as I was walking to work, I really felt alive and close to God. There is a short portion of my walk that goes through a woods, and when I got to that point, all my senses were tingling—the breeze on my skin, the sound of the birds and the cicadas, the million shades of green that I saw. It was all so beautiful. It helped me in making a connection to God, that green is an important color in our liturgy. The celebrant wears green vestments often during the Church year because green is the color of life and of hope. Seeing it reminds us that no matter how bad things get, no winter lasts forever. Life always returns. That was the feeling I had as I walked along that day. I was totally immersed in that moment and enjoying the feast that God had set before me.

There are other days, however, when I hardly notice that bit of woods as I walk by. I am quite certain that on those other days, God is also laying out a feast for my senses, but somehow I am not aware of it. On those days I miss out on the fullness of the life God means me to have.

Usually, when I miss out in this way, it is because I am doing what my mother would call "borrowing trouble." I am thinking about all the things that are going on that day at work or at home, and what I will do if this thing happens or if that thing does not happen. Often this is not very productive mental activity. It is just worry for worry's sake, and its only real effect is to rob me of peace as I walk along. Jesus warns us against getting caught up in this kind of worry, but it is hard to avoid sometimes. If we find ourselves borrowing trouble in this way, maybe we could try offering all those things to God in prayer, allowing him to hold them for us, while we try to focus on the gifts he has placed in front of us right now.

Another thing that can get in the way of our experience of the full and rich life of the spirit that Jesus brings us in the Eucharist is the burdens of the past. If you have a large family, there are probably a few people in it that do not get along with each other, perhaps because of something that happened many years ago. Have you ever been to a party or family gathering with one of those people, when that other person arrives? It can turn a beautiful occasion sour for both individuals. It is very sad. Suddenly, their food is forgotten, and conversations with one or the other become difficult, because each one only has eyes for what the other one is doing. We should pray that we never get caught in a similar trap. With God's help, we can learn to lay down the burdens of the past, all the resentments and pains, and allow ourselves to find the joy of the present moment. In the love of Jesus, we can find the strength to forgive others and even to forgive ourselves, and by doing so, we open ourselves up to be truly alive.

I've talked quite a bit about the deep joy which a hallmark of our new life in Jesus, but it should be remembered that it is not a simple joy. It is rather a rich and complex experience of joy mingled with sorrow. As we open ourselves up to be alive in the present moment, we will find sorrow and pain there, as well as joy.

I don't know why this needs to be so. I do know that we humans can only perceive things through contrast. If everything in a scene is exactly the same color and brightness, we have trouble seeing anything at all. If we cannot hear the silences in between a person's words, we have trouble understanding what is being said to us. So perhaps we would be unable to perceive joy at all if there were no sorrow and pain in our lives. That may be so, but I think there is also something deeper than that going on here. This is one of the great mysteries that lies at the heart of our faith. Ultimately, it goes back to the mystery of the crucifixion, which is an essential part of our Eucharistic faith.

As we begin to come out of ourselves and enter into the new life that Jesus offers us, we also open ourselves to the lives of others and their joys and their pains become our own. This shared pain can be a potent motivator in our lives, pushing us to write letters about immigration policy to our legislators, or urging us into some kind of volunteer activity, or leading us to bake cookies for someone who needs some cheering up. These are all beautiful expressions of our spiritual life.

One final point, in just a few weeks, St. James will tell us in his letter that God is unchanging in his perfection. Theologians have long interpreted this to mean that for God there is no such thing as future or past. Everything for God is one long eternal instant of now. I can't help believing that when we practice living in the now and opening ourselves up to all its joys and its sorrows, we are experiencing something of the life of God in a special way, and we are preparing ourselves well for our life with God in heaven. And the fullness of that experience will give us all the assurance we need that Jesus will continue to be a life-giving presence for us, no matter what lies ahead, and he will truly raise us up on the last day.

24th Sunday in Ordinary Time, Sep. 17, 2006:
DIVERSE IMAGES OF JESUS

(Is 50: 4-9; Jas 2: 14-18; Mk 8: 27-35)

Today Jesus asks his disciples "Who do you say that I am?" It is a piercing question that gets right to the heart of our faith. And today he also aims this question at us: Who do we say that Jesus is?

This is not at all an easy question. One way to begin to answer it honestly is to look back at the different images of Jesus that have been important and helpful in our lives. When I was little, my family belonged to Holy Trinity Parish in Glen Burnie, Maryland. We had a beautiful little church, and behind the altar, there was a half dome that was frescoed with an image of the Trinity. On the right side was God the Father with white hair and long beard resting on the clouds. In the center was a descending dove to represent the Holy Spirit, and there, seated at God the Father's right hand, was Jesus, resting and looking down at everyone with a contented smile.

Jesus held his cross across his lap, but at a funny angle, with the base of the cross extended toward the people. To my childish eyes, it looked like a sliding board. I had the idea that Jesus had just gone down the slide, and there he was smiling at all of us as if to say, "Go ahead, now you try it." That was comforting to one rather timid little Maryland boy who found sliding boards frightening.

As I grew up and received fuller instruction in our faith, I was taught about the many other images of Jesus that can be found in Scripture and tradition. For example, many people are drawn to Jesus as the Good Shepherd. He is the true embodiment of the 23 Psalm: "The

Lord is my shepherd. I shall not want. He makes me to lie down in green pastures." Jesus is that good shepherd who goes out to seek the lost sheep, and lays down his life for them.

Or how about Jesus as the compassionate healer, who had such sympathy for the blind and the lame. He grasps our weak and trembling hand in his strong and steady one, and lifts us up, saying "Rise up and walk." Luke's gospel is a good place to look for this comforting image.

Or Jesus as the teacher. This is an important theme in Matthew's gospel. In that gospel Jesus gives us five great discourses. These include the Beatitudes, the Lord's prayer and many, many parables which tell us in very plain and simple ways what God is like and how we ought to live.

All these images of Jesus from Scripture are good and helpful, and there are many more: Jesus as the just judge, as the suffering servant, as our brother or our friend, as our advocate before the Father. The contemplation of any of these images could be an important part of our spiritual growth.

Today, on Catechetical Sunday, we should note that we learned about all these wonderful images of Jesus from our teachers in the faith, our catechists. Today we honor all the time and effort they put into their teaching. It would be great to say a prayer for them today. We also honor those who are serving in that role in our parish today. They do us a wonderful service, and we are greatly in their debt.

These wonderful teachers opened up a whole treasury of images of Jesus for us, but contemplating this treasury, we might wonder why there are so many different images. We need so many different images, because each one is imperfect. Each one rests on our experiences of a particular human relationship, and those relationships are always less than perfect. None of the images alone can quite capture the full reality of who Jesus is. For this reason, we should not be surprised that our favorite image of Jesus changes as we change. It is not that the old image is wrong, and now we have found the true image of Jesus. No, it is simply that we have moved, and so if we want to look at Jesus we have to look in a slightly different direction than we did before.

In this, I trust in the wise words of Julian of Norwich. She was a mystic and writer of the late thirteen hundreds in England. In the Following passage from her "Revelations of Divine Love" she refers to Jesus both as mother and as father, and then tries to take us beyond all such images.

She writes: "Jesus Christ ... is our true mother. We owe our being to him—and this is the essence of motherhood!—and [we owe him] all the delightful, loving protection which ever follows. God is as really our mother as he is our father. He showed this throughout, and especially when he said the sweet word 'It is I.' In other words 'It is I who am the strength and goodness of Fatherhood. I who am the wisdom of motherhood; I who am light and grace and blessed love; I who am trinity; I who am unity; I who am the sovereign goodness of every single thing; I who enable you to love; I who enable you to long; It is I, the eternal satisfaction of every genuine desire.'" (Chap 59, Para 1)

I think that Julian is saying something very wise here. By putting together all the different images we have of Jesus, we hope to leap beyond them all to that deeper encounter, the "It is I" experience. This is similar to the way we get to know anyone. We might first encounter a person as a coworker, then get to know him as a golfer, then as a gardener, then as a grandfather. But pretty soon, in some mysterious way, we are able to move beyond all those particular images to an appreciation of the person as a person. The same thing can happen in our relationship with Jesus.

So I invite you this week to look back over your life and the different images of Jesus that have been important to you, and see if considering them all together doesn't help you to triangulate through them to a deeper encounter with the real person of Jesus. The final step, then would be to go back to those images we love, and allow them be informed and deepened by that "It is I" experience.

Even the image of Jesus on the sliding board might be saved in this way. Jesus asks us to do difficult things sometimes, no doubt about it, and that's like climbing up that steep ladder. And then, we have to let go and slide, giving ourselves over to the fulfillment of God's will. And everything I have learned about Jesus makes me sure that when we get to the bottom of the slide, we will find Jesus down there waiting to catch us, and give us a big hug and whisper in our ear, "Now, was that fun, or what!"

Who is Jesus? He is savior, brother, shepherd, lord, judge and healer. He is also the guy waiting for us at the bottom of the slide.

BETWEEN ENOUGH AND TOO MUCH

(Wis 7: 7-11; Heb 4: 12-13; Mk 10: 17-30)

I have to admit, right from the start, that this gospel is one that I struggle with. I've got a retirement nest-egg and a house full of stuff, and sometimes I feel a bit like the man in today's gospel, who walked away sad from his encounter with Jesus.

Now, it is a wonderful thing that there are those among us who respond to this gospel very literally. They *do* give everything away to follow Jesus, and become nuns or brothers or priests. What a wonderful example of trust in the Lord they are among us! But God is not calling each and every one of us to that same level of poverty.

Well then, what about us who keep our houses and our cars and all our financial responsibilities—what are we supposed to take away from today's gospel? How are we to take Jesus' warning that it is easier for a camel to get through the eye of a needle than for a rich person to be saved? Here are three dangers among many involving money, that could be at least a part of what Jesus is talking about today.

The first danger is that too much concern over money can make us timid in following the Lord. We end up trusting our bank accounts more than we trust him. I want to share with you an example of one kind of boldness and freedom that the Lord wants for us.

When my wife and I were graduate students back in the seventies, we were friends with a couple named Tom and Diane. Tom studied metallurgy. When we were finishing up our degrees, Tom quickly got a job offer. It was for really good money with a solid company, and he would be working on exactly the kind of molybdenum alloys that he had done his research on. The problem was that the company made munitions—guns and bombs. Now, Tom and Diane tried to be good Catholics, and this fact bothered them a lot, but they also had two little children to think about. The economy was not particularly good at that time in the sort of manufacturing industries that employ metallurgists, and it was unclear how long it would be before another offer would come along.

In the end, Tom and Diane did a very bold thing and turned down the offer from that company. Having kept up with them over the years, I would have to say that from a purely financial standpoint, that was a bad move. After about a year, Tom did get a job with a company that made silverware, but it was for considerably less money and then he was laid off for a while, and so it went. Of course, God's bottom line has nothing to do with money, and I have no doubt that as far as God is concerned, Tom and Diane made the right decision. And to their credit, as far as I know, they have never regretted their decision, and they are happy with the way their life has turned out.

There is great freedom in being able to make a decision that answers to what is in our hearts, rather than to what is in our pocketbooks. God wants us to experience that kind of freedom. One danger of our concern over money is that it makes us timid and cautious, when God wants us to be bold and free.

A second difficulty with having a bit of extra money coming in, is that we can quickly lose sight of what the word "enough" means. How many pairs of shoes are enough? How many cars? How big a house? I can't even tell you how many t-shirts I own, but I do know that there are too many to fit in one drawer, and yet I claim to follow a teacher who said if you own two cloaks, you should give one away. Personally, I am still struggling with the difference between "enough" and "too much".

I have great admiration for those who choose to live a life of voluntary simplicity. People who look at their car, and say, "Yes, it is getting a bit shabby, and it's not quite as reliable as it once was, but, really, this car still has some life left in it. It's good enough for me." Or "A spoon and a knife are enough for the way I cook, I don't need fancy kitchen gadgets." Or "No, thank you, I would rather *not* have my meal super-sized." There is great peace and contentment in knowing when enough is enough. Madison Avenue, of course, has done its best to banish the word "enough" from our vocabulary, but God wants us to know the contentment that a simple life can bring.

If we want to act on this idea this week, one thing we might do is to have a discussion with our loved ones to see if there isn't a better way for us to show our love for one another than buying each other expensive Christmas presents. I can tell you from experience that this can be an uncomfortable conversation to have, but it is nonetheless an important one, and if we are going to do it, now is the time.

The third danger of wealth I want to point out today is really the most serious, and that is that wealth can insulate us from the rest of the world. If we live in what is called a "nice" neighborhood, for example, we may never see poverty close up—never know anyone personally who is struggling to put food on the table or whose utilities might get shut off. We may become so insulated in this life that we can no longer hear the cry of the poor, and that would be a serious difficulty when it comes to getting the camel through the eye of the needle.

We have a great program here at St. Paul's that I hope you are participating in, called the Food for the Poor. There are containers at the entrances for boxed and canned food to be given to the needy in our community. When you think about it, it is a really awesome experience to bring a can of corn, say, to the church on Sunday, and to know that by next Friday that particular can might be on the table of someone who really needs it. The pure physicality of holding that particular can is one way of making contact with the needy in a tiny way. We might even say a little prayer of blessing for the people who will receive them as we put our cans into the container.

We should be careful, though, about exactly how we participate in this program. If we go to our shelf and grab a dusty can out of the back that is close to is use-by date, and say to ourselves "Well, what do they want for nothing?" That is not a good attitude. If our brother came to the house and said "Gee, I'm really hungry, would you heat me up a can of soup?" is that the one that we would give him? Or would we search for a can of soup of the kind we really like and say "Here try some of this! You'll like it!" The needy are our brothers. They are our nephews and nieces and our grandparents. We should give them a share of the best things that we have. There is great joy to be found in sharing generously, and God wants us to know that joy.

God wants us to have enough physical stuff to meet all our needs— not all our desires necessarily, but all of our needs, certainly. He also wants us to have an abundance of freedom, contentment and joy. Money might promise us those things, but in the end, it cannot deliver them, because they only truly come from the Kingdom of God. As we continue our worship this morning, let us ask God to show us the difference between "enough" and "too much," and to give us the freedom, contentment and joy that come from following in the way of Jesus.

32nd Sunday in Ordinary Time, Nov. 12, 2006:

GIVING FROM OUR LACK

(1 Kgs 17: 10-16; Heb 9:24-28; Mk 12: 38-44)

Today's first reading starts out in a desperate state. Drought and famine have been ongoing for three years, and now Elijah, God's prophet, is starving—just like the widow of Zarephath that he meets. It is a dire situation, one that we might have trouble relating to on a personal basis. It seems like something that might happen today somewhere out on the parched plains of Africa, but certainly not here in Princeton.

We might bring the story a little closer to home if we remember that there are many different kinds of hunger in this world; hunger for food is only one of many. If we look deeply into our lives we will probably find that we too have a hunger which is not being satisfied. I feel confident in saying this, because we are all biological systems, and biological systems have the property that they grow until they reach the limit of some critical resource, and at that point, the lack of that particular resource blocks further growth.

For some of us, the resource that is in chronically short supply might be money. For others, it might be respect, either in our work or in our family. Some people feel very keenly a lack of acceptance for who they are or are trying to be. Others feel a lack of control over events in their lives. Young parents can feel that the pressures of child raising leave yearning for a bit of a privacy. So many different kinds of hunger! For me, the critical resource is often time. I often feel that there just is not enough time to do all the things I want to do, or need to do.

We can learn a lot about ourselves by asking what our critical resource is at this point in our lives, and also by watching the way we react to the lack of that resource.

One way I have reacted to my perceived lack of time, is to try to prioritize what I do. For example, in our division of labor around the house, I do the vacuuming. I am embarrassed to say just how far down in my priority list the vacuuming sometimes falls. Please don't tell anyone, but I sometimes decide that it's time to vacuum by noticing how much dust has accumulated on the handle of the vacuum cleaner. I try to check it a couple times per month, just to be sure. On the other hand, science fiction novels are still fairly high up on my list of priorities. Not at the top, of course, but pretty far up the list.

It is amazing how much we can learn about ourselves through this sort of personal spiritual examination, but no matter how we set our priorities, and how we work to secure a steady supply of our critical resource, we all get to a point when we get close to the bottom of the barrel. I know I have felt that way many times. There have been times when I've said "OK God, that's it! You can just send down the chariot for me now, cause I am finished. I am played out and there is nothing left." Then I start feeling sorry for myself, and just like the widow of Zarephath, I start gathering sticks for my last meal.

Possibly, God might answer our prayers in this difficult sort of a situation with some show of comfort. But at other times, he may answer us with the unexpected sort of answer that appears in today's reading. God might send someone like Elijah the prophet into our lives to say to us "I can see that you are at the end of your rope, that's for sure. But before the end, could you do just one last thing for me? Just bake me a little cake! Just a little one, could you do that?"   Sometimes I think that the whole of our lives, the whole of the natural world, conspires to get us to exactly this uncomfortable choice point in our lives. And I believe that the angels in heaven hold their breath to see how we will respond to that request. What will we say?

Such situations come up for people all the time. Here are some examples:

~ You are working on some big project at work, and you are really putting in a huge effort, but you do not feel you are getting any recognition for what you do. This upsets you, and then, to top it all off, a supervisor comes to you and tells you confidentially that one of your coworkers is up for an award, and wants some nice words to write about their efforts. What do you say? You are hungry for praise, and yet are being asked to praise someone else.

~ Here's another example. You are in school, and there is a person that you think is really nice, but that person acts like you don't exist. And there's another person who is sort of awkward and a social misfit, and that person wants to spend time with you. Now, you know that if you are seen hanging out with the awkward person, your social life is done for. Your chances of hanging out with the person you really like are gone. So, what do you do? You hunger for acceptance from a certain person, but are asked to give acceptance to someone else instead.

~ A final example. You are a parent home with a sick child. It has been a long, long day. Finally the kid gets interested in a toy and you hope to put your feet up for a few minutes and read a magazine which arrived a week ago and you have yet to open. But, as soon as you get settled, the kid comes in and asks you to read a story. What do you do? You need some pampering, but you are being asked to pamper someone else.

As painful as such situations can be for us, they can also be moments of grace. In that critical moment, we can follow the example of the widow of Zarephath. When she faced this situation, she saved a stranger. It is in that kind of a moment that we can show that we are not simply biological systems. We are biological systems married with souls—souls that can sometimes give the needs of others priority over our own.

Now don't get me wrong. There are no simple answers in this life, and I don't think our choice in the moment of a resource crisis can always be exactly the same. I know for myself, there are times when I need a night off. I need a cup of herb tea and a good novel, and some down time. We should accept such opportunities lovingly from God, and enjoy them thoroughly. But it is also important that sometimes we give the other answer. That we decide we will bake that cake for Elijah, or as Mother Theresa said, that we give to God out of our need.

It is important that we do this for many reasons, not the least of which is that we learn something very important from the experience of giving out of our need: we learn that we can trust the beautiful promise that ends today's reading: the oil jar will not go empty. Now, we might already believe that up here in our heads (or at least we might want to believe it), but this kind of experience can make us know the truth of it, down here in our hearts.

As we continue with our worship together let us pray that we will always be people of the promise. Let us pray for the insight to identify our critical resources and to learn from the way we react to our hunger for them. And let us pray for the sort of experiences that will show us the truth of the promise that the oil jar will not go empty. For truly, it will not go empty, not until God sends his rain upon the earth, and the earth is renewed.

4th Sunday of Advent, Dec. 24, 2006:

STRESS OR JOY THIS CHRISTMAS?

(Micah 5: 1-4; Heb 10:5-10; Lk 1: 39-45)

So, here's a quick quiz. In the last two weeks have you ever woken up in the middle of the night in a panic attack because you think you have forgotten to buy enough red and green M&M's for your Christmas party? Or, how about a panic attack because you are suddenly not sure that the present you just bought for Uncle Tony isn't exactly the same thing you got for him last year? If the answer to either of these questions is "yes" then you are probably in over your head this holiday season, just like the rest of us. It can be a crazy time of year because of all the burdens we place upon ourselves, and how tightly we pack our schedules.

What a good thing it is that we have this hour to sit quietly together to prepare ourselves internally for the holy day of Christmas. Let's take full advantage of this time together and put out of our minds all the things we have left to do, and concentrate on the beautiful example of Elizabeth and Mary in today's gospel reading —two people who were so very important to the fulfillment of God's plan for the world.

Mary and Elizabeth are both pregnant in today's reading and that can be a wonderful time in the life of any family. It can be a time that gives very concrete and homey expression to the virtues of faith, hope, and love.

First let's consider Faith. In this context, the virtue of faith is not about believing a certain creed, but rather it is about faithfulness, that is, staying true to our commitments. I know that when my wife

Jane was pregnant, we tried to work together to follow all the rules we got from her doctor: take vitamins, exercise, eat well, be moderate, get enough rest. What we were doing was just so important in our lives that we wanted to do everything that we could to make it work. I'm sure the same was true of Mary and Elizabeth.

Mary went to visit Elizabeth to help her get through her pregnancy. Probably that pregnancy was not easy, since Elizabeth was quite a mature woman when she found herself pregnant. I remember when we went to the hospital for the birth of our second child, Jane was wheeled down the hall to the birthing room saying "I'm too old for this!" I can only imagine that Elizabeth, who was of course much more advanced in years than Jane was, must have felt much the same way at times. In her wisdom, Mary understood this, and as soon as she found out about Elizabeth's pregnancy, she was right there to share the burden.

We too in the family of Saint Paul's can think of ourselves as "expecting" in a certain sense. We are expecting our savior, and that process is not always the easiest thing in the world. Maybe we are wondering if we aren't a little too old or tired or jaded for such a change in our life. Our faithfulness to each other can help all of us to prepare for the reality of God-Among-Us this Christmas. We see that happening in our many ministries around the parish, and in our warm greetings and words of concern for each other. I have felt particularly blessed in this way over the last month or so, by your many kind words and prayers for my mother. I am most grateful to all of you. We can all rejoice in the gift of faithfulness so evident in our community this Christmas, and strive to do even more of the same in the year to come.

And what about the virtue of Hope? Pregnancy can be a time of great uncertainty. There are so many unknowns. Will the baby be healthy? How will the family come together in a new configuration? Will we be up to all the new responsibilities? What will the world be like in twenty years when this baby begins to find a place in it?

The example of Elizabeth and Mary shows us that things don't always work out the way we would expect them to in this regard. Consider Elizabeth. As a young man, her son went out into the desert wearing the roughest camel hair clothing and eating locusts and wild honey and talking to God. What ever did she tell her neighbors? It cannot be anything like what she would have imagined for him while she was carrying him. Similarly for Mary. The gospels tell us of one time when a group of Jesus' relatives decided that he was completely off his rocker and went out to fetch him home and set him straight. Mary went along on that trip, and surely her heart was full of turmoil as she went. Such troubles are not what a mother wishes for when she is pregnant.

But what the gospel shows us is that no matter how things in our lives seem to be going down paths that we cannot control, God can turn all of that to glory, just as he did for Elizabeth and Mary. And that is where the virtue of Hope comes in. Hope is our trust in the promise of God, that things will work out for good in the end, even if we cannot understand how that will happen.

Maybe this isn't your best Christmas. Perhaps you are lonely, or there are family members you are worried about, or in some other way, things are not working out the way you hoped. Well, today in this Mass we can join with Elizabeth and Mary and wrap all those worries and troubles and disappointments and hopes and dreams up in a big prayer to God. We can give it all to him saying, "Here it is, God. I've done what I can. I sure hope you can make something out of all of this." Our hope assures us that he can. He can turn all of that broken and confused stuff in our lives to his greater glory. And someday, who knows when, we will see it happen.

Finally, there is the virtue of Love. During pregnancy, this virtue often expresses itself in the most practical and humble of ways. I'm thinking of nest-building sorts of things, like cleaning and painting and preparing the baby's room. I can just see Mary and Elizabeth sitting together and sewing clothes for their soon-to-be-born children. Just by sitting there together, they shared their hopes and their fears. And in that gentle way, in their bodies and by the work of their hands, by all their loving actions, they were making the mystery of Christmas real for all of us.

Now it is up to us to make the mystery of Jesus real for each other. Our loving actions: our patience, our forgiveness, our cheerfulness when things go awry, those are the things that will make this be a season full of love for our family and those we care for. We have Elizabeth and Mary to be our examples.

As we rush headlong into Christmas, maybe it will give us strength to keep the image of Elizabeth and Mary in our hearts. This Christmas maybe we can focus our attention on their homey virtues of faith, hope and love. Holding on to those three, we might be willing to let go of our need for red and green M&M's or for Ooh's and Ah's from our family over presents we've bought. We might laugh off burned pies or a bedraggled Christmas tree. Faith, hope and love are our real Christmas gifts for each other this year. All the rest is so much wrapping paper and tinsel.

CLIMBING THE LADDER OF HOLINESS

(Jer 17, 5–8; 1 Cor 15, 12. 16–20; Lk 6, 17. 20–26)

I don't know about you, but I find the directions for dealing with other people that appear in today's gospel to be very challenging. "Turn the other cheek", "Be good to your enemies." "If someone steals something from you, don't try to get it back." To say the least, these are not easy directions to follow.

One way to approach them is to put them into the perspective of other moral laws that we find in the Bible. In the Bible we find a whole range of standards about how to deal with other people. One of the earliest comes from the time of Moses. It says:

> *When men have a fight… [and] injury ensues, you*
> *shall give life for life, eye for eye, tooth for tooth,*
> *hand for hand, foot for foot, burn for burn, wound*
> *for wound, and stripe for stripe. (Ex 21: 23-24).*

That approach might sound kind of bloodthirsty to us now, but at the time it was actually an advance in human behavior. The prevailing idea at the time for how to get along with others was: "If you do something to me and mine, I will hurt you and yours as much I possibly can, so that you will never hurt me again" The law of Moses is about restraint, and putting limits on such violence. So this law was a step up on the ladder of holiness.

Another rung on the ladder appears in the book of Leviticus:

> *Take no revenge and cherish no grudge against*
> *your fellow countrymen. (Lev 19: 18)*

This rule is a bit more generous in not cherishing a grudge, at least when it comes to fellow countrymen. Foreigners are still a different matter, but that will come. Several rungs higher on the moral ladder is this standard from the book of Tobit. Tobit tells his son:

> *Do to no one what you yourself dislike. (Tobit 4: 15)*

This would be a good standard to live by. It is sometimes called the "silver" rule. It is not quite as good as the "golden" rule that Jesus gives us today: "Do to others as you would have them do to you." The golden rule and the other things Jesus tells to do today are much more active in seeking out the good of the other person, including our enemies. So Jesus' words today represent another couple of giant steps up on the moral ladder.

And the words we hear today are not even the highest rungs on the ladder. Elsewhere in the gospels, we find these two standards. Jesus says:

> *Love one another as I have loved you. (Jn 15: 12)*

> And

> *Be perfect, even as your heavenly Father is perfect.*
> *(Mt 5: 48)*

I think that last one has to be the top rung of the moral ladder, don't you? But notice that at the top of the moral ladder we find our generous and loving God. Isn't that wonderful?

So, the Bible preserves for us the whole range of moral standards that humanity has struggled to follow throughout the ages. And what about us? This Wednesday is the beginning of the season of Lent. This is a time when we take stock of our lives and prepare ourselves, along with those who are to be baptized, to have an encounter with the risen Jesus in the Easter mysteries. It might be a good idea at the beginning of Lent to examine our relationships to other people, and see where they fall on the moral ladder.

Like most people, I suppose, my relationships with other people are all up and down the line. There have been certain times and certain people, when I would have been doing well to stand on the same rung as Moses and limit myself to an eye for an eye and a tooth for a tooth. I'm not proud of that, but that's how it was.

As we engage in a sincere evaluation of our interactions with those around us, we might be a little bit embarrassed to note how many of our interactions come out pretty low on the moral ladder. But that's OK, Lent is a very good time to work on our lives.

Now, I suppose there are some people who might be able to take stock of their life in this way, and if they found it wanting, they would take radical measures to improve. They might decide to move all their interactions with other people right up to the top rung. That would grand thing to do, and I suppose some saints have managed it, but I think that for most of us, that would be a very short-lived resolution. We might not even get out of the parking lot after Mass with that resolution intact! Happily, there is another way to try to make moral progress in this life, and that is to try to move up the ladder one rung at a time. We might just pick a few interactions that especially bother us, and try to move those relationships up a little higher. First let's get to the silver rule, and then to the golden rule and beyond.

As we do this, and concentrate more attention on the people around us, we will begin to appreciate the wonderful truth of the words that we find at the end of today's Gospel: that in the people around us, God gives us an overwhelming amount of blessings "tamped down and overflowing into the folds of our garment."

I love that image of God's generous nature, and when I hear it I can't help thinking of a story my brother-in-law Jim tells of a time when he was little and his family was visiting his Uncle Frank's house. When they got there, Jim went exploring, as little boys will do, and in the living room he found a beautiful cut-glass dish filled with chocolate candies. Jim was standing there transfixed by this vision of loveliness when his uncle came into the room, and said "Oh, would you like to have one?" Jim took one, but before he got it to his mouth, his uncle said "Here, have another." Now Jim had one in each hand, and his uncle said again "Please, have another one." As a lark, Uncle Frank was trying to see just how many Jim would take. He never did find out, though, because Jim kept accepting more and more candies, until he was juggling ten or more in his hands and then Jim's mother came in and spoiled Uncle Frank's fun.

Sometimes, I think that God is just like Uncle Frank. God is generous beyond compare in many ways, but especially in the people he sends into our lives to help and challenge and guide and comfort us. As we take stock of our relationships with other people and work to improve each of them, our appreciation of God's generosity in this way will grow and grow. We will begin to notice that practically every time we turn around God is offering us another person to share the road with us. Just like Uncle Frank, he keeps saying "Here, would you like another one?"

So, as we continue with our liturgy this morning, let us cherish the memories of the people God has given us in our lives, and make a commitment to honor those gifts by reviewing our relationship with those around us right now and attempting to move each of those relationships up the moral ladder toward our loving and welcoming Lord. In that way, we too will be able to greet the Lord with joy and thanksgiving on Easter morning.

4th Sunday in Lent, Mar. 18, 2007:

THE FATHER'S FORGIVENESS ABOUNDS

(Josh 5: 9. 10-12; 2 Cor 5: 17-21; Lk 15: 1-3. 11-32)

Today's parable is a beautiful work of art. It has everything that a good short story needs: simplicity, and finely drawn characters, and elemental human values. It is amazing to me that it was composed almost two thousand years ago, and yet it remains as fresh and relevant as if it had been written yesterday.

It is good that we can appreciate this story for its great beauty, but it is not just a piece of literature. It is also Scripture and that means that it is meant to challenge us in the way we live our lives. We are challenged to bring the story forward out of its context of two thousand years ago, with its Pharisees and prostitutes and tax collectors and let it shine a light on the way we live our lives today. One way for us to do this is to imagine ourselves a part of the story.

Perhaps, today this gospel is challenging some of us to put ourselves in the place of the younger son. Many of us who have been around for a while, have some things in our past that we are not proud of. Really bad things that we did, which we now wish we hadn't, or important things we should have done, and failed to do. But now, like the younger son, we have turned away from those things, and want to return to the Father, taking advantage of the wonderful sacrament of reconciliation to make the transition complete.

Often, the sacrament of reconciliation can help us to move from wrongdoing into a better spiritual place. But sometimes, people in this sort of a situation can get stuck in their remorse for past sins, and never quite feel forgiven. Such people may find themselves continually asking God to give them again the forgiveness that he has already granted.

For those of us in that situation today, this gospel may be challenging us to really accept the forgiveness of God. Try this meditation. Picture yourself down at the end of God's driveway. You have turned away from your sins and started up the road toward his house. See him coming eagerly down the driveway to greet you, with tears in his eyes and a smile on his lips. Feel his arms around you in a great big hug. Smell the clean fragrance of his garments. Hear his words: "My child, I'm so glad you're here. I'm so glad you're safe. Come in! Come in!" When we are bothered by the ghosts of the past, resting in that kind of meditative experience for a time might help us to return to joy. We need to remember that, while it is true that we have done bad things in our life, those actions do not define who we are. We are defined by the way God sees us, and he looks on us with love and compassion.

So, the challenge God is sending for some of us today may be to experience the gospel story as the younger son did. Others of us may be challenged today to experience the story as the older brother. I don't know about you, but like the older brother, there are some people that I have trouble forgiving. Not so much those who have hurt me, but those who have hurt people that I love. Sometimes I wonder what's going to happen if I get to heaven and end up sitting next to one of those people. Will I be able first to say to myself, "Boy, I'm so glad I'm here!" And then be able to turn to that other person and say "and I'm really glad that you're here too!"

Or will I be like the older brother and refuse to go into the feast under those conditions? Will I stand on God's porch and say "Wait a minute God, is this my reward? I've been good my whole life … Well, most of it anyway … Well, I definitely remember one time when I did something that wasn't completely selfish! Well, anyway, I did that for you, and my reward is to sit next to that bum?" That's not going to be an argument that holds much water, is it?

The Church tries to lead the way for us in this regard. Notice that the Church keeps a list of saints. It has looked into those people's lives and what came after and the Church says "We are as confident as we can be that these people are in heaven." But the Church doesn't keep a parallel list of the damned —people that we feel sure are in hell. That is because the Church always holds out the hope that even in the worst of people, God's grace might be working in ways that no one else can see. This applies even to people like Hitler and Stalin and the other great butchers of the twentieth century. We cherish the hope that somehow each one might have had a death-bed conversion and allowed God's mercy to enter his or her life.

Listen to the word of the second Eucharistic prayer from the Mass: "Remember our brothers and sisters who have gone to their rest in the hope of rising again; bring them *and all the departed* into the light our your presence. *Have mercy on us all.*" Have mercy on us all. It is the Church's fondest wish, just as it is God's fondest wish, that all people might be saved; even the people that I don't get along with so well. For some of us the challenge of this Lent might be the challenge of the older brother —to embrace the possibility of God's forgiveness for people that we have trouble forgiving.

Well, if those two challenges are not enough for us, there is yet a third challenge implicit in today's gospel, and that is to see ourselves in the role of the father. St. Paul says as much in our epistle today. We are called to be ambassadors of reconciliation. God wants to plead through our voices for all his son's and daughters to return to him.

Think about that father. His son insulted him terribly by asking for his inheritance early. Essentially he was wishing that his father was dead. But still, after the son left, the father spent his nights wondering how the boy was doing and whether he was safe, and he spent his days gazing out the window and watching for his return. And then comes the fair morning when the father sees his son down at the end of the driveway and bang! he is out the front door like a flash, still in his bedroom slippers, with his robe flapping around his knees. The servants hear the noise and see the open front door and say to themselves in surprise "Where's he going?" and "I don't know, but quick, follow him!" and there they are, all running down the driveway like the Keystone Kops, just to greet that no-account son. How could the father do that? Doesn't he have any pride at all? The simple answer is no, he doesn't. Perfect love drives out pride.

Today the gospel might be challenging us to love like the father. To give up the pride which says "Well, I suppose I'll forgive you, if you kiss my feet." If we are to be ambassadors of forgiveness and reconciliation we are going to have to learn a bit more humility than that.

As we continue with our worship this morning, let us consider what special challenge today's gospel brings to us. And then let us resolve to take up that challenge during the remainder of our Lenten season. Can we really accept God's mercy in our lives? Can we accept the possibility of God's forgiveness for those who have hurt us? Can we let go of our foolish pride? If we can do any of those things, we will make our Lent into a story that is every bit as beautiful as the gospel we share today.

7th Sunday of Easter, May 20, 2007:

FRUITFUL TREES PLANTED BY THE RIVER OF LIFE

(Acts 7, 55–60; Rev 22, 12–14. 16–17. 20; J 17, 20–26)

This Easter season we have been taking one of our readings each Sunday from the book of Revelation. This is a difficult book in many ways, with all its symbolism and dark imagery. But recently, our Sunday selections have been taken from the final chapters of the book, which are more straightforward and easy to interpret.

These chapters portray the coming of the kingdom of God at the end of time. The major image that is used for the kingdom of God is the new and perfect city of Jerusalem. The original city of Jerusalem—the city where Jesus walked and the great temple of God was built—that city was gone by the time the book of Revelation was written. It was destroyed by the Romans in the year 70AD, to put down a rebellion by the Jewish people. Imagine the entire Holy City with every wall flattened, every roof caved in, and every inhabitant either dead, enslaved or a refugee. Imperial Rome wanted to make the fate of Jerusalem an example that no one would forget. What a dark hour that must have been for all who loved God.

So the book of Revelation makes a restored Jerusalem the centerpiece of its vision of the coming of God's kingdom, and the nostalgia and longing that people felt for the city that was lost was an important part of the dynamic of those visions. Our reading today, which includes the very last verses in the Bible, makes it clear that the author's intention in writing about these visions is to awaken in us a hunger and thirst for the return of Jesus and the coming of the king-dom of justice and light and life. As our reading today invites us "Let the one who thirsts come forward and the one who wants it, receive the gift of life-giving water."

These words recall the words of Jesus in the gospels where he makes a similar offer, and they also recall the symbolism used earlier in Revelation. In a part of the book that we did not hear this season, the new and more perfect city of Jerusalem is portrayed as having a river of life-giving water flowing down from God's throne. Now every ancient city needed some source of water in it so that the citizens could be assured of water in time of need, and the old Jerusalem was no different. It had a reliable spring and a great reservoir of water in caverns beneath the city. But the new Jerusalem of John's vision has so much water in it that it spills out in a great river for all to share. What a potent image of God's love that would be for those living in a dry Mediterranean climate! And that's not all, along the banks of this river grow fruit trees that bear fruit twelve times per year.

Now when the first readers of the book of Revelation heard about the river and trees they probably thought about olive trees and date palms. But when I think of abundant fruit trees, I remember a pear tree in the yard of one of our neighbors when I was growing up. It was a big old tree that bore those little seckel pears that are sort of small, but so very sweet. And every year when the fruit was ripe, our neighbor would invite my family to come and take all the pears we wanted. There seemed to be no end to them. We would go out very early in the morning and collect the pears that fell during the night. We had to go early before the yellow jackets really got moving and took over the field. I remember waiting and waiting each summer until those pears would ripen, so that we could go out and collect them again.

It is that sort of memory of waiting expectantly for a time of abundance that the book of Revelation is appealing to in order to try to awaken our hunger and thirst for the kingdom of God. In that sense, we in the modern world are at a bit of a disadvantage in reading this book. Our fruit mostly comes from the grocery store, not directly from trees, and the idea that we might visit the store and find the bins empty is almost impossible to imagine. We now have every imaginable kind of fruit available to us whenever we want it. There aren't even any yellow jackets! The situation is similar with water. Abundant clean water comes out of our faucets whenever we turn them on. The idea of being thirsty and not being able to immediately satisfy that thirst is foreign to us.

It would be hard to say that this physical abundance we have is a bad thing, but it can make it harder for us to really get to know our needs. If we are feeling the least bit needful, before we really have a chance to live with that need and get to know it and put a name to it, we are offered an endless list of things to buy to paper over that perceived gap in our lives. There is a whole industry that tries to make these things seem very enticing, and so it would be no surprise if we were to be seduced into buying some stylish new clothes or the latest gadget before we have the time to sort out whether that is what we really want or need. And if it is not quite the right thing, well that doesn't matter, because as soon as we realize that that wasn't what we wanted, something new will come along to fool us again, until we are so confused we don't know how to identify what we need anymore.

The book of Revelation invites us to consider how much of that unfocused and ill-met need we feel is really a desire to live in the kingdom of light and life. That surely is the desire that brings us all here this morning. It might be a good spiritual exercise for this last week of the Easter season to try to get in touch with that need, get to know it a little better and give it its proper name.

This would be especially appropriate now because our Church is about to celebrate three great feast days on the next three Sundays. The first of these is the feast of Pentecost, in which we celebrate the coming of the Holy Spirit to our Church and to our own lives. The Holy Spirit is our comforter, our advisor, the giver of gifts of courage and prudence, and all the rest. We rejoice in the Spirit's presence.

The following Sunday is the feast of the Holy Trinity, in which we celebrate the strong bond of love which unites Father, Son and Holy Spirit into the unbreakable unity of one God. Through Jesus, this love pours into our lives as well and brings us to unity, and that reveals God's glory, as our gospel emphasizes today.

Finally, we will have the feast of the Most Precious Body and Blood of Jesus, in which we celebrate the wonderful gift that Jesus left with us to assure us of his continuing presence among us. In this gift we receive our bread for the journey.

When I was young, living in Maryland, and friends would invite my family to a party or a cookout or something, it was common to hear them say "Now, make sure you come hungry, 'cause there's gonna be plenty to eat." I think that's the same message we should take away from our readings today. We will want to come hungry to these great celebrations of the Church, for if we know our true hunger, we will find that there is plenty there for us to feast on.

As we continue with our worship this morning, let us try to get in touch with our desire to live in God's kingdom and with all our deepest longing let us pray the short but very moving prayer from the concluding verses of the entire Bible: "Come, Lord Jesus!" And our hearts will respond "Amen, Come, Lord Jesus!"

11th Sunday in Ordinary Time, Jun. 17, 2007:
NURTURING RELATIONSHIPS

(2 Sam 12: 7-10. 13; Gal 2: 16. 19-21; Lk 7: 36-8:3)

We have a wonderful story in our gospel today, about a woman who found her way back to God through Jesus. It is a story that piques our curiosity. We want to know the "back story," as people in the news business might call it. What was her sin? What wonderful thing did Jesus do for her that turned her around and made her so grateful? The gospel, however, does not appear interested in any of that kind of detail. Rather than the back-story, the gospel is interested in what is happening to the woman right now.

We should notice the bottom line of the story as far as Jesus is concerned. He wants Simon to see how much love the woman now has for God. That really is the bottom line in life, for her and for all of us. God wants to be in a loving relationship with every one of us. How we get to that happy ending is much less important, than that we do get there.

Our reading about King David has a somewhat similar message for us. In this case, we do get to know the "back story." King David did some pretty nasty, self-serving things. But listen to what God says to him when he confronts him through the Prophet Nathan. He does not say "Why did you break the fifth commandment and the ninth commandment?" No, he asks "Why did you spurn me?" It is all very personal with God. Like a hurt lover, he is saying to David "I thought we had a relationship. What happened?"

Jesus wanted the host at the party he attended to think about what his relationship with God was like, and we should do the same. In order to get our thoughts moving, I would like to consider three signs of a loving relationship, and how they might apply to us and God.

The first sign of a loving relationship is *Time Spent Together*. The only way I know to build a loving relationship with another person is to spend time together. We do this with God in prayer. Now our Church has many different kinds of beautiful formal prayers, and I hope you take advantage of them frequently, but I'm not actually thinking of those kinds of prayers right now. I'm thinking about prayer as a kind of friendly conversation with God. For example, we might be on vacation and decide to take a walk on the beach. We can invite God to come along on that walk, just as we might invite another family member. "Come with me God, let's look at the sunset together."

Similarly, we might wake up late at night and remember that we have a doctor's appointment with a big medical test coming the next morning. We might say "God, I could really use a hug right now. I'm so scared about tomorrow. I don't know what they'll find. Please sit by my bed tonight and be with me."

Or we might be dressed up in our best clothes and walking into a job interview, and ask "Please God, hold my hand through this interview. If this is the right job for me, give me the words I need to show them that I can do this work."

By inviting God into all the important moments in our lives we allow him to know us better. This sort of invitation to God is a wonderful prayer habit to develop.

A second sign of a loving relationship is *Honest Communication*. Sometimes when someone in a family has a problem, say a problem with gambling, and the communication in the family is not good, the family will not acknowledge the problem. It can get to be like an elephant in the living room that everyone has to maneuver around, but no one will talk about. God does not want that kind of relationship with us. That is what makes the sacrament of reconciliation so important. Again, it is not about telling God the facts of what we did; he knows those well. It is about getting out into the open the thing that is in the way of our relationship with God. We want the problems out in the open where they can be discussed and dealt with honestly.

The third sign of a loving relationship for us to consider is *The Gift of Self*. This is Father's Day, and I am reminded of when I was young and my Dad had a workshop in the basement where he built things out of wood. I loved to be down there with him. He would give me the leftover pieces of wood so I could make projects of my own. That was hard. The hammer was heavy, and I can't tell you how many blades I broke on the coping saw, before I got the hang of that tool. My projects never turned out as good as his, but I liked nothing better than to be down there doing what Dad was doing.

It is the same with us and God. When we love him, we want to be like him. God is kind, and so when we are in a position of authority, we also want to be kind to those under our control. God is forgiving, and so we want to be forgiving of others. God creates beauty in the world, and so, in all the things we do, we want to create beauty too. We want to do more than just finish a job, we want the result of our work to be a thing of beauty for others—whether we are working in the kitchen, or the garden or at our desks.

Now none of those things are easy to do, and we probably won't always succeed at them, but the effort we make is our gift of self to God. It is a gift that cements our loving relationship.

God wants to have a relationship with us that is marked by time spent together, honest communication and the gift of self, but often we seem to be content with something much less. We say to God, "OK, God, just tell me what I need to do to stay out of trouble. Ten commandments, the corporal works of mercy, the spiritual works of mercy. Fine, I'll do all those things, and then you can go your way, and I can go my way and we'll all be happy."

That is not the kind of relationship God wants to have with us. That way of approaching life makes God into a circus master. He sets up the hoops and we jump through them just like trick ponies. But God doesn't want a trick pony. And it is silly to imagine that God would create the world in hopes of someday having 5 billion trick ponies all jumping through hoops at once.

Ah, but to create a world in which God could have 5 billion loving relationships, what would that be like? Each relationship unique, some as soft and tender as a mother's love for her newborn baby, others as tough and resilient as the love of a couple who have been together for fifty years. I can't quite imagine what that would be like, but I can imagine that that would be a world worth creating.

Now don't get me wrong, the ten commandments and the corporal and spiritual works of mercy are very important. But to be life-giving for us, they need to arise out of our loving relationship with God. They are important because they become the measure of our gift of self to him.

So as we continue our worship today, and share the great gift of God's self given for us, let us think about our relationship with God and see if we can't make it deeper and richer, by spending more time together, by sharing honest conversation with him, and by committing ourselves as a gift to him. That would be a Father's Day gift that our Father in heaven will cherish forever.

16th Sunday in Ordinary Time, Jul. 22, 2007:
DIFFERENT PATHS TO SAINTHOOD

(Gen 18, 1–10; Col 1, 24–28; Lk 10, 38–42)

Today's gospel gives us a very human look inside the life of Jesus. Our reading tells us a small part of the story of Martha and Mary, two sisters who were good friends of Jesus. Today, we see their first meeting with him, and maybe things did get off to a bit of a rocky start, but eventually they, along with their brother Lazarus, all became very good friends of Jesus.

From the evidence of today's reading, it seems that Mary and Martha were of very different temperaments. I think I understand that because I have two sisters, and they also have very different temperaments. My sisters shared a bedroom while we were growing up, and for awhile there was a masking tape line right down the middle of their room to mark off each one's territory. I don't know, but I get the feeling that maybe Mary and Martha might have liked to have done that while they were growing up too.

As we reflect on this reading, we might marvel at how these two very different women each found her own way to closeness with Jesus. Mary honored Jesus by sitting at his feet to listen to his word. Martha honored Jesus by inviting him into her home and seeing to his needs, just the way Abraham did with his holy guests. In this way, each one of these sisters found her own particular path to sainthood, her path to holiness.

This might lead us to reflect on the question What is my particular path to holiness? Now, if we haven't thought much about that before, we might wonder if we have such a path, but we can be sure that God has a set up a path to holiness that is just right for our personality, and all we have to do is to figure out what that path is.

For some people in our community, the path to holiness involves a lot of prayer. Daily Mass, frequent recitation of the rosary and Eucharistic adoration might be points along their path to greater holiness. We might think of these people as working toward a Mary-style holiness. And that is really good. Our community needs a lot of that kind of holiness.

There are others in our community for which these particular devotions don't play such an important part in their lives. Points along their path to holiness might include volunteering in the school, or taking communion to the hospital, or helping out with our food donations for the poor. We might say that these people are working toward more of a Martha-style holiness. And that too is very good. Our community also needs a lot of that style of holiness.

Of course, these two ways to holiness are not mutually exclusive (one can do a bit of both) nor do they cover the whole spectrum of possibilities. Singing in the choir, for example, is a path to holiness that is equal parts of prayer, and community action and healthy physical activity. I can imagine both Mary and Martha wanting to be a part of that ministry.

Or we might be called to something that is not part of the Church proper. For example, my mother's path to holiness was lined with zucchini bread. It seemed like whenever anything happened in our neighborhood, someone got sick, a relative died, or someone lost their job, whatever, sooner or later I would be called down to the kitchen and my Mom would say "Here, take this over to Mrs. Schweinburger and tell her we were sorry to hear about her brother." "Aw, Mom!" "Go!" I can't tell you how many times that little scene was acted out in our kitchen, but for my Mom giving a gift of baked goods was a spiritual exercise. Think of it as a prayer with sugar and spice on top.

With so many possibilities to choose from, we might feel a bit overwhelmed, but here are two questions we might use to help us decide if we are on the right track. The first is, is this activity making me feel closer to Jesus? Can we imagine Jesus walking with us on the path we have chosen? He wants *us* to be as close to him as Mary and Martha were. As we pursue holiness, we want to find activities that make us feel as if we are sitting at Jesus' feet, or perhaps that we are sharing our meal with him. That kind of feeling of intimacy with Jesus is a sign that we have found our path to holiness.

The second question we might ask is, is this activity a source of joy for me? Recently, as I'm sure you remember, our parish had its yearly opportunity to help with the Loaves and Fishes program, and take meals down to the cathedral in Trenton where hundreds of poor people can come to get a hearty meal on a weekend after the food stamps have run out. Well, I happened to stop by the school cafeteria on the day before the big day, and I found there six or eight of our fellow parishioners making piles and piles of peanut butter and jelly sandwiches to be handed out after that dinner as a take-home meal. The first thing I noticed when I got to the cafeteria was what sticky work they were doing, but the second and more important thing that I noticed was how much fun they were having doing it together. Most everyone had smiles on their faces, and the place had the feel of Christmas Eve as each sandwich was lovingly made. That kind of joy found in difficult work is a real gift of the Holy Spirit and a sign of being on the right track spiritually.

This does not mean, of course, that everything we try to do to grow spiritually will be a laugh riot. Like anything that is worth doing, our spiritual journey will sometimes be hard work. If we are trying to be more prayerful, we will find times when we have great difficulty concentrating on our prayers. And when we are trying to do some good deed, we will occasionally get frustrated when circumstances seem to be working against us. We should expect those sorts of frustrations every so often, but if we find we are never experiencing joy in what we are doing as a spiritual exercise, then maybe that is a sign that God is calling us onto some new path.

Martha may have been having one of those hard days in today's gospel. But there may also be another problem going on in this particular case. It seems that Martha was trying to force Mary to follow Martha's chosen path to holiness. That is something that really doesn't work. If we try, it will eventually rob the joy for both of us. Certainly, it is a great joy when can we share our path to holiness with someone that we love. And sometimes, we can expect to be blessed with good companions on our spiritual journey, but we cannot make that happen on our schedule; it is always God's gift. We can invite, and we can be welcoming, but we cannot force another person on our chosen path. And even in the spiritual domain, sometimes it is an act of love to put that little strip of masking tape down the middle of the room and carefully mark off yours from mine.

So, today Saint Mary and Saint Martha remind us that our Church is full of different kinds of people pursuing different paths to sainthood. As we continue with our celebration this morning, let us ask the Holy Spirit to guide us onto a path of greater holiness, and as we begin to plan for the fall, let us look for an activity that we can comfortably share with Jesus. And let us also work on training ourselves to recognize the joy in the journey which is the gift of the Holy Spirit.

20th Sunday in Ordinary Time, Aug. 19, 2007:

THE INTENSITY AND PASSION OF JESUS

(Jer 38, 4–6. 8–10; Heb 12, 1–4; Lk 12, 49–53)

If we tried to find adjectives to describe Jesus in most of Luke's gospel, we might choose words like "gentle", "welcoming" and "compassionate". But when we hear today's gospel the first words that might come to mind are "passionate", "unwavering" and "intense". Jesus as we see him today is a little unsettling. He is not a holy-card image; he is a flesh and blood person. This intensity of Jesus is an important part of who he was and is.

I would like to suggest three ways that we might be able to get more comfortable with the Jesus we find in today's gospel. The first of these is to appreciate this passage in its place in the larger gospel. We want to see how this passage functions as a part of the narrative presented to us by the gospel writer. Now, that is not always an easy thing to do when we only hear a little snippet of the gospel each Sunday, and especially when we hear important sections out of order on Holy Days. It really takes some time reading the gospel as a whole.

Here is just a bit of this context. Several chapters earlier in the gospel, right around the middle of it, Jesus decided that his hour had come, and the gospel tells us that at that point "he resolutely determined to journey to Jerusalem". This is a literary turning point for the gospel of Luke, and from then on, the closer we get to Jerusalem, the more the intensity of Jesus comes to the fore.

For example, one Sunday not too long ago we heard about a person who wanted to follow Jesus, but asked to first go and bury his father. Jesus said "Let the dead bury their dead; you go and proclaim the kingdom of God." Wow! That's pretty intense. It shows just how urgent the call of Jesus is. Honoring parents is important. It is part of the Ten Commandments after all, but at that moment, the call of Jesus was even more important. This theme of our urgent need to respond to the call of Jesus carries over into today's gospel.

Also, later in the gospel we will see Jesus sparring verbally with some of the authorities in Jerusalem. That undercurrent of conflict is also a part of the context for today's gospel. Of course, Jesus is intense. Of course, he is passionate. He sees a train wreck coming and he wants everyone to be as prepared for it as they can be.

A second way that we can come to grips with passages such as this one is to delve into the imagery Jesus uses as he speaks. For example, we hear Jesus today say that he has come to bring fire upon the earth. When we hear the word fire, the first thing we might think of is the uncontrolled fires raging this summer in Idaho and Utah and in many other places in the West. It seems that nightly we see images on TV of burned out homes and terrible destruction. Probably, this was not the sort of thing Jesus was thinking about. It is likely that he was drawing on the writings of the prophets, and making reference to fire as it is used in refining metals. Smelting was one the high-tech industries of the ancient world, in which crushed iron ore, say, was subjected to an extremely hot fire, hotter than any normal oven, in order to burn away all the impurities in the ore, and leave behind beautiful pure metal. This was a powerful image that the prophets sometimes used for what would happen at the coming of the Messiah.

So the fire that Jesus is talking about here has a good purpose. Its end is not destruction but purification. And although the process might be distressing for the bits of ore that suffer through it, if they are smart little bits of ore, they want to be pure so much, that they welcome the fire. The hotter the better.

We too want to get rid of the garbage in our lives and become purer. We want a life that is sturdy and beautiful and strong. We want no impurities left in us that might make our lives brittle and undependable. That longing animates today's reading.

Finally, a third way of approaching this passage is to consider it in the context of our own lives. Jesus talks today about his coming creating divisions within families and society. We know what that is like. There are so many serious issues over which our society is deeply divided today. One important one that has been much in the news this summer is immigration reform. What a slug-fest that turned into in the congress!

How does our faith inform the discussion of this difficult topic? Well, in 2003, the U.S. and Mexican Catholic bishops issued a joint pastoral letter entitled *Strangers No Longer: Together on the Journey of Hope*. In this letter, the Bishops proposed a number of principles for immigration reform, that they saw as following directly from our Catholic values. The letter is positive and hopeful in its outlook, but in it they did not try to come up with a wishy-washy compromise position that would paper over all the differences. No, they stood up very strongly for due-process protections for immigrants, and for a permanent residency program, and many other things that some people might describe a "pro-immigrant".

To say the least, these are not popular positions to take in many circles in this country. We should study the letter of the Bishops (which can be found on-line), and if we accept their teaching, we may well find ourselves at odds with many of our work colleagues and even some of our relatives.

It is this painful process in which our religious values begin to take hold in every corner of our lives, that Jesus is talking about at the end of today's gospel. The divisions within families are not something that he particularly wants to have happen. Jesus would be much happier if all people would be immediately persuaded by the wisdom of his words. But he knows that is not going to happen. Fallen human nature just doesn't work that way. We, however, cannot wait for everyone around us to see the wisdom of Jesus before we take up his call. The issues are too important and too urgent to allow us such leisure.

So, today we have a real encounter with the intensity and passion of Jesus. We should feel a bit unsettled by this encounter. To follow up on this experience, it might be a good idea to read and meditate on Jesus' journey to Jerusalem as found in Luke's gospel. We should make sure we have a Bible with good footnotes, so that we can get all of the imagery, and try to savor the different emotional flavors of the stories that are presented. Or even better, we might want to join up with our St. Paul's Bible study group which will be starting up again in September. As it happens, they will be working through Luke's gospel and they will be using the three techniques we explored today. They will study the literary context of each passage, the sources for its imagery, and its connection to our own lives. You are most cordially welcome to join the group.

But however we decide to act upon this aspect of our faith, as we continue with our worship this morning, let us make the most of this encounter with the passion and intensity of Jesus, and let some of that passion infuse our thinking on the important issues of our day.

24th Sunday in Ordinary Time, Sep. 16, 2007:

HIS MERCY ENDURES FOREVER

(Ex 32: 7-11. 13-14; 1 Tm 1: 12-17; Lk 15: 1-32)

Today we have one of those rare occasions when all three of our Sunday readings share the same theme. Normally, the middle reading, usually from a letter of St. Paul, moves along according to its own schedule. But today its theme is God's forgiveness, just like the other two readings, and it gives an interesting perspective to the discussion.

First, recall what we know about Saint Paul's life. During the early years after the death and resurrection of Jesus, he was a zealous defender of the Jewish faith and persecuted the followers of Jesus in every way he could. He was present at the stoning of St. Stephen, the first martyr of the Church, and even if he was too young at that point to be one of the ones actually throwing stones, he was a willing participant in that terrible deed.

Then, after a good number of years of this sort of persecution, while on the road to Damascus to arrest some Christians, Paul had an encounter with God that turned him around completely, and made him into a devout Christian and eventually made him a saint. What a miracle that was! And the question addressed by today's epistle is: Why did God bother? Why would God forgive someone who was doing so much harm to the Church? Why not just squash him like a bug and let the Church get on with its work?

Well, in today's epistle, St. Paul offers two reasons for this remarkable generosity on God's part, but I think that neither one of these reasons really gets to the heart of the matter. The first thing St. Paul says is that he used to be a blasphemer and a persecutor and an arrogant thug, but God forgave him for all that because he did it all out of ignorance. Well, let's think about that. Surely St. Paul does not mean to say that God would not have forgiven him if Paul had known what he was doing at the time. Remember what the Church teaches about mortal sin. There are three criteria for an action to be a mortal sin. First the moral issue has to be serious. Second, we have to understand that God forbids us to do the thing we want to do. And third, we have to give a free and complete consent of will to doing that very thing. It sounds like St. Paul is saying that what he did was not a mortal sin because of his ignorance, and therefore God was willing to forgive him. But we know that God forgives mortal sins all the time. That is one beautiful property of our sacrament of reconciliation. So, St. Paul's ignorance of what he was doing can't be the main reason that God forgave him for what he did.

A few verses later in the today's reading St. Paul says that he was the worst of all sinners, and God forgave him so that he would stand as an example of God's great patience and kindness. We are all supposed to think, "Well, what I have done in my life may be bad, but it is not as bad as what Paul did, so if God could forgive him, he will surely forgive me too." Paul hopes this example will increase our trust in God.

Now, that would be a very good result to come out of God's forgiving Paul, but it cannot be the main reason God did it. We are not to imagine God sitting around considering the matter saying, "Well, I want to make a good example of my forgiveness, and I could forgive that bum the High Priest Caiaphas, or I could forgive that other bum, Paul of Tarsus. I don't want to forgive both, so which one would be a better example for the people?" The idea is silly. God does not use his mercy as a marketing ploy; his mind is not so convoluted as all that. His mercy is mercy pure and simple.

No, the real reason that God forgave Paul was neither of these two. It is something altogether simpler and much more profound. God forgave Paul because he loved him. That's all. He loved him with a love so strong that it burned.

In this way God is like the shepherd that Jesus describes in our gospel today. The shepherd had one hundred sheep, and one got lost. But it was that one lost sheep that occupied the mind of the shepherd. He worried about him out there in the wilderness getting his coat all full of burrs stumbling around in the darkness. He worried that the stupid little guy would fall off a ledge, or maybe he would bleat so loud that the wolves would find him. The shepherd could not rest knowing that the lost sheep was out there all alone, and so he went to find him. Economically, that was a silly thing to do. It would have made much more sense to cut his losses, rather than to risk 99 to save one. But love has its own calculus, and that is the point of the story. The shepherd could not live with himself if he did not go and try to rescue the lost sheep. So it was with God and St. Paul. God wanted him back so much that he went out there and tried to get him back.

The really important thing for us to get out of today's reading is that God has that sort of intense love for each of us, the same kind of love he had for St. Paul. He wants us to be with him, in just the same way. So, if there is something that we have done that is getting in the way and keeping us away from God, we can be sure God will be continually searching us out and giving us every opportunity to be reunited with him.

I suppose that, sometimes, these opportunities for reunion with God might come in visions, as they did with St. Paul on the road to Damascus, but more likely, I think, they are mediated by another individual, as when Moses came down the mountain and confronted the people about what they were doing with the golden calf. Or it might be some circumstance in our life that suddenly makes us wake up and see our life in a new and more honest way. But however they come about, they represent a wonderful moment in which God is reaching out to us, and hoping we will respond by rushing into his arms. As a meditation this week, we might want to look back over our lives for events like that, where we had a real turn-around in our life and give thanks to God for the way he pursued us when we wanted nothing to do with him.

This meditation might take on an even more pointed focus, since today is Catechetical Sunday and it would be especially appropriate for us to consider the many times God has reached out to us in the person of a teacher of our faith. I remember a high school teacher I had, named Brother Paul, oddly enough. He was a substitute teacher, who was only with our class for a few weeks. I don't really remember anything in particular that he taught. But I do remember being deeply impressed by the great joy he took in his faith. More than anything else he helped me understand why one might want to be a follower of Jesus.

Our community is blessed with many people who share their faith every week with the children of our parish. This is a wonderful ministry and so important for the spiritual health of our community. We are deeply indebted to all of them. Probably, if we were like most kids, we never quite gave our own teachers the thanks they deserved. As we continue with our celebration this morning, let us thank them now in prayer, and maybe if we see one of the teachers of our parish after Mass today, we can give them a big "Thank You" for all the time and effort they are putting into their work this year.

33rd Sunday in Ordinary Time, Nov. 18, 2007:

GOD WITH US IN GOOD TIMES AND BAD

(Mal 3: 19-20; 2 Thes 3: 7-22; Lk 21: 5-19)

The Church is very wise in the way it tunes its theological reflections to the rhythms of the natural world. We are coming to the end of harvest time, and for farm workers, that means the end of a summer of hard labor. And matching that, we have the Church's meditation on the return of Jesus in glory and the ingathering of God's people into the harvest home of heaven. That is a very comforting theme to enrich our Thanksgiving celebration.

But there is more to the season than that. This is also the time when the weather turns colder and we lose the leaves from off the trees, and in this season of shorter days and longer nights, the Church also meditates on the much less comfortable idea that there are difficult times ahead for us before the fullness of God's kingdom appears. Our gospel today explores this second theme. It presents a sobering list of possibilities: insurrections and plagues, earthquakes, betrayals by loved ones, and kangaroo courts—almost as scary as the things we can read about in today's paper! But here too, the Gospel message is one of hope and trust. If we trust God and persevere, we will be saved.

Today we celebrate this promise of God's abiding love. The calamities listed in our gospel are not presented to make us feel frightened about the future. Rather, they are presented to us so that we can make sure that our confidence about the future is centered in the right place: in God, and not in our human institutions or even in our own resources. Any of those earthly things might fail tomorrow, but God's love will not fail.

The life of our patron saint, Saint Paul, is a good example of how this works out in practice for a person of faith. We know that Saint Paul dared many dangers to spread the good news of Jesus. And he survived much: he was robbed. He was flogged in public. He was imprisoned, attacked by mobs and shipwrecked. That's more exciting stuff than I hope ever happens to me! But in his letter to the Philippians, Saint Paul summarizes his experiences by saying that he had lived through good times and bad, and he had learned the secret of being at peace no matter what came his way. You know what his secret was? He held onto this one idea: "I have strength for everything, through him who strengthens me." And what a wonderful thought it is for us to cling to in our own times of trial: "I have strength for everything, through him who strengthens me."

Notice that God's promise of protection did not mean that Saint Paul could avoid all the difficult moments in his life, and God does not promise us that we will never face painful times in our lives. But he does promise to be there with us in our pain and give us his strength and assistance to get through it all.

Studying the lives of the saints and their writings is one good way for us to come to a fuller assurance that God will be with us in all our trials. But that sort of an understanding is up here in our heads, and in order to really trust in God's promise, we also need to believe it down here in our hearts. And to gain that sort of trust, we are going to have to look a little closer to home. We might begin by looking back at our own lives at some of the hard times we have faced, and see if we can't begin to see the hand of God working in those situations. Maybe God sent us just the right person when we really needed help, or he might have given us a little push in the direction we needed to go, or sent us a song or image that brought us comfort in sorrow. Recalling that sort of experience in our own lives or seeing it in the life of a loved one, is the best assurance we will ever find that God will be there in our need.

Some time ago, when my new family was living in the rural part of Northeastern Connecticut, my wife and I and our new-born baby were driving home late one evening, and as we were going down a lonely country road, the muffler fell off our car. Well, it sort of fell off—what it really did was part way fall off and drag along the road making an awful racket, especially added to the noise of the unmuffled engine.

We had to stop, and I got out to see what could be done while Jane comforted our startled baby. The night was as dark as a cave, and the flashlight from the glove compartment was completely dead. I could see one little light in the distance showing someone's house, but from that direction also came the loud barking of fierce-sounding dogs. Just to complete the image, I will remind the younger folks here that this was way before the days of cell-phones, so we were really stuck.

As I stood there unable to imagine what to do next, I saw a light approaching from the direction of the house, and soon a man appeared behind it. He was huge—about six-foot-five and 300 pounds, and he said "I wondered if you might be needing this.", holding up a hacksaw. Well, working together, we cut through the tailpipe of the muffler and soon my little family could make its way back home. That was twenty-five years ago, but to this day whenever I try to imagine an angel, I see a guy who is six-foot-five and weighs 300 pounds, and is carrying a hacksaw. (Swing low, sweet chariot!)

Well, we can look for signs of God's care in extraordinary circumstances such as these, and we can also look for him in more ordinary parts of our daily life. Surely Saint Paul did not begin his life of trust in God with some grand adventure! He began as we all do with little acts of trust, that grew as time went on. We can have a similar experience by challenging ourselves in doing good works. I am thinking here of good works which draw us out of our comfort zone a little bit. I don't know what that might be for you, but it could be taking communion to the sick in the hospital, or sharing faith with the children of our religious education program. Or perhaps it might mean volunteering down at Martin house in Trenton, or bringing a faith-based perspective to the public discussion of some important topic like fair housing or immigration reform.

The thing about trying to do some good work like that in a situation in which we feel awkward and out of place is that we cannot count on our own abilities to get us through it. We need to rely on God. No matter how many times I try to do this, I find that I am usually reluctant to go, while on the way in, and then on the way out, I'm usually glad I went. Over time, if we are observant, we will begin to see the hand of God helping us along in this sort of situation and we will become more confident that God is really there with us and bringing out of that particular situation whatever good he means to have happen through our presence.

We should try to keep a balance between the twin themes of this season: the looking forward with joy to the fullness of God's kingdom, and the acknowledgment of our need to trust God and persevere until that time. Let us now bring our hopes and fears for the future to the table of the Lord, where we will be nourished with the ultimate sign of God's loving care for us. Let us give thanks this week for all our blessings, including the times when God sent us angels bearing hacksaws, and finally let us challenge ourselves, asking: "How am I willing to dare myself for God this week?" So that we may know more fully the truth of the words of Saint Paul, that "I have strength for everything, through him who strengthens me".

4th Sunday in Advent, Dec. 23, 2007:

I SEE YOU, I ACCEPT YOU
AND I LOVE YOU

(Is 7: 20-14; Rom 1: 1-7; Mt 1: 18-24)

The story we hear in our gospel today is one that is so familiar that we may miss the outrageous claim that it contains: that the little baby son of two working-class parents living in a small Mediterranean country two thousand years ago is the true fulfillment of Isaiah's prayer and prophesy, which we hear today. Jesus really is "God with us".

Even if we accept in faith the whole story we just heard with its dreams and angels and everything, how do we get our heads around the claim that God could come among us as a little baby? Think about that for a moment. God is all-powerful, but a little baby is almost powerless. God is all-knowing, but a little baby lacks even the most basic understanding of the way the world works. How could Jesus have had both of those natures at the same time? How can those two ways of being be compatible?

We call this tenet of our faith a mystery. But we have to be careful how we understand that term. A mystery of our faith is not a puzzle that we try to solve, and then after we solve it, the whole thing seems ordinary and unsurprising to us. Rather, a mystery in the Catholic faith is a wondrous fact that we contemplate and explore and celebrate, never expecting to get to the bottom of it. Unlike a puzzle, a mystery becomes more wondrous and precious the more we study it.

On this gray and rather soggy day, let's explore the mystery of the incarnation together in pre-Christmas joy. I mentioned earlier some differences between the eternal God and a human baby, but there is also one very important respect in which a baby can be an excellent image of the eternal God, and that is in its capacity to love unconditionally.

One time, soon after our first daughter was born, I awoke in the middle of the night hearing her crying in her crib. She could not have been more than a week old at that point, and when I looked up at the alarm clock I could see that it was still about an hour before her next scheduled feeding. So, to let my exhausted wife sleep just a little bit longer, I got up quietly and carried the baby around our dimly-lit apartment, singing to her, and trying to calm her down.

Well, after a while, she got very quiet, and I continued to wander through the apartment groggily, assuming that she had fallen back to sleep. When I finally looked down at her, I saw that her eyes were open, and with a face as calm and serene as the Buddha's, she was staring up at me. This was quite a shock, because up to that point she had never really opened her eyes for more than a few seconds. I was immediately struck by a couple of things. The first was the recognition that I was holding a tiny person in my arms, not a hungry little diaper machine, and the second strong impression I had was of the love in her eyes. Her expression told me clearly that there was nowhere else she would rather be right then, and nothing she would rather be doing than simply looking at me. And instantly, I felt exactly the same way.

When our second daughter was born, I was a little more prepared for this wonderful experience, but it was just as thrilling when it happened again. It was different, as the girls themselves are different, but still there was that look of heavenly peace and an open loving expression. With her look, she seemed to be saying "I see you, I accept you, and I love you."

Contemplating an experience like that, it might not be so hard to believe that Jesus could bring a deep love and peace into the world as an infant, and that, even as an infant, he could be the perfect image of the invisible God.

But, of course, it didn't stop there for Jesus. As the gospels tell us, seeing people in this special way was a thing that Jesus did throughout his life. He saw people that others could not or would not see: a blind beggar by the roadside, a crippled old woman in the synagogue, or a poor widow in the temple. Always, his reaction to them said "I see you, I accept you, and I love you." Even during his crucifixion, he saw the good thief and promised him that they would be together in paradise, and he saw his mother and St. John at the foot of the cross and gave each of them into the other's care. That was Jesus all over. St. John tells us "God is love." He may *have* power and knowledge and glory, but he *is* love. Jesus showed us how this works through his life, from beginning to end.

Now, we are not as innocent as little babies any more, and love is a much more complicated experience for us. But this Christmas, I hope that you can find some time to be with each of the people that you love. If you can, try to find a quiet moment to linger in eye contact and in whatever way you do such things in your family, make sure they get the message "I see you, I accept you and I love you." That is the real gift of Christmas, and if you give that gift, it really doesn't matter how many presents are piled up under the Christmas tree, or even that you have one at all.

Now that may sound easy. It does mean that there is no need to fight the last minute shoppers and dig through picked-over merchandise to find one more gift which has so far eluded us. But on the other hand, we also know that it is not always easy to communicate our love effectively and when we do, it is far from being a cheap gift. When it is done right, it is worth your life to love that way.

For the kind of love we are talking about here is not without pain. For example, when our loved ones hurt, we hurt. It is a terrible feeling to have a loved one in pain, and not being able to do anything about it. Also, separation hurts. Maybe the kids grow up and move out. We want them to soar like eagles, but it still hurts to let them go. And it also hurts when we have to let go of our loved ones at the end of their lives.

Perhaps you are in the midst of one of these painful loving experiences this Christmas. Be assured that God knows that pain well, for that too is part of the incarnation. Maybe you feel that there is nobody around to gift you with acceptance and love. But there is hope even for those of us in such difficult straits. For Jesus wants to be "God with us" this Christmas too. We can receive the gift of Jesus in prayer and meditation. Sometimes a holy card or other image can help make this experience feel more real. I have a reproduction of a painting of Jesus at home that I have grown very fond of. It is an image of the Sacred Heart. And I suppose it isn't a very good likeness of Jesus. Certainly He doesn't look very much like a Mediterranean carpenter in this painting. In fact, he looks sort of Polish, which is where the painting comes from. But when you get to the eyes, I am confident that the artist got the image exactly just right. Jesus looks out of that painting and says "I see you, I accept you and I love you."

Jesus wants to come to each of us today, just as surely as he came to the people of Galilee. He will come to us even when we are blinded by our pride, or crippled by our past or spiritually impoverished by our material wealth. He comes to be with us, to heal us and to save us. This is our Christmas joy.

During the Christmas season, we are invited more deeply into the wondrous mystery of the incarnation. At this altar, beneath this crucifix, we are all invited to share the great gift of God's love. Come to the table and receive the gift prepared for you from ages long ago —a gift that says "I see you, I accept you, and I love you."

Mary, the Mother of God, Jan. 1, 2008:

OUR INHERITANCE FROM GOD

(Num 6: 22-27; Gal 4: 4-7; Lk 2: 16-21)

We are now celebrating the third of four feast days which commemorate the birth of our Lord. We began with the feast of the Nativity. Then, Sunday, we celebrated the feast of the Holy Family. Today we celebrate the feast of Mary the Mother of God, and then finally, on the coming Sunday, we will celebrate the feast of the Epiphany, when Jesus was revealed in a special way to the wise men and also to all of us. Having four feasts in twelve days fills up the Christmas season with joy. Each of them gives us a slightly different view of the wonderful mystery in which God came to live among us as a little baby.

It is a wonderful thing to remember that God chose to come among us a little child surrounded by the love of a working-class family, and not as a king surrounded by rich and powerful people, or as a general surrounded by his army. And the great love of the Holy Family gives us a good example for how we are to live our own lives in our families. We should try to trust God as they did, and follow in his ways. For example, in today's gospel reading we hear that Mary remembered all the good things that happened to her family and saved all those things in her heart. This reminds us that the stories of our families are also important. We should treasure them and share them. It is especially important for the grandchildren in the family to know the stories of their grandparents. They should know as much as possible about how they lived and the problems they faced and overcame. Then they will know how good is the stock that they come from, and will be proud of their background, and confident when they face difficulties in their lives.

However, these feast days that we celebrate are more than a source of good examples for us. Saint Paul tells us today that there is much more here to celebrate. He reminds us today that we are the adopted children of God. That makes us, in one sense, also members of the Holy Family. When I think about this, my first response is that "I'm not worthy." And perhaps you may feel the same way. It is true that we are not really worthy of this great gift. Nobody ever could be, but because of God's great love for us, we have nevertheless been invited by God into this special relationship with him. We are called by him to be his children, and this is a part of our Christmas joy. It is a good Christmas meditation to think about Jesus as our brother and Mary the mother of God as our mother. When we are far from our natural mother, or after she goes to be with God, we still have a mother near to us to talk to in prayer and who will be able to comfort us in all of our daily problems.

And there is even more joy to be found in the reading from Saint Paul. He tells us that because we are God's children we will receive an inheritance from him. That is a another marvelous idea to consider; everything that God values will someday come to us.

Recently, I was looking through a box of my things at home, and I found a coin that my grandfather gave to me when I was a little boy. It was a silver dollar from the year 1923. It is a large coin, and I can still remember how heavy it felt in my small hand when he first gave it to me. I could tell that this was "real" money. It felt very different from the small coins that I used to take to the store to buy milk or bread for my family. My mother told me to keep the coin safe and treasure it, and I am glad that I did, because when I hold that coin now, I am filled with memories of my grandfather, and feel much closer to him.

The inheritance that we have from God our father in heaven is something like that. It is much more weighty and precious than the ordinary things of everyday life. The promise of an inheritance from God applies first and foremost to our life with him in heaven after we die. That is very important, but I think that this promised inheritance is not just about some time far in the future, it is also about what we have from God today.

There are many different ways that this inheritance can be a part of our life today. I will describe three of these ways. I mentioned earlier that Mary saved the stories of the Holy Family in her heart. Well, the family of God has been preserving its stories for many generations, and we have them today recorded for us in the Bible. This collection of stories is our precious remembrance of all that God has done for us. We should get our Bibles out often, and read these stories for our comfort. When we do, we will feel closer to God in the same way I feel close to my grandfather when I hold that coin that he gave me so long ago.

A second part of the inheritance that we have from God is the twelve fruits of the Holy Spirit, which we receive in the Sacrament of Baptism and even more fully in the Sacrament of Confirmation. When we truly live a spirit-centered life, these will be the fruits that sweeten our lives. The first three of these fruits are: love, joy and peace. Then come patience, kindness and generosity. Then faithfulness, gentleness and self-control. Finally, we have modesty, moderation and chastity. Each one of these wonderful fruits is like a little bit of heaven that we can experience right here and now. They make our lives better, no matter what our physical circumstances may be. Just take one of these, gentleness. Life can really be rough sometimes, but think about how good it is when someone we love treats us with gentleness. Isn't that a little touch of heaven? And when we choose to treat other people that we meet with gentleness, we are that much closer to the gentle little baby that we see lying there in the manger.

A third part of our inheritance from God is the sacraments which we experience in the community of faith. In the sacrament of the Eucharist, God gives us bread for our journey. We receive the strength we need to face the new week. In the sacrament of confession, we are helped to overcome the things in our lives that are separating us from God and making it difficult for us to experience the love, peace and joy that God wants us to have. We experience these sacraments within a community of other people who are also striving to live spirit-centered lives, and that too give us strength. When we become friends with these good people and learn the story of their faith journey, it helps us to keep going.

So, as we continue with our worship this evening, let us remember with joy that we are God's children, and that we have a rich inheritance that can make our lives better right here and now. Let us resolve to live a spirit-centered life so that we may more fully enjoy all the fruits of the Holy Spirit, including peace, love and joy.

May you have a healthy, prosperous and happy New Year that is full of God's many blessings!

THE GATE TO HEAVEN STANDS OPEN

(Ezek 18: 21-28; Mt 5: 20-26)

I don't know if it is something that we are born with, or something that develops in early childhood, but it seems that just about everybody is walking around with a strong sense of what is "fair" and what is not. They may not always live up to it, but they know what it demands.

I remember one particular situation when my younger daughter was about four years old. She had discovered that we were going to allow her older sister to do something that she was not allowed to do. She stormed into the room with all the gravitas of a disappointed four-year-old and told us in no uncertain terms "That's not fair!" No prophet in Israel ever spoke with more conviction that he was standing on the moral high ground. And the attack worked for our daughter too. My wife and I felt compelled to defend ourselves against the charge of being unfair. That sense of fairness is a very good thing. It is a little spark of the divine, a little breath of the Holy Spirit, that enriches our lives.

But I think what Ezekiel is trying to tell us in today's reading is that innate sense of fairness that we are born with still needs to be educated. Just as in my little daughter's case, our sense of fairness needs to grow as we grow. And as it does grow, we hope that it will be leavened with love and understanding and come to approximate God's sense of what is fair, as Ezekiel describes it today.

There are a number of ways in which the fairness of God exceeds ours. The one I want to focus on tonight is that our sense of fairness is often very much focused in the past, while God's is focused on the present. We do tend to get hung up on the past, don't we? We mull over what he did and what she did. William Faulkner expressed our human attitude very well in a letter to a friend. He said "The *past* is never dead. It's not even *past*." Think about that "The *past* is never dead. It's not even *past*." Boy, what a prison that is.

When we drag all that past along into the present, it can get to be a problem, because the past is unchangeable. What ever we did, be it good or bad, we cannot go back and fix it. So if we keep beating each other up about what happened in the past, there is no way out of the situation. No way anything can ever get better, and truly, that is not fair.

God, however, is much more focused on today. He wants to know what are we feeling, what are you doing today? We can bring our past, all of it to the sacrament of reconciliation, acknowledge what we have done and then Let It Go! What freedom there is in that gift from God!

That is the good news of Lent. It is not too late. One of our stained glass windows (the one way in the back on Mary's side) has an image of Jesus preaching, and up at the top of the window there is a representation of the door of heaven. And the door is open. It is thrown wide by Jesus' preaching. Isn't that wonderful? The door to heaven is open. This Lent it is open for all of us, no matter what we did in the past.

Imagine a virtue that we admire in other people: maybe courage or humility or cheerfulness or honesty. This Lent we can pray about that virtue, we can train our eyes and our ears to be sensitive to it in other people. We can study the life of a saint known for that virtue. We can begin to practice it ourselves little by little. And pretty soon, maybe even by the time Easter comes we could be living a life that is full of that virtue. Wouldn't that be a wonderful way to greet the Risen Lord on Easter?

The Good News of Lent is that it is not to late for us. No matter what we have been through, no matter what we have done, it is not too late.

THE VIEW FROM THE MOUNTAINTOP

(Gen 12: 1-4; 2 Tim 1: 8-10; Mt 17: 1-9)

In today's gospel, Peter, James and John were given an opportunity for a deeper insight into just who Jesus was. They had been with him for a while, walking the roads of Galilee and it was easy to see that he was a powerful preacher and a really holy man, but now they saw much deeper into the matter. First, they saw that he was a partner to Moses and Elijah, two of the guiding lights of their faith, and then they learned that he was the very Son of God. This must have come as a welcome reassurance for people who had left everything behind in order to follow him.

It is worth noting too, that as wonderful as that experience must have been, the Apostles could not just stay up there on that mountain top. They had to come back down and get on with their lives. And as the gospels show us, even after this singular event, the Apostles were often as confused as the rest of us about what was going on around them.

As I try to understand what that whole experience might have been like for the Apostles, I think about the times when I was a kid and I used to do some hiking in the Appalachian mountains in western Maryland. Although these mountains seem quite big when you are trying to climb one of them, they aren't really very big as mountains go, and most of them are tree-covered right to the top. So as you hike up the trail it is easy to lose track of just where you are and how high you have climbed. But then, every once in a while, the trail will run close to the edge of a cliff, and the trees clear away and then you can see for miles. Maybe you can see back to the parking lot where you started the hike, or off in the distance to the town where you hope to have lunch. That sort of thing can be a marvelous moment on a long hike, a time to rest and reflect and enjoy the view. But eventually, of course, one has to take one last look and then get on down the trail.

I think of the story of the transfiguration as that kind of experience in the journey of faith of the Apostles. They could see back to the founding days of their faith and forward to the glory of the resurrection, but not all the steps in between. Meditating on their experience can bring us some comfort as we contemplate our own faith journeys. We too have our "mountain top" moments when we are granted some insight into our faith, and then there are a lot of other times when we have doubts and questions and have to muddle along as best we can.

As we continue on our Lenten journey, it is helpful to remind ourselves of these moments of insight, and so I would like to share with you three aspects of our faith that are particularly relevant to the season of Lent, in which some people, including myself, sometimes have trouble seeing the deeper insights that our faith provides.

The first concerns the crucifixion. It is very easy to see the violence and cruelty of that event. It also seems like something that Jesus could have easily avoided, if only he would have toned it down a bit and not been quite so in-your-face with the authorities. He could have swung a deal, but he didn't do that. Jesus did not step out of the way of trouble, but rather chose to be true to the person that he was. Our faith sees this willingness of Jesus as a critical part of this event, and acknowledging that, we can see this terrible tragedy as a great act of love. It was not a cutting-short of Jesus' life, but rather its apex and its culmination. It is a gift of love from Jesus to his Father in heaven, and to all of us.

It is this deeper insight into what was really going on in the crucifixion that allows us to venerate the crucifix and hold it as the sign and symbol of our faith. It also encourages us to celebrate the stations of the cross, as we do here on Fridays during Lent. We are not glorifying pain, we are returning love for love.

The second item I would like to consider is our celebration of the Mass. It is easy to see this as a beautiful social gathering. We come together from our different lives, and share an hour of prayer together. We bring all our concerns to that prayer and support each other in our daily struggles. That's a very good thing, but it barely scratches the surface of what is really going on here, and our faith gives us a deeper insight. In the first letter to the Corinthians, Saint Paul describes the bread and wine of the sacrifice as our participation in the body and blood of Christ. Our faith tells us that this is not just a metaphor, but a solid fact. It may be hard for us to see sometimes, but how it deepens our experience of what we are doing when we finally get it! Our unity with Christ in the Eucharist fosters our unity with each other, different as we may be.

The third item that I would like to talk about today is perhaps the hardest of all to see, maybe because it is the closest to us. It concerns this gathering here. Us. It is easy to see our surface, with all its flaws. "Oh that deacon! He is so full of himself!" Or "Oh those parents! Why can't they control their kids during Mass?" Or "Oh, those teenagers! Can't they find something a little more suitable to wear to Church?" We all have our faults and foibles, but here too our faith gives us a deeper insight. It calls us "children of God", "members of the body of Christ". It calls us "saints", or "holy ones."

I grant that this may be a little hard to see sometimes, but I have learned a few of the stories of the people of our parish, and I've seen more than enough to be sure that each one of us is the hero of a story of faith. Maybe not an untarnished hero, or an undefeated one, but a hero nonetheless. And some among us are great heroes indeed. I am sure that there are some people here today who have struggled mightily with demons and have the scars to prove it. There are others here who have been forced by life's circumstance to carry heavy burdens —heavier than one person can possibly manage, but somehow they have struggled along, sometimes for years on end. Those are true heroes; they have followed Saint Paul's injunction to "bear your share of hardship for the gospel". And if we could see them now as they will be revealed on the Day of Glory, we would be overwhelmed. We would tell our grandchildren that we used to share Eucharist with them here every weekend. It would be our pride and joy if we could say that we had once done a favor for one of them.

But we should also note that all of us here have made at least a beginning of our own heroic story, and although we may have not accomplished quite so much, even to have begun such an adventure is no small thing. We are like Abram in our reading from Genesis. We have taken the first steps in a journey of faith, in response to God's call. I am sure that's true, because it is God's call that has brought us together here today. Having thus begun, we can be sure that God will lend us his strength when we bear our own hardships for the gospel. The example of the great saints among us give us that confidence.

As we continue with our worship today, let us thank God for those precious moments of insight he has given us in the past and treasure them in our hearts. Let us ask God to continue to be with us in those times of insight and in all of those other times in between, when we feel like we are just muddling through. May God lend us his strength and help us to make of our lives a beautiful story of love and fidelity —a story with a really happy ending.

5th Sunday of Easter, Apr. 20, 2008:
THE INTERIOR CASTLE

(Acts 6: 1-7; 1 Pt 2: 4-9; Jn 14: 1-12)

During the Easter season, the Church often takes its Sunday readings from John's gospel, which is particularly rich in its theological reflections. Today's gospel is a good example of this. It abounds in so many interesting ideas, that I would like to focus our attention a little bit by considering one particular question that the gospel raises: What exactly does it mean when Jesus says that *he* is the way to the Father? How can a *person* be a *way*?

The gospel itself gives us several ideas to get us started in thinking about this. The first comes when Jesus tells Philip that to know Jesus is to know the Father. Because they are so intimately related, as we come to know Jesus better, we automatically come to know God the Father better. That is clear enough, and it certainly is true, but we need to be careful about how the word "know" is being used in this verse. Knowing in this sense means something more than just knowing facts about Jesus. The sort of knowing we are talking about here really means being in a relationship with him. We want to know Jesus the way we know our best friends. That may sound very appealing to us, but it is also much harder for us to achieve that kind of knowledge of Jesus, than it was for the apostles who ate and drank with him.

It is harder for us because the sort of knowing we mean here really requires communication. Personally, I am a quiet sort of person, but one thing I have definitely learned in my 32 years of marriage, is that if you want to be in a committed relationship with someone, you need to talk with that person. A Lot. More than you might imagine if you're a quiet guy like me. You need to listen carefully to what your loved one is saying to you and you need to be willing to share your own thoughts and feelings. Well, the same thing is true with us and Jesus, and with Jesus, we do this sort of sharing in prayer.

How best to go about this sort of prayerful communication is something that the Church has meditated on for a long time. For example, Saint Theresa of Avila wrote a whole dissertation on prayer that is based mostly on today's gospel. Recall that Saint Theresa was a Carmelite nun, which is a contemplative order, so she did a lot of praying. Near the end of her life, around 1570 or so, she wrote a book titled "The Interior Castle" to teach the sisters of her order how to pray better. The castle of the title is the soul of the believer. She imagined that the soul of the believer is like a beautiful castle in which God dwells and in this castle are many different dwelling places, just as our gospel today tells us. In our different moods and stages of growth we visit different rooms of the castle.

For Theresa, the soul is a rich landscape to be explored. Here's one of the things she says "The things of the soul must always be considered as plentiful, spacious and large; to do so is not an exaggeration. The soul is capable of more than we can imagine." Prayer sounds sort of exciting, the way she describes it. How wonderful it would be to explore the inner castle of our soul in prayer and get to know both ourselves and God better!

So, prayer *can* be something elaborate and even mystical, as Saint Theresa describes it, or it can be something very much simpler and down-to-earth. A very good place to begin is with the "Our Father." That is a prayer that most of us know, and it is a very good spiritual exercise to say that prayer slowly and thoughtfully each day. Sometimes, because we know it so well, we might be tempted to just rush through it, but it is a much better prayer if we savor each word and phrase. We might find five minutes of quiet, maybe just after we get up, or just before bed, or when we take a break from our daily chores with a nice hot cup of coffee. We could invite Jesus into that quiet moment and say the prayer that he gave us as a gift.

Notice that we often call this prayer "the Lord's Prayer". That is more than just a name. It really is *his* prayer, because it reflects his life so very well. In fact, Pope Benedict, in his recent book on the life of Jesus, reminds us that this prayer "aims to form our being, to train us in the inner attitude of Jesus." Wouldn't it be great to always say the Lord's Prayer with the goal of aligning our lives with the life of Jesus!

Our consideration of how praying the Lord's Prayer might change us to be more like Jesus brings us to a second sense in which Jesus can be our way to the Father. He is our example of what it means to be a child of God. The last verses of today's gospel also reflect this understanding, when Jesus says that his followers will do the same sort of works that he did, and then Jesus adds the really amazing prediction that his followers will even do greater works than he himself did.

Isn't that an exciting thought: if we are faithful followers of Jesus, we might be able to do even more wonderful works than Jesus did! But then, what do you think the greatest works of Jesus were? The first thing I think about when I hear those words is the miracles he performed. Those were certainly very important and I suppose we might feel very important if we could do that sort of powerful deed, but I wonder if Jesus really thought of those as the most wonderful thing that he did in his life. Recall that often we hear Jesus saying to the person he just healed "go on your way, your faith has saved you." It seems from this that Jesus saw himself as more of a catalyst for miracles, but that the hard work of the miracle happened inside the people being healed, because of their faith.

Surely the *most* wonderful thing that Jesus did in his life was his crucifixion, death and resurrection. In particular, the way he accepted his suffering, transformed a senseless act of violence into a wonderful act of love for all of us. That would be a deed worth imitating if we could!

I was talking to an older woman a while ago, and eventually we got around to talking about the problems of growing old. She suffered from Parkinson's disease, which as you may know is a slow degenerative disease of the nervous system without any known cure. Finally, she said to me. "Well, you know, when you think about it, Jesus got off pretty easy. Yes, he had to carry his cross, but he only had to carry it for one day. Us older folks, we carry our crosses for years and years!" Now my first reaction when she said that was that she was being a little sacrilegious, but the more I think about today's gospel, the more

I think she had it just right. To carry the cross of a debilitating disease, and in spite of that to stay faithful to God, is truly an amazing thing. Like this woman who just offered it all up to God. Now there are many kinds of crosses, of course, not just illnesses, and not only old people who carry them, but when we can find a way in our hearts to transform our carrying of a cross into an act of love for someone or something, it can become a beautiful act of faith.

As we continue with our worship this morning, let us resolve to follow the way of Jesus, all the way to our heavenly Father. Let us take courage from the wise words of Saint Theresa, that our souls are capable of more than we can imagine, and let us try to make the Lord's prayer our prayer, so that, always, where he is, we may also be.

Most Holy Trinity, May 18, 2008:

MAY THE EYES OF OUR HEART BE OPEN

(Ex 34: 4-6. 8-9; 2 Cor 13: 11-13; Jn 3: 16-18)

In today's reading from the book of Exodus, Moses climbs up to the top of Mount Sinai and has an encounter there with God. Just before this in the story, Moses asked God to show him his glory, and today God responds by passing before him, revealing himself as "the Lord, the Lord, a merciful and gracious God, slow to anger and rich in kindness and fidelity." It is not clear in the text whether it is Moses who says these words or God himself, or if it is an angel chorus, but it is very clear that this was a life-changing experience for Moses and for the people that he led.

That scene up there on the mountain is one that lends itself to the imagination, as anyone who has seen Cecil B. de Mille's *Ten Commandments* will remember, but I wonder what we would have seen if we had really been up on that mountain that day with Moses. The descriptions in the Bible make Mount Sinai seem a lot like an erupting volcano. Would the scientist in us have seen only the smoke and heard the thunder? Would we have been so unsettled by the power of the magma rumbling beneath our feet that we would miss completely the power of God's love that was revealed that day?

About five hundred years after the time of Moses, the prophet Elijah was on the run from the police of Queen Jezebel, and as he fled, he climbed up that same mountain. Again God revealed himself, but God was not in the noise and the pyrotechnics of the mountain. God revealed himself in the quiet of a whispering breeze. Again, what would we have seen and heard?

In thinking humbly about this question, I am drawn back to the epistle that we heard on the Feast of the Ascension. In that reading, St. Paul gave the people of Ephesus a benediction, wishing for them that *the eyes of their hearts* might be open to see all of the wonderful things that God was doing in their lives. I love that phrase "the eyes of our hearts". It says something important about how we come to know God. We may not be able to see God with the eyes of our bodies, but he does reveal himself to the eyes of our hearts, if only we will open them to see him.

It is not always easy to keep the eyes of our hearts open, though, especially when we feel like we are standing on an erupting volcano. I remember a time last Fall, when I was in the hospital for some surgery. Everything worked out with the surgery as well as I possibly could have expected, but still it was not an easy experience. There was one particular night that was really difficult. Everything seemed wrong. I was worried about some tests I had to have the next day that would decide when I could go home, and I really wanted to sleep, but I had gotten a new roommate that day who was hard of hearing and he was playing his TV unmercifully loudly and even my bed seemed terribly lumpy all of a sudden. I could not rest. I could not pray. I could not even think clearly, so I got up and paced the halls of the surgical ward, going around and around. As I walked I complained to God: "Why are you doing this to me? Couldn't you have arranged for me to have a quiet roommate for one more night?" There was a lot more of that, but I'm sure you get the idea. My focus was all on me.

Anyway, as I walked, there was one picture on the wall that kept attracting my attention. It was photograph of one of the bridges leading into Manhattan. Finally I just stopped and stared at it, trying to figure out what was so attractive about it. After looking for a few minutes, I noticed that the stonework of the bridge looked just like the outline of the windows of a cathedral. It was at that point, I think, that I stopped seeing that photo with my physical eyes and started seeing it with the eyes of my heart, and it became a comfort to me. Now, don't get me wrong, spending a few minutes in front of that photo did not solve all my problems that night. The tests were still hanging over me, and the blaring TV was still there and even the lumps in the bed were still there. But, I knew then that in oh-so-subtle a way, God was telling me that he was there too. Nothing was different, but everything was changed by that realization.

"The Lord, the Lord, a merciful and gracious God, slow to anger and rich in kindness and fidelity." God invites all of us to open the eyes of our hearts to see him as he truly is. We should be prepared to be surprised if we do open our eyes in this way. That is the amazing thing about vision. It shows us things that are more real than anything we can dream up in our heads. Today we celebrate the Feast of the Holy Trinity, in which we recall the mystery that God exists as a community of love. Father, Son and Holy Spirit are so tightly bound in love that they exist as one God. And yet, somehow, in that unity, they do not lose any of their individuality. This is a marvelous truth that we can only appreciate by seeing it with the eyes of our hearts.

We rejoice especially in this mystery today, when we remember that we are made in God's image and likeness. That means that we too are meant to live in a community of love. Maybe if we open the eyes of our hearts today we will be able to recognize all of the different communities of love that we are a part of. Perhaps because we are so humanly imperfect, God provides us with many different possibilities. There is our birth family, and our extended family, and our parish family. There is the community of our school, or our place of employment. There is the community of our neighbors and our friends. Most importantly, if we are in a long-term committed relationship, that is where we should look first for a sign and symbol of God's community of love. Today we might pause to reflect on how these different communities have supported us at different points in our lives. We might trace the development of those communities to see the hand of God at work, and give thanks for the nurturing that we found there.

Of course, every one of the communities that we are a part of is only an imperfect image of the love of God, and it must be said that sometimes they can be painfully imperfect, and even destructive of God's love. But even when we are in the midst of that pain, we should never doubt that it is always God's will that we should live swaddled in a community of love, which supports us richly and yet, mysteriously, also allows us to grow into the unique individual that we are meant to be. Exploring this mystery here on earth helps us to experience the mystery of God's inner life. Maybe, if we open the eyes of our heart today, we will see the potential for one or another of the communities that we are a part of to grow and develop. We might be shown something that we can do this week to enrich the spirit of one of these communities, making it a better reflection of the love that is God.

"The Lord, the Lord, a merciful and gracious God, slow to anger and rich in kindness and fidelity." Such is the glory of our God and we his children. As we continue with our worship this morning, let us thank God for revealing himself to us as Father, Son and Holy Spirit, bound tightly in a community of love. Let us ask God to help us to open the eyes of our heart to see the community of love that he means us to be a part of now, in this phase of our journey toward him, and how we can reach out in love to make that community a more perfect union.

11th Sunday in Ordinary Time, Jun. 15, 2008:

SHARING IN THE COMPASSION
OF JESUS

(Ex 19: 2-6; Rm 5: 6-11; Mt 9: 36-10: 8)

Today's gospel paints a beautiful portrait of the community we call Church. This is a very important theme in Matthew's gospel. He presents several stories about the beginnings of the Church. This first one shows us a Church that is centered on the Apostles, with a mission that is grounded in the compassion of God. At the end of the gospel the Apostles will be sent out to baptize the whole world, but here they are sent out to heal the hurting and rescue the lost .

Notice the way the story begins. It says that Jesus was "moved with pity" for the crowds of people that flocked to him. The Greek word that we translate as "moved with pity" is a real tongue-twister: "esplangxNISthei". The word refers to a very strong emotion of sympathy, literally "gut-wrenching". This is a very important thing for us to notice, because in Jesus' response to this situation we see God's deepest desire being acted out. God greatly desires that all people should be healed, and comforted, and live in peace. And we and the Apostles have a part in that response. We are not simply sent out to carry out this mission of Jesus, we are also invited into that emotion of compassion for those in need.

I am thinking back to 9/11, and how many people wanted to donate blood at that time. Much more blood was donated than could be used effectively, but what a beautiful gesture that was! Many people felt that they needed to do something very concrete and personal to respond to that tragedy. Or, more recently with the earthquake in China, or the cyclone in Myanmar, think of all the stories we read or heard of the tremendous outpouring of aid from around the world.

When we hear of such tragedies and our heart goes out to the victims and we experience a desire to be of some assistance, we are experiencing the best of what it means to be human, and we are also experiencing the deepest desire of God. We may not be able to know the mind of God very well (why these things happen; how they fit into God's plan, and so forth). That's hard. But it is much easier to know the heart of God, because our own hearts quiver in response to his. We can feel it. So, one important thing for us to do when we feel that rush of compassion is to notice the experience and rejoice in it, because it is then that we are fully connected to the heart of God.

The second thing to do when we have that sort of desire is to act on it in some way. We should try never to let that feeling die in our hearts. I know that's not always easy to do. Walking the streets of New York or Philadelphia, it is not possible for us to act on a desire to help every homeless person that we pass, but we can save up that desire and act on it later by supporting a shelter for the homeless in some way.

Or, to take an example that I struggle with, what are we to do about all the requests we get for donations? One thing I do around the house is go through the mail. Well, we have been living in our house for more than 20 years now, and we have given to a lot of different charities over that time, and I don't think any one of them has ever forgotten where we live. On a normal day we get three or four letters from different kinds of charities. I try to look at them all, including the ones with pictures of beautiful little children in dire circumstances, and it does pull on the heart-strings. I have to admit though, that even though they are good causes, we can't give to them all. If we did somehow contrive to make even a small offering to every one of them, I have no doubt that the next month the number of letters would double and each one would be asking for fifty dollars rather than fifteen.

Perhaps you are in a similar situation. So what are we to do? One thing that would be a bad thing to do, is to put up a wall between us and those problems that tug at our heart strings. One kind of wall we might build is a wall of cynicism. We convince ourselves that most of the letter writers are scoundrels, or things are not as bad as it seems in the pictures. It is not a good thing for us to allow that kind of cynicism to grow in us. Of course it is true that there are scoundrels out there, and we do have to be careful. We have to use our heads as well as our hearts, but we don't want to build a wall that blocks us from feeling the deepest desires of God.

A better thing for us to try to do with that strong emotion of compassion that we sometimes feel is to allow it to power us to do the hard work needed to be of real help. That's what our emotions are supposed to do for us; they motivate us to act. We can let that emotion take us to the internet, where we can go to one of the sites that evaluates different charities, and find one, like Catholic Relief Services for example, which has a very good record of actually getting help to the people who need it. When we find one that fits the bill, then we go write the check. In this way our hearts and our heads will no longer be pulling us in two different directions. Instead, we will have our heads working in the service of our hearts, which seems the right way round.

There are, of course, things we can do to express our compassion that don't involve money. I mentioned earlier how many people gave blood right after 9/11. Well that really is a deeply personal way to express our compassion for the sick. We are giving a part of our selves so that others might have a chance at better health. And we don't have to wait for a blood drive to come around to do it. The Medical Center has an office where we can make an appointment pretty much any time, and right across Route 1, on Alexander road, the Red Cross has a donation center. It is perfectly safe if you are in reasonable health, and the need is ongoing and very great.

The last thing I would like to suggest that we might do to act on these deep feelings of compassion that we sometimes feel, comes from the last line of today's gospel: "Without cost you have received; without cost you are to give."

Perhaps we might think back to a time in our own life, in which we were in some difficulty: job-loss or difficulties with a relative, or a loss of confidence in what we were doing, whatever it might be; and in that difficult place, eventually, some way, somehow the Love of God found its way to us and improved the situation. That sort of difficult experience puts us in an excellent position to help other people who are going through the same sort of problem right now. It would be good to meditate on this for a while, and ask if it isn't time to find a way to give back what we received through God's grace. Our parish and community have many, many ways for us to give back. Our Loaves and Fishes program next weekend is just one example. There are the hospital visitors and Pre-Cana, and the religious education program—the list goes on and on. Any one of those programs would be eager for additional help, and could be an excellent way for us to express the compassion of God that we feel in our hearts.

Let us now bring to the table of the Lord, our joy and thanks for the opportunity to know the heart of God in all of its compassion, and ask the Holy Spirit to guide us as we seek to give freely of what we have so gratefully received.

16th Sunday in Ordinary Time, Jul. 20, 2008:

TO BE THE YEAST OF GOODNESS IN SOCIETY

(Wis 12: 13, 16-19; Rm 8: 26-27; Mt 13: 24:43)

The gospels tell us that one of the most important parts of Jesus' preaching was "change your hearts, for the kingdom of God is at hand." It is clear that some people had trouble understanding this message, in part because the kingdom of God, which Jesus was talking about, was unlike any kingdom that the people had any experience with. It was not to be represented by armies and palaces, but was to be expressed in people's hearts and in their everyday activities.

Jesus explained this new sort of kingdom by using parables: simple stories about everyday things like farming and cooking and commerce. The word 'parable' means to set one thing down beside another, in other words, to make a comparison. A parable compares something that we know, with something that we want to know more about.

The parables Jesus told worked very well for the people of his time, because their lives revolved around farming and housekeeping. It may be a bit harder for us to get into these stories, because most of us live lives that are focused on office work and broken air conditioners, and the price of oil, and lots of other things. We are further from the land, so we really need to exercise our sacred imagination to get the benefit of the stories. We have lots of opportunities to practice, because last week, this week and next week, we hear seven different parables from Jesus, all concerning the kingdom of God.

To get us started, I would like to concentrate on just one of the parables we heard today: the one about the yeast and bread making. Baking bread is one of those wonderful kitchen activities that I wish I had more time for. I have wonderful memories of the aroma of baking bread in the house where I grew up. When you think about it, it does seem almost magical, the way you can take simple ingredients off the shelf and put them together in just the right way and create something that is so different in form and substance from the original ingredients, and so tasty, too! The raised-dough recipe that is a tradition in my family begins with five cups of sifted flour and one package of dry yeast. In Jesus' telling the case is even more extreme: his recipe includes more than 100 cups of flour. It is hard to believe that a small amount of yeast could make any difference at all with such a large amount of flour, but it clearly does. All you have to do to prove that to yourself is one time to try to make bread using an old package of yeast that has been sitting on the shelf since who knows when. Instead of two loaves of nice light bread, you end up with a couple of paving stones! I can attest to that.

So how is the baking of bread like the kingdom of God? Well, the gospel of Jesus with its radical call to love of neighbor is the yeast for the world. It is a tiny idea which makes all the difference for whether the world is going to be a lightly-baked place of peace and joy, or a heavy lump of misery.

To show you how this works in practice, I want to share with you the story of a man I had a long conversation with a few weeks ago. He is a wonderful, gentle man in a good marriage now, but as a teenager he lived in a rough part of New York City, in the middle of the gang culture. As a kid, he had a tough life; his family situation was not good, and he was full of anger. He couldn't even trust other people well enough to join a gang! In his mind, it was always him against the world. As a teenager, he knew something was missing in this sort of life, and he yearned for something more. One of the places he looked was the youth group at a nearby parish, but it only took him a few meetings to see that the kids in that group only cared about socializing. Finally, at one meeting he blew up at the other kids and confronted them about this and then walked out.

Well, as he was walking home, he noticed that someone was following him. It was one of the guys from the youth group. This guy caught up with my friend, and tried to tell him about a different youth group in another parish that was much better. My friend was having none of it and just wanted to be left alone. But the guy was insistent, and told my friend that he would pick him up on Saturday to take him to the other group. And sure enough, come the next Saturday, he was at my friends door, and dragged him off to this other youth group. And to my friend's surprise, he liked the other group and found the support he needed there.

Now this new experience did not turn my friend's life into a bed of roses by any means. He even spent some time in jail before he got his life turned around. But as he looks back on his life now, it was that first guy who reached out to him and would not take "no" for an answer, who helped him to escape from a life that might easily have left him dead on the street. That encounter on the street corner in New York City was a little bit of the yeast of the kingdom of God that lifted the loaf of my friend's life.

We are called to be yeast for the world in a similar way. That may seem like an overwhelming responsibility. There are so many things wrong with our world. But when we feel oppressed by this task, maybe that is the time to get out the sifter and the baking pans and remind ourselves what a tablespoon of yeast can do with five cups of flour.

As we meditate about this, it would be helpful to keep two pieces of advice in mind. The first comes from Mother Teresa. It can help us to determine what God wants us to do, because we are not all called to walk the streets of New York City looking for teens to rescue. Personally, I don't think I would last more than two minutes in that environment! Mother Teresa's advice to us is: "Do what's in front of you." That family across the street with the troubled marriage, that kid in the neighborhood who doesn't have many friends, that park that we pass every day that is in disrepair. Those are the places that we can make a very important difference.

The second piece of advice comes from an unlikely religious philosopher named Andy Warhol. His advice is that "ninety percent of success is just showing up." We don't have to worry that we wouldn't know what to do in some particular situation. We should remember that we are not called to be the baker in the kingdom of God, we are called to be the yeast, and that is a much easier job. In any situation we might find ourselves, God, who is the consummate baker, will make a heavenly confection, if only we will provide him with the missing ingredient. We can rest assured that God will accomplish whatever he means to have happen by our presence. We may not be there to see it, but it will happen.

It is just like the yeast. All it has to do is get into the dough and then just be yeast—just do what yeast does best. We just have to be willing to get involved, and then do what humans do best, which is to love one another. Therein lies the kingdom of God.

So as we continue with our liturgy this morning, let us try to exercise our sacred imagination and see the gospel of Jesus as the yeast for the world's needs. Let us ask God to open our eyes to the task that he has placed in front of us, and to give us the courage to show up when and where God needs us to be. If we can do those things, then we can be sure that when we reach the end of our days, we will awake to see a table before us loaded down with all the heavenly confections that we helped to create.

GOD IS NOT A CANDY MACHINE

(Is 56: 1, 6-7; Rm 11: 13-15, 29-32; Mt 15: 21-28)

The picture of Jesus that we find in today's gospel is hard to reconcile with other images we find in the gospels, as when in Mark's gospel a leper approaches Jesus as he is praying the desert and says to him "if you wanted to heal me, you could", and Jesus simply says "I do wish it." and immediately heals him. In comparison, today's Jesus seems aloof and uncaring about the plight of the distraught mother.

We may find this image of Jesus all the more distressing if we feel that God has sometimes treated us the same way. I remember that when our daughter Anna was little, we had a particular tree in our front yard that she loved to climb in. The only problem was that the tree was dying and we could do nothing to save it. Well, our daughter bravely prayed night and day that that tree might recover. But it eventually died anyway, and we had to cut it down. Now, why would God fail to answer the prayers of an innocent little girl like that? What cosmic harm would have been caused by one tree living a few years too long? Perhaps you have asked similar questions about even more weighty problems than this.

But the hard fact is, that God does not protect us from all pain and sorrow, no matter how hard we pray. Why this might be is worthy of our meditation, but today I would like to focus on the implications of this hard fact for our prayer life. Why do we bother to make prayers of intercession, prayers in which we ask things of God? What is this kind of prayer all about anyway?

It is a good thing for us to focus on this question, because this particular kind of prayer is often misunderstood, even by thoughtful Christians. We sometimes fall into the trap of thinking of intercessory prayer as being something like a candy machine. When we have a good candy machine, we put in our coins and press the right button, and out comes the candy bar we want. If it is a bad candy machine, then maybe a turnip comes out instead, or perhaps nothing at all. Well, intercessory prayer can sometimes be viewed similarly. We make our prayers, we ask God for something, and the only interesting question is "Did we get what we asked for?"

To say the least, this is an inadequate view of the powerful role that intercessory prayer can have in our lives. I would like to suggest three important considerations that can lead us to a more spiritually-sound view of intercessory prayer.

The first idea for us to consider is that intercessory prayer is an expression of our relationship with God. Jesus taught us to view God as our father, and the parent/child relationship gives a very good framework for thinking about intercessory prayer. We come to God with our needs in prayer just as a child might run to a parent with a broken kite or a skinned knee. Sometimes, the response of our parent might be to help us to fix what is broken, or it might be to administer a stinging antiseptic, or it might be to give us the hard news that that is just the way the world works, and we have to try to be strong.

When I was little, I decided one summer that it would be a great idea for us to build a pirate ship in our back yard. Nothing too big, twenty or twenty-five feet long would have been plenty. My imagination soared when I dreamed about how wonderful that pirate ship would be. Wisely, my parents didn't say "yes" to this marvelous plan, but then neither did they say "no". What they said was "We can't do that today". Instead, my mother helped me make a pirate flag out of an old pillow case, and my father helped me make a pirate cutlass out of plywood, but that was as far as the idea ever got.

Different parental responses are appropriate in different circumstances, and we, as the children in the relationship, may not know which one we need at any given time. But God is the perfect parent, and we can be sure that the right one will be administered along with a dose of parental love, which will help us to grow from our experience. Intercessory prayer is one important part of our parent/child relationship with God, and we lose something if we try to consider it separately from the rest of that relationship.

A second consideration to keep in mind when thinking about intercessory prayer, is that it is an expression of who we are as a community of faith. Some of you may remember that I was seriously ill with cancer last year. Well, the community of faith was overwhelming in its support of me in prayer. And not just here locally. I can't tell you how many people told me "I'm praying for you, and I asked my mother, or my friends or my prayer group, to pray for you too." It felt like there were a million mirrors surrounding me, all focusing God's love my way.

One result of all those many prayers, you see before you today. God has granted me more time to be among you, for which I am exceedingly grateful. But the really important thing for our consideration here today is that even if God had responded to all those prayers in a different way, that would not mean that those prayers were any less important or effective. Even now I look back at some of the rough patches that I faced over those months and ask "How did I ever get through that?" I am absolutely sure that it was the support of the community that gave me the strength I needed. You will never know how much that has been appreciated by me and my family.

My story is far from unique, of course. This sort of shared burden of prayer is a very common and a very beautiful part of the spiritual life in a faith community, and it is another very important aspect of intercessory prayer that is left out when we think of this sort of prayer as a kind of candy machine.

Finally, intercessory prayer is an expression of our hope in the kingdom of God. In a few moments, we will say the prayer of the faithful together as a community, and as usual, one of those prayers will be for world peace. Now, our parish is over 150 years old and I dare say that in all those many years, every week some prayer for peace in the world has been made from our altar. Given all the hot spots there still are in the world after those many thousands of prayers, one might wonder why we don't just give it up as a bad job. God is clearly not going to let that particular candy bar out of the machine. But of course we don't give up our prayers for peace, even though we understand that perfect peace will only come with the fullness of the kingdom of God. Praying this way expresses our longing for peace, and makes us work all the harder to achieve it, accepting that for the foreseeable future, the results will be partial and incomplete. The situation is the same for world hunger, and refugee relief, and the other problems that face our world. It is not always easy to continue with this work without losing heart, but in the letter to the Romans Saint Paul describes the attitude that will help us to keep going in this long-term effort. He says to "Rejoice in hope, be patient in trials, and be persistent in prayer."

So as we continue with our worship, let us celebrate the place of intercessory prayer in our lives, as an expression of our relationship to God, as an expression of our solidarity with the community of faith, and as an expression of our hope in the kingdom of God. Let us resolve together to follow the good advice of Saint Paul and always "Rejoice in hope, be patient in trials, and be persistent in prayer."

25th Sunday in Ordinary Time, Sep. 21, 2008:

LATE HAVE I LOVED YOU, O BEAUTY EVER ANCIENT, EVER NEW

(Is 55: 6-9; Phil 1: 20-24, 27; Mt 20: 1-16)

The parable in today's gospel is one that can sometimes cause us some confusion and consternation. It might have been *kind* on the owner's part to give all the workers the same wage, but it doesn't seem like a particularly *wise* thing for him to do. My wife, practical woman that she is, said, "You know what would happen if somebody really tried such a scheme. The very next day nobody would show up for work until right before quitting time! And then what would happen to the harvest?"

But, on second thought, would that really work, do you think? What would have happened in the parable if a person was sitting around in the plaza of the town and the owner came over and offered him work, but he said "Well, I'm not ready to work right now. Come back in the afternoon, and if I don't get a better offer, I'll come work for you then." How do you think the owner of the vineyard would respond to such a suggestion? Not very happily, I don't suppose. That sort of question refocuses our attention on this parable, not so much for what is says about fair wages, but for what its says about God's call, and how we respond.

A real life example that we might want to consider in this regard is Saint Augustine. You know, I suppose, that he lived in the late Roman empire and until he was well into his adulthood, he pretty much followed the ways of his pagan father and rejected the faith of his Christian mother. Then some time in his thirties, God finally got through to him, and Augustine turned his life around and embraced Christianity. He eventually became a monk, then a priest and finally a bishop. In a way, he was like the kind of worker my wife was worried about. He was one who refused the first call, or even the first several calls, to enter God's vineyard, but then decided to enter the vineyard in the afternoon of his life.

So how did that work for him, do you suppose? Did he congratulate himself, saying "Oh isn't that sweet! When I was young and full of spirit, I got to live a life of worldly pleasures, and now that I'm a bit older and tired of that sort of thing, I get to live a holy life and be with God! I got the best of both worlds!" Not really. Here is what he actually had to say about those times in his memoir:

> *"Late have I loved you, O Beauty ever ancient,*
> *ever new, late have I loved you."*

Hear the regret in his words. "Late have I loved you." He realized, once he finally did enter the vineyard of the Lord, how much he had been missing in all those years when he thought he was having fun. He probably would have given much to get those years back and start over, but those chances, those opportunities, those particular invitations from God were gone. I think we can appreciate the sadness of that realization.

Now, in the parable, the owner of the vineyard goes out quite frequently to look for workers, and similarly, God is often coming to us with an invitation to share in his creative labor in the world and in that way to enter into a deeper relationship with him. It is up to us to decide how we are going to respond. God's invitation might come in any number of ways. For example, it might come when we are reading the paper and a little child comes to us with a book and asks us to read a story. It is no good saying "Well, come back when you're twelve and I'll read to you then". That particular invitation is for that moment, and if we ignore it, it will be gone, and we will be the poorer.

I think I know something of the regret that Saint Augustine was expressing. I only knew one of my grandparents. The others died before I got a chance to interact with them. But that one Grandfather I did know was very special. And he loved me very much. I mean, he loved all his grandkids, of course, but you can always tell who the favorite is, can't you? I was the oldest grandson, and I was the apple of his eye. When I was little, we did things together, like going duck pin bowling and playing pool together in his basement. But by the time I got out of grammar school and began to make more choices for myself, I didn't make much time for him in my life. I wish now, that when I was in high school or in college I had gone and sat with him, and asked him to tell me the story of his life. But I didn't. God was reaching out to me in my grandfather's loving care for me, but I paid no attention, and so I missed an opportunity that won't come again this side of heaven.

Perhaps you can look back at your own lives and see similar missed opportunities. I don't bring this up just to wrap us all in the sadness of our wasted youths, but rather to impress upon us all that we should search carefully for the invitations that God is offering us today. They are different from yesterday's but still very good. We can't go back, but we can go forward.

And what will it be like if we do answer today's call? Augustine's memoir also says something about his experience in this regard too:

> *"You called, you shouted and broke through my*
> *deafness.*
> *You flashed, you shined and you dispelled my*
> *blindness.*
> *You breathed your fragrance on me; I drew breath*
> *and now I pant for you.*
> *I tasted you, now I hunger and thirst for more.*
> *You touched me, and now I burn for your peace."*

Wow! That sounds like really being alive. If that is what it means to enter the vineyard of the Lord, show me how to sign up! I am sure that God will be trying to get through to each one of us this week with just such an offer. I don't know how it will happen, for our God is endlessly creative and surprising, but I'm sure it will. Here are just three possibilities out of thousands.

Today is Catechetical Sunday, when we honor all those who serve our community by sharing their faith with our young people. Those are good people, and if you know one of them, you should say "thank you". We owe them a large debt of gratitude. Well, perhaps God is calling some of us today to be classroom helpers in the religious education program here at Saint Paul's. Now there is a calling that is hard work, but also giving great rewards.

Here's another possibility. At the end of our Mass this evening, we will have someone here to talk to us about the Saint Paul's youth group. Maybe that presentation is the invitation that God is extending to you today. It could be a great thing to join with a group of other young people who are serious about understanding their faith better, and also serious about sharing fellowship and having fun at the same time.

Or here is one last possibility. This is a time when we may be beginning to make plans for Thanksgiving or Christmas. Maybe there is a particular relative on our mind that we feel compelled to visit with, even though they aren't the most pleasant person to be with. What would happen if we didn't wait for the Holidays to get together with them? After all, we don't know if that person will be around then. We don't even know for sure if we will be round then. We could invite them for next weekend, and make them the center of attention. It would be work, but who knows what we might learn, or worlds might open up to us?

God invites us to be workers in the garden of his love. We will find honest toil there, as well as a share in his many blessings. Just like Saint Augustine, the more often we take advantage of his invitation, the more eager we will be for the next opportunity.

LOOKING IN THE RIGHT PLACE
FOR CHRISTMAS JOY

(Is 45:1. 4–6; 1 Thes 1: 1–5; Mt 22: 15–21)

The people portrayed in today's gospel come to their encounter from very different perspectives. From the Pharisee's side it is a story about conflict and trying to trap Jesus in an impossible situation. They supposed that no matter how he would answer their question, Jesus would get in trouble with somebody —either with his power base or with the authorities. But as he usually did, Jesus came to this event with a very different perspective. He refused to be distracted by any practical political considerations and examined seriously the theological question that was the bait in the trap.

The gospel story doesn't make it very clear, but knowing the background of the times and reading between the lines a bit, we can see that there was a serious theological question to be addressed. It involved the coins used to pay the tax. Roman coins minted during this time bore the likeness of the Roman emperor Tiberius. Now, right away that's a problem, because images of people were forbidden under the Law of Moses, as a part of the commandment against idolatry. Things were made even worse by the inscription on the coins, which, when you unpack all the abbreviations, read something like this: "The Great Tiberius, emperor and son of the divine Augustus". It is hard to exaggerate how offensive such coins were to devout followers of Moses. It would be as if our money had dirty pictures on it, or something like that. As much as possible, the Jews tried to avoid handling such coinage, but they couldn't always do that, since that was the coin that was needed to pay the Roman tax, among other things.

Jesus' response today speaks to this underlying ethical quandary. He says essentially, "Look, get real. Nobody believes that stuff about Augustus being divine. You didn't make the graven image and you cannot commit idolatry without meaning to. Tiberius might be committing idolatry, but you're not. So just hold your nose, pay the tax and move on."

That was good brotherly advice. But then, Jesus adds the second half of his answer, which is the part that can make us step back and think today. He adds "But repay to God what belongs to God." Now *that* is a question to make us think: What do we owe to God? Right here, today.

As I think about that question, I find it kind of ironic that Roman coins had such an offensive saying on them, and Jesus told the people not to worry about that, and on our money we have such a wonderful motto, and hardly anybody ever thinks about that when buying and selling things. You know the motto: "In God we trust." I think Jesus would tell us we *should* try to remember *that* motto more often, because that is one of the things that we owe to God: we owe him our trust in his promise, and our trust in his guidance over our lives.

We have many examples of this kind of trust that we might imitate. Today is World Mission Sunday, and so, today we honor the many people that have trusted in the Lord's promise well enough to leave everything behind and go to another place to bring the Good News of Jesus to people who would otherwise not hear it. We honor their commitment, and pray for their success and try to contribute to their work in whatever way we can. And in these uncertain financial times, it does take a level of trust in God on our part to make a nice contribution, but we know that we can trust in God's promise that he will be with us, no matter what kind of hard times lie ahead.

So that is one important way that we can follow Jesus' advice and practice our trust in God, but we might also feel called to examine our lives a little more personally, to see how we can offer up to God our trust in him. We have a good opportunity for doing that during the current financial difficulties.

If we have been worried by the current financial uncertainty, that might be showing us that unconsciously we have been putting our trust in money rather than in God. If we worry excessively about our 401 kays turning into 301 kays or 201 kays or even no kays at all, that worry might be laying bare our unconscious assumption that if we had less money, we would necessarily be less happy. Now, in the extreme, that is true. It is hard to be happy in life if we have no money at all, but I think that most of us (especially if you're like me and have lived a pretty soft life so far) most of us misjudge how little money we could have and still be happy. This is a particularly important thing for us to think about now as we begin to think about Christmas, since Christmas can often turn into a celebration of "new stuff", rather than a celebration of our Lord's birth.

I remember that when I was a kid, just around Thanksgiving time each year the Montgomery Ward's catalogue would arrive at our door. It was a big thick catalogue full of clothes and kitchen wares and other boring stuff, but somewhere in the middle was about 20 pages of bikes and sporting equipment and toys. Each year my parents would invite me to look through the catalogue to see if there was something that I wanted Santa to bring me that year. And there always was, of course. The hard part was choosing what it would be.

As I look back at it now, there was a lot of anticipation in looking through those pages, but somehow the reality never quite lived up to the promise in the catalogue. Either something would break or get lost as soon as I got it or it was not nearly as good as I dreamed it would be. I remember a Cape Canaveral Spaceport set with a real rocket launcher that was a particularly bad choice. One tiny black mark on the living room ceiling, and that rocket launcher went away forever! I mean, what is the point of having a spaceport without a rocket launcher?

Well, I was looking in the wrong place for my Christmas joy, and I think I was probably not alone in doing that. The thing that will really make us happy this Christmas is to work on our relationships with those we love. If we can get those right, then it won't matter what we have under the tree.

Now you may think that I am rushing the season a bit to be talking about Christmas already, but if we want to try to simplify and refocus our own Christmas celebrations this year, now is the time to have that conversation with our loved ones. Once December comes all the events will be in motion, and it will be very difficult to make changes, and people might have their feelings hurt if we try.

Of course, it is a risk to try something different during a season that is so wrapped up in family traditions, and it isn't easy to go against the popular culture and design a Christmas celebration that is more people-centered and less thing-centered. It is a risk even to start the conversation with some people. I know. But that is where our trust in God can come to our assistance. God wants us to be happy, truly happy, and he knows that acquiring more things is not the way to go about it. If we trust to God and take the risk, we can end up with a better, more peaceful Christmas. Wouldn't that be a fitting way to celebrate the birthday of the Prince of Peace?

In God we trust.

EXERCISING OUR TALENTS

(Prb 31: 10-13, 19-20, 30-31; 1 Thes 5: 1-6; Mt 25: 14-30)

When I was in high school, I didn't know what I wanted to do with my life. And because of that, I remember as a junior in high school dreading going in for the required yearly interview with the school guidance counselor. Well, the day came eventually, and in an effort to help me focus on where I was headed in life, my counselor asked me this question. He said "What are your talents?" At the time, I found that question kind of intimidating. In that moment I couldn't think of any in particular. I did know that I had an uncanny ability to fall asleep while listening to rock music, but I didn't think that was the kind of thing that my counselor was thinking about.

Although I found it to be an intimidating question when I was sitting in the guidance office, that question doesn't need to be so intimidating for us here this evening, sitting among our friends and loved ones. And that question is a good starting point for a serious consideration of today's gospel. So, what are your talents? To ask that question of ourselves occasionally and to make a mental list of the things we can do well is not necessarily just an ego trip, as long as we can humbly acknowledge the true source of our gifts: they all come to us from God.

That word "talent" that we use to describe some special ability that we have been given by God, came into our language directly from today's parable. As it is used in the parable, the word refers to a large sum of money. It was equivalent to about twenty seven pounds of pure silver. Now even in the days before spiraling commodity prices, that was a hefty chunk of change. To make a connection between that kind of money and some particular gift or ability that we have shows just how precious those gifts are in the sight of God. So, one thing we might do as a first step in confronting today's gospel is to meditate on the gifts that God has given us and rejoice in them, for they are very precious indeed.

We shouldn't stop the thought process there, however. In order to follow the lead of today's gospel, there is a second question we should be asking ourselves. I don't remember if my guidance counselor asked it of me, but he may have. Actually, I'm not sure I was listening very carefully after his first question. But the second question we should ask ourselves is this: "What does God want me to do with this gift he has given me?" Each talent God gives us is like a tool, a hammer maybe, and once we realize we have been given a hammer, it is natural to go looking for a nail that needs hammering in. So, when we bake a tasty pie, or make a really insightful posting to a blog, or saw a board in perfectly straight line, we should first pause and notice just how good the thing was that we just did, and then take the next logical step and ask, "How can I use this particular gift in God's service?" That is what today's parable asks us to do

We don't need to use our gifts in God's service, of course. The talents we have been given are true gifts. If we want to, we can do nothing with them in particular, or we can use the gifts for our own good alone. God hopes we won't do that, but he won't stop us if we do. On the other hand, we won't really get the full pleasure of the gift we have been given until we start to use it for someone else's benefit. Eating a pie we just made is one kind of pleasure; if it is a good pie, it can be a very enjoyable thing. But offering a fresh-baked pie to someone else and seeing their enjoyment of it—that is a pleasure of a wholly different order. Many people would say it is a deeper and richer pleasure. So we should be happy when we have named our talent and also started to do the thing God wants us to do with it, because "Things worth doing are worth doing well."

So that's the basic story our faith tells us about our talents, but I would like also to address two possible misconceptions about these gifts of God in our lives. The first misconception is that we always begin by figuring out what our talents are, and then figure out what to do with them. Sometimes for me anyway, it happens the other way round: we see a need and realize that God is calling us to answer that need, long before we have a chance to take stock of any talents we have that might be useful.

Experiencing that kind of call can be just is as scary as a visit to the guidance office. We see the nail that needs hammering in, but we have no idea where the hammer is going to come from. That's a time when we need to really draw on our trust in God. We need to trust that he will give us whatever we need in order to accomplish what he wants us to do. And it is not an uncommon experience in ministry to get done some event and feel surprised and pleased at the way things turned out, after all the worry about it going in. That's a pleasurable "Hey, I'm not so bad at this!" phenomenon. And even if things don't seem to turn out so well every time, we can still trust that God is accomplishing what he wants. I said before that "Things worth doing are worth doing well", Well, it is also true that "Things worth doing are worth doing badly." If no one else is stepping up to the plate, then anything we can do is an improvement.

The second misperception that I might have left you with at first is that we exercise our gifts in a vacuum. As if we were all "lone rangers" who get a gift from God and then go out and apply it. Certainly, it is possible that we might need to strike out on our own sometimes, but more often, we exercise our gifts in conjunction with others. Our parish community is a good example of this. One person comes forward with the gift of great compassion, another with a gift for organizing, another with a gift for being a dependable worker, and out of all those individual gifts, something greater arises: the gift of our community. As a parish, we should be asking those same questions: "What are our gifts?" and "How are we to apply them?" and in this way we can become the imitators of the "good wife" who is praised so highly in our first reading today.

I was away on business for a part of last week, and as I was flying back into Newark airport last night the ride got very bumpy. Well, they lashed us into our seats early and during our long and uncomfortable descent, a strange thing happened. It got very, very quiet in the cabin of the airplane, as each of us faced that difficult situation alone. It was never really dangerous, but I think many of us had the feeling that it could have been. And what I realized in that moment was that there was no community there. We were all just individuals who happened to be stuck in the same bumpy plane ride.

It can't be that way for us as Catholic Christians. Here tonight, we are not just 300 people who all happened to attend the same Mass on a particular Sunday night. We are called to something so much greater and more beautiful than that . We are called to become a community of faith. We are called to join our gifts together and become "the Church", the bride of Christ who is praised for her good works and generosity.

So as we continue with our worship this evening, let us give thanks for our talents, and search diligently for opportunities for applying them to benefit others. Let us remember the invitation we have right here at Saint Paul's to join with others who love God and want to serve him. We are, all of us, a people who long to hear God say "Well done, my good and faithful servant. Now, come and share your Master's joy".

OPENNESS TO GOD'S SURPRISING GIFTS

(2 Sm 7: 1–5. 8–11. 16; Rom 16: 25–27; Lk 1: 26–38)

Advent is a joyous season that offers us a sweet mix of remembering and anticipation. We remember the long time of waiting when the people of Israel longed for the coming of the Messiah, and we combine that with our own longing for Jesus to return in glory at the end of time. Also in this season we remember with joy the gift that Jesus is in our lives today, and in response we give generously to others. Perhaps you have made or picked out a gift for someone special in your life and are counting the days until you can share it with your loved one. That wonderful feeling of a joy that is coming so close that you can almost taste it, is an important part of Advent. I think that's how God experiences Advent, and we should be quick to join in.

I remember a time, not long after I met the woman who would some-day become my wife, when I had that kind of experience. We were both in graduate school at the time and I wanted to get her a gift that would show how much I cared for her. I knew that there was a hard-to-find reference book in Latin that she wanted for her studies, and I decided to get it for her. Now that might not sound like a re-ally exciting gift to you, but when you're in graduate school, things seem different. Unfortunately there was no amazon.com back then, but eventually I located the book with an academic book seller and ordered it by mail. Actually I went overboard a little bit and ordered a four-volume set of books for her, including both Latin and Greek texts, and the amazing part was that the whole thing was really inex-pensive too. I felt very shrewd!

Well I waited and I waited and I waited. I began to get worried, but finally, just a few days before Christmas, the package arrived. But something was funny. The package was way too small for four books. At first, I thought they must have sent them in four separate shipments. But no, when I opened it up all four books were there. They could fit them all in one package because the books were only three inches high! Somehow they forgot to mention that part in the description of the books. So, the surprise Christmas present ended up being an even bigger surprise for me, but a great laugh for Jane, and it all worked out in the end, because she married me anyway.

What I find memorable about that story is that I was waiting for something that I thought was going to be wonderful, and in the middle of it, there is a part that was not at all what I expected and that led to a moment of panic, but then in the end of the story, it all worked out just fine.

The Bible gives us lots of such stories of waiting and anticipation, which get fulfilled in surprising ways, by our ever-surprising, ever-loving God. In our first reading we heard part of the story of King David. That was a story with lots of surprises. When David was young, the tribes of Israel were in trouble. They had powerful enemies, but they had no king to unite them and lead them. The first person who tried to be king didn't work out very well, and so God sent the prophet Samuel to pick a new king from among the sons of Jesse. David was one of those sons, but he was the youngest of the eight brothers. At first, Samuel was sure God wanted one of the older guys, because they were all so big and handsome. But no, God had a surprise in store for everyone. David, the youngest of them all, was to be the king. And he did a pretty good job of it, too.

In our reading today he has already defeated all his enemies and is living in a grand palace, when he decides to give God a gift: a beautiful temple to be his house, just as grand as David's own palace. That sounded like a good idea, but God surprises him and says "no". In fact, it would be the opposite way round. God was going to build a "house", that is a royal dynasty, for David, and what's more that dynasty would last for ever. And there were more surprises on the way. People assumed that God's promise meant that David's sons and grandsons would make good kings, but that didn't happen. Most of his descendents turned out to be lousy kings. In the end, it took a thousand years before God's promise would really be fulfilled, and that fulfillment was Jesus. Didn't that happen in a surprising way! What kind of king gets born in a stable, and sleeps his first night in an animal's food trough? What a surprising gift-giver is our God!

The surprises continue in our gospel today. At the beginning of the story, Mary was waiting for something special, but it was not a visit from an angel. Our reading says that she was "betrothed" to Joseph, but that is not quite an accurate description. We don't have the right word in English, because marriage customs were different back then. Mary and Joseph were already married, but Mary was still living in her parents' house, waiting for Joseph to prepare a place for them to live. The wedding celebration would happen when Joseph would come in a joyous procession of friends and relatives to lead his wife to their new home. That is when they would really start their married life together, and that was the very good thing that Mary was waiting for. We can be sure that she was eagerly anticipating being a good wife to her new husband.

But our ever-surprising God had a different gift in mind for her. It was a gift that must have seemed very strange. In her very straight-laced society, an inexplicable pregnancy was a really difficult challenge. But God also gave her a good husband, and in the end it worked out well for all of us.

And what of us, here in Princeton, just a few days before Christmas? What are our hearts full of expectation for, and how is our gospel challenging us today? I think God is inviting us this morning to follow in the footsteps of Mary in two ways:

The first is to wait peacefully, with an attitude of openness to whatever God is doing in our lives. Like Mary, we want to be quiet in our hearts so we can hear the whispering wings of God's messengers, and we want to be ready for God to surprise us with the fulfillment of his promise in his own way and his own time.

The second thing we might do is to listen carefully to the words of the angel Gabriel today, and trust God's action in our lives, because we have seen how it is playing out in the lives of others. Just as Mary was given the example of Elizabeth, we have been given the Scriptures, and the people of faith that we know in our own lives.

These two invitations from God are especially important for those of us who are right now in the difficult part of our story —the part in which it seems to be taking a thousand years for God's promise of peace and joy to be fulfilled. Maybe we wish our family could be more like a Norman Rockwell painting, but we are beginning to suspect that it never will be. Or maybe there is someone far away that we dearly wish could be with us. Perhaps our hearts are aching for a person who has already gone home to God. Maybe our health is not good, and only seems to be getting worse. In those sorts of difficult situations we can be so focused on the impossible thing that we wish we had, that we miss the unlikely thing that our ever-surprising, ever-loving God wants to give us for our comfort. If we were wise we wouldn't expect to be able to guess what gift God will be giving us this Christmas. It could be anything from a set of three-inch-tall reference books to a palace in Jerusalem. But in any event, with Mary to guide us, we can find the courage to say "may it be done to me according to your word!"

Mary, the Mother of God, Jan. 1, 2009:
THE MYSTERY OF JESUS

(Num 6: 22-27; Gal 4: 4-7; Lk 2: 16-21)

We celebrate a very important feast today. We honor the Virgin Mary and give her the title "Mother of God". This title that we give to her points to a very great mystery. We do not know how it is possible for Mary, who is one of God's creatures, to be the mother of that same God, but we accept in faith that that is exactly what happened. Here are two reasons that it would be good for us to think about what we are celebrating today and to meditate on this mystery that is being presented to us: first, because it leads us closer to the mystery of who Jesus is, and second, because it leads us closer to the world that Jesus loved so much.

First, consider the mystery of who Jesus is. We believe that Jesus truly is God. He is one of the three persons of the Holy Trinity. As God, he is an important part of the creation of the universe. At the same time, we also believe that Jesus was truly human. He was born and he died. He was a person like us in all things except sin. We do not understand exactly how those two natures could co-exist within one individual, but we are confident that they did. We know this from our reading of the Bible, and also from our own experiences of God and Jesus in our lives.

The important contribution of today's feast day to our understanding of this great mystery is that it teaches us that there was never a time when Jesus was a man but not God. Long ago, some people had the idea that Jesus was born a man, but somehow he "became" God, through his great goodness and through God's good will. That is not what the Church believes and teaches. Through all of his life on earth,

Jesus was both God and man. He was both God and man when he taught us to call God our Father. He was both God and man he healed people of their illnesses. He was both God and man when he died on the cross. We learn from today's feast that he was both God and man even while he was in his mother's womb. One reason that we value today's feast day is that it leads us more deeply into this important mystery of our faith.

The second important aspect of today's feast day is that it can lead us closer to the world. It is true that Jesus was born only once through the power of the Holy Spirit in the life of the virgin Mary. But there is another sense in which we also bring Jesus to life in our world, whenever we act as he would have done. In Spanish there is an expression for giving birth that I like very much. In Spanish they say literally that the mother "gives her baby to light".

I think we can learn a lot by thinking about how we can "give Jesus to light" in our own lives. One way we can do this is through the way we act toward the people in our family. Jesus accepted people for who they were and loved them all: saints or sinners, in sickness or in health. When we accept the people in our family and love them even with all their virtues and faults, we are acting as Jesus would do.

Similarly we can give Jesus to light in our workplace or school. When things are difficult in our work, and there is much anger or jealousy or fear, we can try to remember the peace we find here in church and share that with others, just as Jesus would do.

Just as he did many years ago, Jesus wants to be present to the world of today, with all its pains and imperfections. We are privileged to have a part in making this happen, just as Mary his mother was privileged.

On behalf of Msgr. Nolan and Father Rene, and all of my brother deacons here in the parish, I wish you a new year that is full of peace and contentment, and a year in which you come to more fully appreciate the great mysteries of God, and in which Jesus truly is given to light in your life.

2nd Sunday in Ordinary Time, Jan. 18, 2009:
WHAT ARE YOU LOOKING FOR?

(1 Sam 3: 3-10, 19; 1 Cor 6: 13-15, 17-20; Jn 1: 35-42)

There are only a handful of times in the gospels when Jesus asks a question of someone, and when we look carefully at those places we notice that most often when he does this, his purpose is not so much to gain some information, as it might be for us, but rather Jesus' main purpose is to make people think harder about the question he is asking. He is inviting them to re-examine the question in their own minds, and come up with a better answer than might first fly off their lips. For example, in one place in the gospels, Jesus asks the Apostles "Who do the people say that I am?" and that question starts off a discussion in the group that finally draws out of Peter his personal faith affirmation that Jesus is the Messiah, the son of God.

In today's gospel Jesus also asks a question. He asks it of the two disciples who followed him down the road. On the face of it, it seems like an innocent little conversation starter: "What are you looking for?" But when we think a little more about it, this question is actually very deep. And when it is asked of us by the Son of God, it is a question that is big enough to take our breath away. It is a question without limits, and it strikes us dumb as we consider it.

The gospel writer has been very clever too, in this little story. He has only given us the name of one of the two disciples that Jesus spoke with that day. Some say that the reason for this is that the other person was the gospel writer himself. Now that may be, but the lack of another name is very convenient for us, because it allows each of us to imagine that we are the one standing there with Andrew on that dusty road, staring into the welcoming face of Jesus and hearing him ask us that deep question "What are you looking for?"

What are we looking for from Jesus? Sometimes, I think, we are not quite sure ourselves. My wife tells the story of a woman she knew long ago, who was taking a trip through Europe in the Spring of the year. As it turned out, this woman was going to be in France at Easter time, and although she wasn't a very religious person, she decided that she wanted to do Easter right that year. She decided that she wanted to attend midnight Mass at Chartres cathedral. Wouldn't it be wonderful to participate in the greatest liturgy of the Church year in one of the most beautiful shrines in Christendom! Well, unfortunately, this woman ended up disappointed by her Easter experience. The church was very crowded for one thing, and from where she was seated way off to the side, she couldn't see the pageantry or smell the clouds of incense. The crowd noises blunted the beauty of the music, and all in all she wished she'd stayed in her hotel.

Probably we could have warned that woman that pageantry and beautiful music was the wrong thing to be looking for in the Easter vigil, but if it isn't to see a colorful pageant or hear beautiful music, then why have we come to this holy place today? I suppose that if we were to take a poll of all the people in the church this morning, we might get lots of different answers. I would like to share with you three needs that I have at various times brought with me to the Mass: the need for hope, peace and consolation.

We might have come here in order to refresh our hope. You probably noticed that we are back in our green vestments today, after two months of wearing either purple or gold. Green in the color of hope. In these bleak winter days, the color green is supposed to remind us that even now the world is turning toward spring. We may not be able to see it yet, but it will surely come eventually. And just as surely as spring will come again, Jesus will come again in glory. This is our faith and our hope and our joy. We come here on Sundays to celebrate that hope together.

Alternatively, we might be coming here this morning looking for peace. The world can be so full of chaos and craziness sometimes. Whenever we watch the news, it seems that our living rooms fill up with scenes of senseless violence, or senseless greed, or senseless financial markets. But here it is different. Here in this quiet place we find rituals that we know and love. We say again the prayers that we have said a million times. We hear readings that we almost know by heart. We hear the priest recite again the words of consecration that bring us the bread of life. Here we find sustenance and timeless truth that can restore our peace.

Finally, we may have come to this place today looking for consolation. When we are feeling the pain of loss or separation, loneliness or illness, we can come to this place and find friendly smiles and concerned friends. We hear again the comforting words of Scripture, which remind us of God's abiding concern for our welfare. Those comforting messages can console us in our pain.

Hope, peace and consolation—three things we might be happy to find here this Sunday. Of course, we don't always find these wonderful things here when we come looking for them. Sometimes when we come here looking for hope, we might be confronted instead with the needs of other people. We might be asked to dig down into our pockets, to give some stranger the gift of hope, when we feel the need of hope for ourselves. Sometimes instead of peace of mind, we may leave church disturbed, confronted with a pressing need to change our lives to become better followers of Christ. Sometimes when we come here looking for consolation, we are instead confronted with the grief of others, to which we are called to respond. Note that when this happens, the situation is different from that of the woman at Chartres. She left the liturgy untouched. We *are* being touched by God, just not in the way we had expected when we were coming into the experience.

I think that we can get more comfortable with the unexpectedness of this situation if we think about the answer to Jesus' question in that way: what we are really looking for today is God's touch in our lives. That touch might be the gentle caress of a loving father, or it might be a gentle shove in a direction we need to go. We don't know which we will receive, because God is not a force of nature that we can control, he is a living being with whom we enter into conversation as we pray. How that conversation will turn out depends both on us and on him.

Our word "sacrament" embodies this idea. The older Greek word for the same thing is "mysterion". It refers to a situation which is fundamentally outside of laws of nature, because God is interacting with us. Today we are invited to enter into the mysterion, the sacrament of this liturgy, and allow ourselves to be touched by God. In that touch, we may hope to find the peace beyond all understanding, and also the power to make a real change for the better in our lives. Like Samuel, the little boy in today's first reading who in his dreams heard the voice of God calling his name, we are invited to respond "Speak Lord, your servant is listening."

6th Sunday in Ordinary Time, Feb. 15, 2009:
JESUS IN THE IN-BETWEEN TIMES OF OUR LIFE

(Lv 13: 1–2. 44–46; 1 Cor 10: 31–11, 1; Mk 1: 40–45)

At the end of today's selection from Mark's gospel, it says that the people had to go out into the deserted places in order to be with Jesus. We needn't think of the "deserted places" that Jesus spent so much time in as an actual desert. The Greek word used here could mean a desert, but it could also simply mean a place without any people in it. Sometimes the word is translated as "lonely places". Imagine being so keen on the idea of being with Jesus that you would hike out into the wilderness to seek him out in such a place. What would that journey be like?

Even today we may feel that same desire, but where can we go to find Jesus? One place that our faith tells us we can have an encounter with Jesus is here in the Mass. We believe that he is present in several different ways every time we gather to celebrate. He is present first of all in the gathered assembly. He told us "wherever two or three are gathered in my name, there I am also." This is a promise and a fact, not just a pious wish. He is also truly present in the proclamation of Scripture and in the person of the priest. Finally, of course, he is present in the Eucharist itself.

I hope that you experience all those different modes of Jesus' presence often, because they are a great blessing, but these ways of encountering Jesus, many as they are, do not exhaust the possibilities that are open to us. In keeping with today's gospel let's explore some other opportunities that come to us in the "in-between" times of our lives.

Here's an example of what I mean. On Monday morning I happened to get up early, before dawn in fact, and while I was doing my morning prayers, for a moment I put down my prayer book and just noticed my surroundings. The window in the room where I was sitting looks to the east, and I could see the beginnings of the sunrise. The house was very quiet. The only sound I could hear was the cooing of a mourning dove outside the window. That very gentle and repetitive cooing seemed to be laying down the beat for the dance of the planets. It was a very peaceful moment to just be with the creator and enjoy his works.

In that moment I was resting in between the night and the day. Sometimes in the night I wake up and think about things. All right, sometimes, I worry. I worry about the kids, my work, the world. And then in the day, more practical things like work schedules absorb my attention. But at that moment I found myself blessedly in between those different distractions.

We all have such in-between moments in our lives. There is the time when we transition between home and work, for example. Commuting can be that sort of in-between time, or maybe you have the kind of job in which you can take a moment when you arrive at work to get a cup of coffee and gather your wits before diving into the day's work. Perhaps you have young kids, and you treasure the time right after the kids are tucked in bed, and you can catch your breath before tackling the last chores of the evening. Such in-between times are precious and we should not rush through them. We should accept them as a gift from God and linger in them, savoring his peace. I'm not suggesting that we try to fill those times up with some activity. I'm suggesting that we notice them and enjoy their emptiness and lack of distraction.

Sometimes it is not so easy to make the time to do that, of course. Often, our lives seemed to be scripted down to the millisecond, and things are made even more complicated by the way everybody in the family has interlocking schedules. Well, God still has his ways of trying to get through to us with his gifts. Sometimes it may happen that a snag will develop in all that complicated scheduling and we may find ourselves waiting for ten or fifteen minutes for someone or something. Maybe we are ten minutes early for some event because the traffic wasn't as bad as we thought it would be, or maybe the person we are meeting is unexpectedly going to be fifteen minutes late.

Such interruptions in the flow of our day can be annoying, if we let them get to us. But we don't need to let that happen. Instead of just staring at our watches, or dreaming up sarcastic remarks to say to the person who is making us wait, I wonder if we can try to re-imagine that little bit of time of waiting as an in-between time, and accept it as a gift from God. It is an invitation from God to just sit quietly with him.

Now often when we get into such a situation, we might be in a crowded or noisy place where it is difficult to find any peace of mind. Nevertheless we may be able to step aside mentally into a place of peace. It might help if we can imagine a place that we have visited in the past, a place where we have known some peace.

When I was a teenager, I worked at a summer camp. It was hard work, and I really loved it. But the thing that I loved most of all about working at that camp was the few days at the end of the summer after all the campers went home and the staff remained behind to shut the camp down for the winter. It was a true in-between time: summer camp was over, but the school year still seemed far away. It was beautifully quiet and peaceful, and when I try to think of a place of peace in my life, that's where I go. We might want to meditate this week on a time and place in our past where we have known peace. If we can keep such a place and time firmly in mind, then, when we hit a scheduling snag in our day, instead of feeling frustrated, we can settle back and reconnect with that peaceful place.

Clearly, situations in which we are forced into an in-between time can be more difficult to deal with spiritually than when we choose the in-between time for ourselves. And there are even more difficult examples to consider. Some people feel thrust into an in-between place when they end a long-term relationship. It might be a relationship with another person, as when a loved-one dies, or a marriage breaks up, or it might be a relationship with a company, when our employment is terminated. Those can be very difficult sorts of in-between places, as we try to figure out what might fill in the empty place we feel, or even if anything ever could.

Other people feel they are in an in-between place when they suffer a debilitating illness. We know that our daily routine has been knocked for a loop, and we don't know when or how it will settle down again.

The leper in today's gospel was certainly forced by his illness into an in-between place that was not of his own choosing. He was stuck in between the desert where he could not live, and the town where he was not allowed. But then, something marvelous happened to him: he had an encounter there with the love of Jesus. While in that in-between place, he asked for healing and received it through Jesus' loving touch. His experience can speak to our experience. When we are in such a situation, if we ask Jesus, he will touch us with his love.

As we continue with our worship this morning, let us ask God to make himself known to us in our in-between times. Let us commit ourselves to noticing all of the in-between times of our lives and by accepting them as his gift, allow them to become for us a source of grace and peace.

Friday after Ash Wednesday, Feb. 26, 2009:

FINDING JOY IN THE LENTEN SEASON

(Is 58: 1-9; Mt 9: 14-15)

The season of Lent offers us many opportunities to become closer to Jesus. For example, in a few minutes we will pray the Stations of the Cross, and meditate together over Jesus' suffering and death. It is not that we glory in the pain that he suffered, but we do glory in the beautiful act of self-giving love that the various Stations of the Cross represent.

Praying the Stations of the Cross is a good thing, but in order to really feel closer to Jesus this season, we should follow the good example of our patron, Saint Paul, and also try to imitate Jesus' self-giving love. There are many ways that we can do this. We can do it as loving parents, and we can do it as dutiful children. We can try to be more giving and forgiving with our spouses and coworkers.

This will not be painless. For example, if we have had angry words with someone, it is difficult to be the one to make the first move and say "I'm sorry for what I said yesterday." This is especially true when we really feel deep down in our heart that it should be the other person who asks for forgiveness first. Being the one to make the first move could be a little cross that we carry in humble imitation of Jesus, and if we do that with love in our hearts, we will really come to know him better, and feel closer to him.

Extending ourselves in this way is an important thing for us to do, and Lent is a wonderful time to work at it, but there is another aspect of Jesus' life that we should also be trying to imitate, which is hinted at in the gospel we just read. That is, Jesus as the Bridegroom of the Church—the one who invites us into the great festival of God's love. It is clear from the gospels, that Jesus enjoyed his meals, and the company of his friends. He loved all of God's creation, and he infected others with that joy. We will learn a lot about him, and feel closer to him, if we also try to do the same. The gospel hints that we should not be glum while the bridegroom is with us. And my brothers and sisters, here he is still. He is with us in the blessed sacrament on our altar. This knowledge can be a fountain of joy which fills our lives and overflows into the world.

My mother was a person who really understood this. She did not have an easy life, but she was a relentless optimist, and always tried to keep a cheerful perspective. The rain we have this evening reminds me of one time when we were kids, and we went for a picnic in the mountains of Western Maryland. It was sunny when we left home, but soon it got cloudy and began to spatter rain. As the rain got heavier and heavier, my father wanted to turn back, but my mother wouldn't hear of it. She said "Well, at least the park won't be crowded," and we all groaned.

When we got to the park we were further disappointed because the park was closed for restorations, but my mother led us to a scenic overlook that we had passed on the way in. As we sat in the car eating our sandwiches she said "Well, at least we have a nice view." And then as the clouds rolled in around us she said "Well, at least it's not snowing."—which made us kids look out the window, wondering who would see the first flake. Finally on the way home she shared a final bit of wisdom, and said "Well, at least we are all together." She was right, of course. That was the best part. I can see that clearly now as an adult with kids who are off on their own, but wisely she waited to share that last observation with us until we had stopped and gotten ice-cream cones!

Perhaps this Lent Jesus is calling us to know him better as the bridegroom. To try harder to be people of hope and bringers of joy to the people around us. Here we are together to pray and meditate on this blessed night. It may be raining outside, but at least we're together. Thanks be to God!

ZEAL FOR THE KINGDOM OF GOD

(Ex 20: 1–17; 1 Cor 1: 22–25; Jn 2: 13–25)

When I was a boy, I joined a troop of Boy Scouts. It was interesting, but a little bit dull, until our old scout master retired and a younger man replaced him. With refreshing informality, the new scout master asked us to call him "Mr. Ken". He was enthusiastic and fun to be with, as well as being a great outdoorsman. He was very strict about some things. Uniforms had to be worn to every meeting, and all badges had to be sewed on straight. But the most amazing thing was that he really believed in all that stuff that they teach you in Boy Scouts, things like "do a good turn daily". He believed deeply in those principles and he made us believe too. He was a real leader and we would have followed him anywhere.

Sometimes I wonder what it must have been like to be with Jesus when he walked the earth. The best I have been able to do is to imagine him being sort of like a larger-than-life Mr. Ken. Jesus really believed all those prophecies in Scripture, like the ones from Isaiah about blind people seeing, and those who can't speak, singing for joy, and those who can't walk, being able to dance. He rejoiced in all those promises of God and he went about making them happen.

Jesus had a burning desire to see the coming of the kingdom of God. In today's gospel we see him acting very directly to protect the honor of God's temple, but he expressed that same love for the things of God in many other ways as well. It was there in his tireless crisscrossing of the Galilean countryside preaching and healing. It was there in his breaking through cultural barriers to seek out lost souls and take meals with sinners. His attitude left him discontented with the status quo in the world, but hopeful and enthusiastic about what it could become.

It is that hopeful, enthusiastic attitude toward the things of God that we call "holy zeal." When they sensed that appealing quality in Jesus, the apostles jumped off their fishing boats and followed him. That same zeal is also a part of our call as Christians; it is our inheritance through the saints. This doesn't necessarily mean that we are called to go around overturning the tables of all the money changers we meet. We have no evidence that the Apostles ever did any such thing in their imitation of Jesus, but we certainly are called to imitate Jesus' hope and his enthusiastic love of God and to spread those around to others.

Now there are any number of reasons that we might feel reluctant to participate more fully in Jesus' zeal. One is that being filled with holy zeal might be confused with being "wired" all the time; as if we all have had so much coffee that we can't sit down. Perhaps zeal does mean living our lives a bit more consciously and intensely, but it doesn't mean being frantic. Zeal allows for resting as well as for acting, but all for the greater glory of God.

Another potential problem with zeal is that it is a virtue that mixes very badly with political power. In history we have many examples of groups who have gone overboard in their religious zeal when they got in charge of things and ended up creating a grim and intolerant society. The Taliban is just one extreme example of this tendency. We certainly want to avoid falling into such a terrible trap. We want to imitate the zeal of Jesus and also his gentleness.

There is a final danger in giving ourselves over to zeal, and that is that if we are not careful, it can lead us to be swept away by religious fads. I think that danger is what today's gospel is talking about at the very end. Jesus accepted the people who flocked to him when they saw the signs he was performing, but he knew human nature, and he knew that their enthusiasm might be short-lived. Many of them might very well be swept away at any moment to follow the next exciting personality to hit the streets of Jerusalem.

Well, so far you may think that I have not really been a good salesman for the virtue of religious zeal! I hope you haven't been scared off though, because zeal is a virtue that has been a beautiful part of many of the lives of the saints, for example Saint Francis and Saint Teresa of Avila. These saints and many others have avoided the dangers inherent in this virtue. By allowing their zeal for the things of God to direct their lives, they ended up making an important difference in the world.

If we do want to try to increase our participation in the virtue of holy zeal, we can do that little by little, beginning by working up a greater enthusiasm for our faith. There are numerous ways that we might do this. One thing that we might do is to immerse ourselves more deeply in our Catholic culture. Reading some of the lives of the saints, and seeing their holy zeal in action can give us a push in the right direction. We might stop by our parish library, and pick out one of the many books on the saints that they have to offer. There other books that might also increase our zeal. One good one is called "I like being Catholic". This is a book of quotes and short essays that celebrate our Catholic traditions, particularly those of the United States over the last century. I think our parish library is going to get a copy of this book, but they might not have done so yet. But you can Google it, of course. Just search for "I like being Catholic". One more very useful book that one you might Google for is "the Catholic Home", which was written by Meredith Gould, who is a member of our parish. This book gives some great ideas for making our faith a more integrated part of our lives.

I have to say, though, that the one single thing we can do to improve our Christian zeal is to sing hymns more often. Every morning I pray Morning Prayer, and that begins with a Hymn. Now, most mornings I am still a bit groggy when I begin; my first cup of tea has not kicked in yet. And maybe for that reason I miss some of the notes, and I might change keys a couple of times before I'm done, but by the time I'm done singing "This day God gives me/strength of high heaven,/sun and moon shining, /flame in my hearth." ... by the time I finish, I am in a very different place, physiologically, psychologically and spiritually. There really is a flame in my hearth again.

If you want to get started, you might pick one of the hymns we sing in church this evening. Pick the one you like best and let that be the song in your heart this week. Sing it out loud in the shower; sing it in the car. Just let go and sing it as if nobody's listening. Except God, of course, and he loves to hear your voice raised in song. Try it and see if that doesn't lift your level of hope and holy zeal this week, and see if that doesn't sweeten your interactions with other people.

It's important, because our world has so much need for hope and enthusiasm these days. This never-ending financial crisis we seem to be in is wearing lots of people down. Our help and hope can console such people. Many are feeling shaken by it all. It is causing some people to wonder if greed is such a good principle to build our society around. Imagine that. Some people have even been heard wondering aloud if accumulating material goods really brings us happiness. Our faith provides such a strong alternative to the bankrupt ideals of consumerism. If we can be a presence of hope and enthusiasm to people who are feeling overwhelmed by the financial uncertainties, we will draw people to our faith, and in our own way, that will be helping to bring about the Kingdom of God.

SUFFERING, FORGIVENESS AND PEACE

(Acts 4: 32–35; 1 Jn 5: 1–6; Jn 20: 19–31)

There is a couple that my wife and I are friends with. They are not members of this parish, and I'm pretty sure you don't know them, but just to be safe, I'll call them "Mary" and "John". I'm deliberately using common names because what happened to them could happen to anybody. John and Mary are both good people, but a while back their marriage ran into a rough patch when John began to have trouble controlling his drinking. It was never terrible trouble, but it was quite bad enough, and it was clear to Mary at least that things were getting steadily worse.

One day it got to be so bad that Mary couldn't take it anymore, and she just got into the car and left home. Not knowing what to do or where to go, she just drove around until finally she ended up in the parking lot of Herrontown Woods. And there she sat for a long time, trying to figure out what she was going to do next.

Mary knew she still loved John, but she had run out of excuses for his behavior. She knew deep down that he couldn't really control what was happening to him and what he was doing, but that didn't matter to her anymore. It didn't matter whether the drinking problem was caused by stress at work, or something in his upbringing, or by bad genes. There were just too many broken promises, and too much pain.

Now, Mary had a strong faith, and she knew that she ought to try to forgive John for what he was doing, but she just couldn't do it. The hurt that his drinking was bringing to her and to the kids was just too deep. She had forgiven John in the past, and some part of her wanted to forgive him again. She even prayed for the strength to do so one more time, but that strength wasn't what she received in answer to her prayer.

What did come to Mary as she prayed, and the thing that allowed her to leave that parking lot, was a sort of a truce with God. Mary knew that she couldn't forgive John herself, but she decided that she would allow God to do so, if, in his infinite wisdom, he would choose to do that. She couldn't sort out all the causes and effects of John's drinking, but she would allow God to sort it all out and to assign guilt and innocence where it belonged. That was the best that Mary could do at that time, and that small light of grace was enough to guide her to her next step.

I think that Mary and John's experience give a particularly important perspective to today's celebration of Divine Mercy Sunday. God is generous in mercy, but we humans often have a really hard time being equally generous. Most often, when we are hurt we desire justice more than mercy. Our faith tells us that God does listen attentively to those calls for justice, and he sends us Jesus to be our judge.

You probably know that in ancient times, most of the judging of disputes between people was not done in a formal court of law, as might be done today. Two people who had a dispute about something would choose a person of honor whom they both trusted and respected, and ask that person to judge who was right and who was wrong. Because both people deeply respected the person they selected as judge, they would feel honor-bound to accept whatever judgment was forthcoming.

When we are injured in some way by someone and we go to Jesus asking for justice, we can trust that Jesus will truly understand the pain that we have suffered.

In an oblique way, a reading that we heard in church a few weeks ago makes this point. The letter to the Hebrews says this about Jesus:

Son though he was, he learned obedience from
what he suffered; and when he was made perfect,
he became the source of eternal salvation for all
who obey him. (Heb 5, 9)

It is kind of mind boggling to think that Jesus might need to be made perfect in some way, but in light of today's celebration we can say that Jesus' own suffering made him the perfect judge for humanity, because it gave him the credentials he needs to be trusted by those victimized by sin. Were *we* hurt by someone *we* love? No worse than Jesus was. Were *we* betrayed? So was Jesus, by almost everyone. We can all trust that Jesus will do the right thing as judge, both for the one who got hurt, and for the one who has remorse for hurting someone else. We are not asking for justice from some distant deity up in heaven who forgives everybody because he thinks that the things they did are trivial in the cosmic scheme of things. We are approaching Jesus, who knows, who really feels, our pain personally.

In today's gospel, Jesus shows us the depth of God's merciful love in the way he interacts with his disciples. We all know that he had the right to go in there and say "So where were you? I was stretched out on the cross, and you were curled up in a corner some place! Couldn't you have at least come and stood by me?" But he didn't say that at all. He understood the apostles' remorse, and his first words when he entered the upper room were "Peace be with you." And "Whose sins you forgive are forgiven them. Whose sins you hold bound are held bound." I use the older translation here, because the idea of sins being bound or loosed is a powerful one. It is important to remember that it is not *only* the one who sinned who is bound. When we cannot let go of a hurt that we have experienced, we too are bound by that fact. Jesus so wants us to be free! He suffered and died and made himself the perfect judge so that we might be free. It is very appropriate that Divine Mercy Sunday comes so soon after our celebration of the passion, death and resurrection of Jesus. The two are intimately related.

And what happened with Mary and John? Well, the peace that Mary found by praying while sitting in that parking lot empowered her to go back and to watch for a time when she could get through to John about the seriousness of his drinking problem. Not in anger, not with recriminations, but with all firmness she confronted him and told him "I can't take it any more. Get help, or get out." And, by the grace of God, those words got through to John and he finally realized how close he was to the edge of the precipice, and he did get help. It has not been easy for him, but he has now been sober for more than 25 years, and their marriage is as good now as it ever has been. In the midst of their pain, John and Mary were visited by God's mercy and love.

We celebrate today the joyous fact that the mercy of God comes to all those who ask for it. Mercy for those who are hurting, and mercy for those who are remorseful for hurts that they have caused to others. It is a deep mystery how God can make both those things happen at the same time, but we wait for them both with Christian hope.

Like so many mysteries, this one finds its best expression in poetry rather than in prose, and in that spirit, I would like to leave you with some verses from Psalm 85, which sum up our desire as children of our loving God:

> *I will hear what the Lord God has to say,*
> *A voice that speaks of peace.*
> *Peace for those who are his friends*
> *And those who turn to him in their hearts...*
>
> *Mercy and faithfulness have met;*
> *Justice and peace have embraced.*
> *Faithfulness shall spring from the earth*
> *And justice look down from heaven. (Ps 85: 9-12)*

LOVING THE PEOPLE WE DO NOT LIKE

(Acts 10: 25–26, 34–35, 44–48; 1 Jn 4: 7–10; Jn 15: 9–17)

When I went to graduate school, long ago and far away, I spent my first several years living in a dormitory for grad students. In the room to my left lived a guy named Bob. He was a likeable fellow—the sort of person who would laugh at a good joke, and a person who would do you a favor at the drop of a hat. The person living on my right (I'll call him Percy), was a different sort of person. Percy was not a happy guy, and apparently had no interest in socializing. He did not like guitar music, at least not the 60's-style folk music that I usually played—In my room—Right next to his. So, that was probably the biggest bone of contention between us, but there were many others as well. He even complained because I liked to keep the door to my room propped open whenever I was around the dorm. Eventually, even the tiniest perceived slight was enough to cause offense between us, and our conversations, which were never very long to begin with, got shorter and shorter and less friendly. Finally we stopped talking entirely. I don't think either of us was happy with the way things ended up, but the whole thing felt like it had tumbled out of my control.

Our gospel today shines a very challenging spotlight on that very common situation: being thrown together for a time with someone we really don't like. How do we act out of love toward such a person? It is possible to do so, because the "love" we are talking about here is not the "warm cuddly" feeling that we get when we think about the people that we like to be with. That warm feeling is an emotion, and we can't ordain our emotions by an act of will. We can't turn them on, and we can't turn them off. That is not what Jesus is asking us to do. The love that Jesus talks about here is the active concern and sense of responsibility that a good shepherd feels towards his sheep. That sort of active love means self-sacrifice always, and sometimes even giving up of one's life for the beloved. It might give us a whole new slant on this gospel, if we were to read it through again, but everywhere we see the verb "love", put in "act lovingly toward".

Now, being a loving friend to Bob, the easy-going guy, wasn't very hard at all for me. We would share freely the raw materials of student life, like paper and pens and pretzels, and do small errands for each other. But I never once said to Percy "Hey, I'm going to the library. Got any books that need to go back?" I'm not sure he would have trusted me with them, and I don't think he would have been eager for the privilege of taking my books back to the library either!

So how *do* we go about acting out of love toward people we don't like? That is a hard question that each of us might meditate on in the coming week. Thinking about it in preparation for this homily, I was led to Saint Paul's famous hymn to love in the first letter to the Corinthians. You probably know the one; it is proclaimed at many weddings. For our purposes here today, let's focus in on the middle section, which tends to get a little bit lost in between the glorious beginning and ending of the reading. Here is what Saint Paul says in verses five and six of chapter 13:

> *Love is not rude,*
> *It does not seek its own interest,*
> *It is not quick tempered,*
> *It does not brood over injury,*
> *It does not rejoice over wrong-doing but rejoices*
> *with the truth.*

A little bit mundane, you might think, but these are good things that we might train ourselves to offer in love to people that we don't particularly like. They are certainly things I wish that I had offered more of to Percy.

There are several things to notice about Saint Paul's little list. One is that these are things that *we can do*, even if the other person is not playing by the same rules. When we read in the gospel that Jesus says "love one another", it is clear that he is speaking to a group, and that everyone in the group is to live by the same rule. That observation might lead us to wonder if this "law of love" even applies to other situations, but then we read a few words further, where Jesus says "as I have loved you". So, how did Jesus act toward the people who didn't act lovingly toward him? He did not stoop to their standards, but kept to his own. And so, we can continue to be civil even when the other person seems to us to be behaving rudely. In fact, it will give us a greater sense of control over the situation if we know that we have chosen, out of love, to act differently.

A second thing to point out about this list, is that it mostly seems to be asking us to cut the other person a bit of slack. So, can we lighten up on that loud obnoxious person who has the really annoying laugh, or that know-it-all who has strong opinions on every topic from fine wines to the secret Vatican archives and the inner life of the wooly mammoth, or finally, how about that gloomy person who sees behind every silver lining a dark storm cloud that people are probably not paying enough attention to? That's just a part of my list, yours might be different. Yours might even include deacons with silly beards, I suppose. But whoever is on the list, for whatever reason, we don't need to let such irritations get under our skin quite so easily.

One way to gain a bit more of an emotional distance in such a situation is to try to see the person as more than just a walking instance of the thing that annoys *us*. Most people do the things they do because of some need inside themselves, not because they are trying to annoy us. Recognizing that the other person is acting out of a need of their own, even if we will never know what that need is, can help to depersonalize the interaction that is bothering us. Of course, if they are doing something hurtful, that doesn't excuse what they have done, but it does put the act at a different distance from us personally.

Another line of thought that might give us a bit of additional emotional distance from behaviors that annoy us is to do a little self-examination about why some good people seem to be able to put up with a certain person, but we can't. I know with my kids, for example, the thing that used to annoy me most is when they would fall victim to the same faults that I saw in my own personality. Knowing why we are so bothered by some particular behavior can help take the heat out of an uncomfortable encounter.

If we can, by one means or another, gain a little bit of emotional distance on the troubled relationship, that might make it easier for us to follow through on some of Saint Paul's five modest principles of loving.

> *Love is not rude,*
> *It does not seek its own interest,*
> *It is not quick tempered,*
> *It does not brood over injury,*
> *It does not rejoice over wrong-doing but rejoices*
> *with the truth.*

This is like love one point zero, right? There is more to true loving care and concern, but with some people we should probably try get this part right first.

Today Jesus calls us his friends. What an exciting invitation. As he says, taking up that invitation in all its parts will fill us with great joy, but it will also be hard work. We need to keep trying to follow his commandment and make progress on acting lovingly toward *all* the people in our life, including the ones that we don't particularly like.

FINDING GOD WHEN WE FEEL ADRIFT IN LIFE

(Job 38: 1, 8-11; 2 Cor 5: 14-17; Mk 4:35-41)

Reading today's gospel puts me in mind of the times when my family used to do a lot of fishing and crabbing on the Chesapeake Bay. We would go out in a rented rowboat propelled by a bright red second-hand outboard motor that my father had bought from a friend. One particular time, when I was about eight or nine, we were on our way back to dock at the end of the day and we had to cross a wide inlet. The current was pretty strong with the changing tide, but we made good headway until suddenly the motor conked out, and we began to drift out toward open water.

Now I knew that beyond our inlet was the bay and beyond the bay were the seven seas, and beyond the seven seas was China. And I began to get a little bit worried, because I knew that in China they only ate vegetables and rice, and I didn't like either of those. But then I began to watch my father working away in the back of the boat. He had his toolbox out and was fussing with the motor and muttering to himself. Probably it is for the best that I was in the prow of the boat and I couldn't hear what he was saying, but I could see him calmly doing what he needed to do to get the motor going again.

Seeing him, I felt very secure because I had a child's utter confidence that there was nothing my father could not fix if he had the proper tools. And sure enough, after what seemed like an hour, but was probably only about five minutes, the motor sputtered to life, and we made our way back home without further difficulty.

So that is my Father's Day tribute. Thank you to all you Dads out there, whether you are a natural father, or someone who has volunteered to be a father in someone's life. You do so much to keep things going in the family—stuff that generally only gets noticed when it doesn't work. Today we acknowledge your many gifts and thank you from the bottom of our hearts.

My story is also one that fits with today's gospel, if it helps us understand better the odd mixture of helplessness and confidence that the Apostles experienced while crossing the Sea of Galilee. There are times in life when we too find ourselves thrust into some scary situation, and we long for someone who can fix what's broken.

One way this can happen is when we or someone we love contracts a serous illness. Some of you know that I am fighting cancer again. I can tell you, that that's a feeling of being out of control of what's happening in your life. It can feel just like being swept away to China against your will. That's often true for the people who are ill, and also for those who share their lives.

There are other ways that we can feel set adrift in life. For example, our department might be downsized or out-sourced, and unexpectedly we are out of a job. Our society places so much emphasis on employment as a measure of worth, that a person without a job can begin to feel valueless and without purpose in life. That is incorrect, of course, but it's hard to fight that impression. Even the worry that such a thing *might* happen can be very scary.

Or perhaps we have lost the person that was our life companion. Now suddenly everything seems out of place and off key. We have a need that feels like it will never be filled. A similar emptiness is sometimes felt by those still waiting to find a life companion. In both cases we see people happily in love, and say "But what about me? Why can't I have that kind of happiness?"

In all of those different life situations, and many more like them, we might feel thrust into a place that is scary and lonely and full of uncertainty. In the context of today's gospel, I wonder if we can't begin to approach such situations as if Jesus is saying to us, just as he said to the Apostles: "I need you to get in the boat, and begin to row across the sea." We might want to object to Jesus that the boat is leaky, or that we see a storm on the horizon, or that we don't know how to row very well, only to have him repeat: "Still, I need you to get in the boat and begin to row across the sea."

In the situations I just outlined, of course, we might not feel we have much choice in the matter. We are already in the boat, so to speak, but still we can make the faith choice to see our current difficulties as a part of God's will in our lives and go along with them willingly.

There is mystery here. As we will hear next week, the Book of Wisdom affirms that "God did not make death, and he does not rejoice in the destruction of the living." So God does not want us to suffer. And yet, when suffering is unavoidable, our willing acceptance of it can be a source of grace. It is not easy to make the decision to accept such a situation. It takes faith and hope and courage. And where will we find those virtues when we need them?

Well, the good news is that Jesus does not send us alone into the boat; he gives us companions to be our source of hope and courage. Maybe it will be some of our relatives or friends, or members of our faith community, but somewhere there are people who will help us on our journey, if only we will allow it. It's just like today's gospel; the Apostles set out together. Now some of them knew the sea well, and at least at the beginning, it wasn't so scary for them. But others, like Matthew the tax collector for instance, didn't know prow from stern or port from starboard. He needed the others to help him along. Whenever we get stuck in a similar scary situation we should begin to look around for the companions God is getting ready for us.

Companions can help with practical details, and also by sharing their stories with us, especially when the stories are what I will call "leaky boat" stories. We may be gifted with a story about our friend in a difficult situation, when he or she was very worried, but somehow God made it turn out OK. Perhaps not the way the person hoped for at first, and maybe there was pain and difficulty along the way, but in the end it turned out "Good Enough." Such stories can give us hope that our story will also have a happy ending.

So companions that God sends us can be a great help, but it gets even better than that, because Jesus himself promises to come with us. He gets right into the boat beside us, which is even better than having your Dad and his toolbox along. It is just like it happened in today's gospel. In our fear, we may sometimes wonder if Jesus is really paying attention to what is going on in our lives, but never doubt that he is there. In fact, hurting as we are, we have the special privilege of bringing Jesus into scary places like hospital rooms and unemployment offices, where he may otherwise be an infrequent guest.

Finally, we can be encouraged because Jesus has his own leaky-boat story to share with us. That story is what we have just gotten done celebrating. We began in Lent with Passion Sunday, and then came all the highs and lows of Holy Week, and finally the fifty glorious days of the Easter season. Now there is a leaky-boat story to beat them all. As we come to appreciate it better because of our own difficult experiences, that story too can give us hope and confidence and courage.

So as we continue with our worship this morning, let us ask God to bless all fathers, both natural and volunteer, and give them the reward of their labors. Let us also make an effort to recognize all of the other companions that God has sent to help us on our way, most importantly our brother Jesus. Let us collect and treasure all the leaky-boat stories we hear so that they can be our courage when we have to climb into the boat ourselves.

4th Sunday of Advent, Dec. 20, 2009:

SAYING "YES" TO GOD IN THE MIDST OF UNCERTAINTY

(Mic 5:1–4; Heb 10: 5–10; Lk 1: 39–45)

Some of you may know that I have been in and out of the hospital several times over the last six months, and in that time I met a lot of people and learned a lot of things. I would like to describe for you a very special person that I met on one of those visits. His name is Rod and he and I were hospital roommates for a while. He has been fighting cancer for more than eight years now and has had five major operations in that time. You might expect after such a long roller-coaster ride of raised and lowered hopes, that Rod would be feeling tired and bitter about his life, but in fact, when I met him, he seemed to be quite happy. He made jokes with all the nurses, and took delight in the food on his lunch tray, and he was openly thankful for his wife's help in washing his face and brushing his hair.

Now, at first I thought that he was just putting a bold face on in all his trials, but I soon learned differently. We were together night and day, and it happened more than once that in the wee hours of the morning, when some piece of equipment was beeping and the nurses were nowhere to be found, we would both be awake and we would talk in the dark. I realized then that Rod had come to accept the fact that many details of his life were out of his control—the disease was calling the shots. But Rod had made a conscious decision to give up his expectations about what was going to happen weeks and months from now, and had decided to concentrate all his attention on being thankful for the small joys that came his way each day. It was that attitude, that personal decision about how he wanted to live, that allowed him to be happy in most circumstances.

I bring up the example of Rod today, because, even though he was not a religious person, his attitude toward life is the closest I have come yet to understanding the attitude of Mary, the mother of Jesus. When she made her "yes" to God, at the time of the Annunciation, she gave up control over many aspects of her life. She ended up with an unexplainable pregnancy in a society in which that was a completely unacceptable situation. That could not be what she dreamed of when she was younger. Then, when she was nine months pregnant, she had to make an eighty mile journey on foot and on donkey-back all the way from her home in Nazareth down to Bethlehem. Surely that was not something she wanted to do for the fun of it. Then in Bethlehem, tossed in among so many strangers, she gave birth to her first child in the back of a barn among the pungent smells of domestic animals. Surely she would have much preferred to be at home, with all her kinswomen and loved ones around her.

Yet, despite all those unexpected twists and turns in her life, Mary maintained the attitude that is expressed so well in the Magnificat, the hymn that follows in Luke's gospel, right after the words we read today. The words that Luke records are a summary of her attitude toward life: "My soul magnifies the Lord. My spirit rejoices in God my Savior, for he has looked with favor on his servant in her lowliness." Now it is likely that Saint Luke made her words more formal and poetic when he put them in his gospel, but the basic attitude behind those words is all Mary, of that I am sure.

When I look at the example of my friend Rod, and even more importantly at the example of our Mother Mary, I say "Wow! That is the way I want to live my life. I want to be able to rejoice in God my savior, no matter what difficulties come my way."

I think that part of the answer in getting ourselves from where we are now to that more favorable position, is to foster an attitude of thankfulness in our life. We want to make it our habit to notice the good things that God is doing for us each day, and give thanks for every one of them. There was a time when I was in the hospital that I was feeling a bit sorry for myself. "Why would God give me a broken liver?,

I wondered. In order to try to change that negative cycle of thinking, I decided to enumerate for myself all the parts of my body that were working correctly, from my eyes and ears down to my ankles and toes, and thank God for each one. It turned out to be a long list, and by the time I was done, my mood had changed, and I could sleep more easily.

So, one thing we can do to make ourselves better able to accept difficult situations is to make a habit of noticing and being thankful for all that God gives us each day. A second thing we can do is to try to let go of our expectations about the future. It is especially appropriate for us to be considering this idea in the week leading up to Christmas, because Christmas Day can become the intense focus for our expectations. We want the food to be perfect, the decorations to be perfect, and everyone to happy all day long. We spend lots of time in the Fall imaging what kinds of gifts to give and what we might receive. All those expectations can turn into a terrible burden, if we are not careful, and make it almost impossible for us to be really happy on that day. This is true especially if our expectations are about things that are out of our control. We may think "We'll all sing Christmas carols around the piano, just like when I was small" Or "I know that my boy friend really loves me, and I'm sure he will come up with a really great gift that shows just how much he cares."

Sometimes we have expectations about the good things we hope will happen, but other times we may be burdened by negative expectations. Even today, some of us may feel that our Christmas holiday is already busted. Maybe the person we wanted to be with won't be here, or the presents we wanted to give were unaffordable this year, or for whatever reason, we feel we have nothing much to look forward to on that day. We may not be as bad off as if we were waking up on Christmas morning in a barn, but we might feel this Christmas is going to be that kind of unwelcome surprise.

If we can let go of our expectations, both the good and the bad, we open ourselves up to recognize the unexpected gifts that God wants to give us each day. By giving up such expectations, we allow ourselves the possibility of being surprised by joy. This happened to my friend Rod one day they upgraded his menu from clear broth and Jell-O, and allowed him to have some ice cream. You can't imagine what pleasure he found in that little four-ounce paper container of chocolate ice cream.

I'm sure that Mary too was surprised by many joyous things in her very eventful life. For example, think about the visit of the shepherds with their glorious stories of the sky full of singing angels. Now if Mary and Joseph had met up with a rich relative in Bethlehem, and had their baby in a bedroom in a grand house, they would never have met those shepherds. No way would a bunch of shepherds fresh off the hillside and smelling of sheep be allowed into a grand house to visit a new baby, but they could visit that baby in a barn. Later in the gospel it says that Mary "treasured all these things in her heart." I'm sure the those memories brought her joy for a long time.

So, as we continue with our worship, let us commit ourselves to noticing all the good things that God sends our way, and make a habit of giving thanks. And let us make the effort to let go of our expectations about what we "need" in order to make this season joyous. It may be that at the end of Christmas day, and for many days to come, we will be able to rejoice with Mary and say "My soul magnifies the Lord. My spirit rejoices in God my Savior, for he as looked with favor on his lowly servant."

2nd Sunday in Ordinary Time, Jan. 17, 2010:
SPIRITUAL GIFTS

(Is 62: 1–5; 1 Cor 12: 4–11; Jn 2: 1–11)

Tonight, as we gather at the Lord's table, our hearts go out to the suffering people of Haiti. The earthquake and its aftermath may challenge us in several ways. We are challenged to figure out how best to help the people of Haiti, and we also may find that our faith in a good God is tested by observing this terrible event. "Where is their God?" is a question that skeptics and believers alike might ask. "What kind of God could allow such a thing to happen?" Philosophers and theologians have pondered such questions for centuries. They are bound up in the general problem of where evil comes from. A dry philosophical answer to the problem of evil is unlikely to be of much comfort in the face of such terrible human pain, but here are two observations that might be helpful as we meditate on this particular tragedy.

The first observation is that this natural disaster was made unimaginably worse by the poverty of the people of Haiti. Shoddy construction practices, the lack of adequate roads and water supply, the sprawling urban slums—all of these factors have turned a bad situation into a horrific one. And we certainly can't hold God responsible for those parts of the problem. God did not make the poverty. The poverty of the people of Haiti is the result of human actions, some taken centuries ago, and some of much more recent vintage. There is a long history behind this poverty, going all the way back to the founding of the nation of Haiti by escaped slaves. We cannot undo that long history, but we can say without a doubt that the scale of this disaster is a testament to the weakness of the response by the human family to the great needs of that nation, which have been with us for many years.

A second observation is that if we want to look for God in this human tragedy, the place to look is not in the power of the earthquake, but rather in the power of the human response to it. The great out-pouring from all around the world is truly a sign of God's love at work. The heart-felt compassion that we experience when we see or hear of the events happening there is a very human response, but it is also a very holy one. It is a gift of the Holy Spirit, and we should act on that impulse.

We hope and pray for the people of Haiti, that someday soon the words of the prophet Isaiah that we hear today will be fulfilled for them: "No more shall people call you 'Forsaken,' or your land 'Desolate,' but you shall be called 'My Delight,' and your land 'Espoused.'" *That* is God's will for the people of Haiti, and as loving Christians we need to redouble our efforts to make it a practical reality.

So if we want to learn something from this tragedy about what God is like, that promise taken from Scripture is a good place to start. In general, whenever we feel confused about God, Scripture is a good place to turn to. Our readings today show us even more about what God is really like. In the gospel, Jesus finds himself in the midst of an awkward social situation, and he shows us that God wants us always to have an abundance of good things. The wine of gladness will be poured out for us.

In the letter to the Corinthians, we see another great outpouring of God's love in the many spiritual gifts given to the community of faith. These gifts are the means by which we can come together as a community to answer great challenges like the disaster in Haiti, and are also the means by which we answer the smaller challenges we face every day. Our appreciation of these many gifts should bring us comfort as we face an uncertain future.

As we look more closely, though, St Paul also presents a challenge to us today, because, if we are not careful, the gifts that the Holy Spirit brings can sometimes be a source of strain. The people of Corinth had allowed the gifts of the Holy Spirit to become a source of personal pride and this caused discord within the community. In his letter, Saint Paul is trying to make the Corinthians understand that all the different gifts of the Holy Spirit work together, and all are necessary to the life of the community. All of them come from the *one* God, and their purpose is to create *one* community.

The problem of how we appreciate the different gifts that people bring to our community is still an issue for us today. This is true even in the smallest of human communities: the family. For example, my wife and I bring different gifts to our relationship. My wife hates to see anything go to waste, so she is a great saver—shoe boxes and paperclips, and scrap paper, and anything else that might possibly be useful at some time in the future. So if you ever need a paperclip and you are at our house, we've got you covered. In fact, if you need to make an Eiffel Tower out of paperclips, we can probably help you out!

I, on the other hand, like to have all the cupboards and shelves be neat and organized, and if it should happen that the shoe box collection, for example, starts to overflow the space allotted for it, I am ready to be ruthless and pick through them and save a few of the best, and put all the rest of them into recycling.

When we were first married, these two contrasting gifts caused some friction between us. We each tended to see the other's behavior as a problem that needed to be solved. But now, as our relationship has matured, we have come to respect what the other person is trying to do. We each try to value what the other person brings to the relationship as a gift from the Lord that balances the gift that we bring.

Certainly, interpersonal relationships are complicated things and this particular aspect is only a small part of our relationship. But in this and in so many different ways, many married couples come to understand the gifts they bring as distinct and complementary, and they understand that their different gifts are necessary to the smooth functioning of the relationship.

This need to recognize what another person is doing as a gift from God is present in all our human relationships: among our siblings, in the workplace and even in committees and groups within the church. It is easy to get annoyed when someone seems to be getting in the way of what we are trying to do, but we will be happier, and more in tune with Saint Paul's letter, if we can at least ask the question of whether this behavior that is annoying us isn't a gift of the Holy Spirit, intended to balance the gift that we bring to the situation. It is important for us to learn how to use our gifts in concert and in peace, because it is only by bringing our gifts together and using them as God intends, that we will be able to master the many challenges that the world presents to us.

So as we continue with our worship this evening let us pray for the people of Haiti, those who have died and those who are still struggling against seemingly insurmountable odds. Let us commit ourselves to recognizing and encouraging the spiritual gifts that the Holy Spirit brings to our community, so that we can work together to relieve human suffering wherever we may find it.

JESUS JUDGES US WITH COMPASSION

(Deut 26: 4–10; Rm 10: 8–13; Lk 4: 1–13)

The first time I ever got into trouble in high school was when I was a freshman and got caught in the halls when I wasn't supposed to be there. The result of getting caught red-handed in this way was that I got sent to the vice principal's office to explain myself to Mr. Ulrich. As I made my way down to his office, I was more than a little worried about how that meeting might turn out. Even his name sent shivers down my spine: "Mr. Ulrich". I only knew him from hearing the lecture that he gave to our class at the beginning of the year about how important it was for us to know and follow all the rules of the school. Beyond that, I had only seen him walking the halls with a stiff back and a stern face and eyes that seemed to be able to see all the secrets of your soul.

By the time I knocked on his office door, I had convinced myself that my pitiful excuse would never be accepted, and that I would probably be in detention until my senior year. To my surprise, though, our meeting was completely different from my expectations. Mr. Ulrich was a real person and treated me like a real person. He listened to my story and, while he didn't give me a blessing for what I had done, he did let me off the hook. I went away in great relief.

This experience of expecting a stern judgment, but receiving an understanding hearing, helps me as I think about Jesus. He too is a real person. We know that Jesus will someday return to judge the living and the dead, and we even have an image of what that will be like from Matthew's gospel. In that vision, the Son of Man comes on a cloud of glory and in a grand assembly, he separates the sinners from the saints as easily as a shepherd can separate sheep and goats. There is no pleading at that point, just thumbs up or thumbs down.

When we feel that we have been hurt by someone, that image of a coming judgment might give us some comfort, but it can also be an uncomfortable image for anyone who has ever done anything they are not proud of, which I suppose includes most of us here—it certainly includes me.

Somehow we have to put the image of Jesus the just judge together with the one we hear described today, in which Jesus goes alone into the desert and is subject to severe temptations. In thinking about today's gospel, it is important to recognize that the temptations that Jesus faced were real and strong. He was tested to the very limits of his human endurance. We might imagine that, since he was God, he could never really be tempted by the lies of the great deceiver, but that view would rob this story of any meaning. No, the temptations that Jesus faced must have been at least as beguiling to him as ours are to us, and there must have been the real possibility that he might have chosen not to be faithful to his Father in heaven.

In the gospel, the temptations are presented in a somewhat abstract and symbolic form. They seem to be more of a debate than a serious attempt at seduction. That may make them seem less relevant to the temptations we face, but notice that at the end of the story, the situation is left unresolved. It only says that the devil departed from Jesus "for a time". Just like us, Jesus faced temptation in moments of weakness throughout his life.

When Jesus was eating with his friends at the end of a hard day, did there come a time at the end of the meal when there was just one piece of pie left, and Jesus felt tempted to say "Well, I put in a really hard day, so I deserve that last piece of pie"? Or when the committee of religious leaders came down from Jerusalem to check out Jesus' ministry, and they decided that it was through demonic powers that he was casting out demons, did Jesus feel a desire to slap their silly faces over the insult they were giving to him and his Father in heaven? Or when April the fifteenth came around, and it was time to pay the tax to the temple in Jerusalem, did Jesus ever feel like saying "Those guys in Jerusalem are just skimming off their ten percent and then wasting the rest, so why should I pay my taxes"? Jesus was a man of flesh and blood, and he surely faced such temptations, and many others besides. And although we may think that our temptations in the modern world are very different from his, we need to remember that all temptations really come down to the same thing: the desire to put ourselves at the center of the universe, and to use everyone and everything around us for our own selfish ends.

The thing that sets Jesus apart, of course, is that he did remain faithful to his Father. He never skimped on his legal obligations. He did not resort to violence when he felt insulted, and he never, ever ate the last piece of pie. This is an important difference, because it leads us a third image of Jesus that we find in Scripture. Along with the image of Jesus as the just judge, and the image of Jesus as a man of many trials, we need to consider the image of Jesus as the perfect high priest.

Back in the time of Jesus, a Jewish person who did something that was against the law of Moses and later repented and wanted to be forgiven for it would go to a priest and ask him to offer a sacrifice to God to make amends to God, and so gain forgiveness. For a priest to serve in this capacity, he had to be a holy person, so that God would accept the sacrifice from him and listen to his pleading, but the priest also had to be someone who was approachable—someone that you could go and talk to about what you had done. Well, after the resurrection of Jesus, his followers began to think of Jesus as the perfect priest. Here is what the letter to the Hebrews says about him:

> *"For we do not have a high priest who is unable to*
> *sympathize with our weaknesses, but one who has*
> *been similarly tested in every way, yet without sin.*
> *So let us confidently approach the throne of grace*
> *to receive mercy and to find grace for timely help."*
> *(Heb 4: 15-16).*

My dear brothers and sisters, Lent is a wonderful opportunity to take advantage of this offer from God: let us confidently approach the throne of grace to receive mercy and to find grace for timely help. We can confidently approach Jesus when we are feeling burdened by our sins, because he knows what it is like to be tempted. He knows just how difficult it is when we are feeling weak and so much want to take the easy way out. He will listen to us with compassion, and help us to find the forgiveness of God. The sacrament of reconciliation is a wonderful way to approach Jesus in this way during this season of grace.

In just a few weeks, when Easter comes, we will all stand together with those who are now preparing to enter our communion, and we will renew our Baptismal promises. The priest will ask us "Do you reject evil?" and "Do you reject the glamour of evil?" Now is the time for us to make sure that our response to those questions will be more than just lip service. Even if we have sometimes failed to reject evil in the past, we can be reconciled to God and receive the graces necessary to make a new start in our life. With these graces we can show with our deeds that we do reject evil and all its glamour. Today God offers us mercy and grace for timely help. Let us accept those gifts with joy.

THE TREASURE OF KNOWING JESUS

(Is 43: 16–21; Phil 3: 8–14; Jn 8: 1–11)

When I get to heaven (if I get to heaven), one of the things I want to do is to have a nice long chat with Saint Paul. And one of the questions I want to ask him is what he meant by the reading we have heard today from the letter to the Philippians. It comes from a highly emotional part in the letter, so maybe he is saying a little more here than he really means, but still there are a number of things in this short passage that scholars have debated about for ages. For example, what exactly does he mean when he says "I consider everything as loss, because of the supreme good of knowing Jesus Christ my Lord." He follows this up by saying that everything that he had given up as a follower of Jesus is to be counted as "rubbish." The Greek word, *skubalon,* that we translate as "rubbish" is very strongly negative. It could also be used when talking about sewage, so he is making a very forceful statement about how he values the things of this world.

And yet we also know that Saint Paul believed in the basic goodness of creation, and considered some things useful. For example, at the end of the second letter to Timothy, St. Paul asks Timothy to join him, and when he comes to bring along Paul's cloak and some scrolls and parchments that he had left behind. From this request, it doesn't seem to be true that Paul felt that everything in the world was useless rubbish in some absolute sense, but rather that everything in the world was to be valued by whether it helped or hindered Paul's main goal in life, which, as he says today, is to "know Jesus and the power of his resurrection." Things that help that goal are worth keeping around, and things that hinder it are best gotten rid of.

By "knowing" Jesus, it is clear that Saint Paul means something more than knowing facts about Jesus. Many of us know any number of facts about President Obama, for example, but not many of us can say that we really know the president. Saint Paul wanted to know Jesus as we might know a friend or a brother. We might join Saint Paul in that holy desire, but also wonder if that goal is within reach of us living in the modern world. Surely it is within our reach, as the lives of many saints have shown. Even Saint Paul himself never actually met Jesus in the flesh. He came along somewhat later in the story and he only knew the resurrected Jesus, and yet he was able to form a deep personal relationship with him. We can do so as well.

One way that Saint Paul and many other saints, have come to know Jesus is through the witness of the disciples who did walk with Jesus. We find their experiences recorded in Scripture. Today's reading from John's gospel is a good example. Perhaps sometime this week you might find a half hour to sit quietly and read this story through again and meditate on it. You will find the exact reference for it on page 10 of our bulletin. To use this beautiful short story to get to know Jesus, we have to engage our sacred imagination as we read. We will make the situation more real for ourselves by imagining what it must have been like to be there on that day. We can begin by setting the stage. Perhaps it was sunny and hot that morning, or perhaps a cool breeze was blowing in from the west. Maybe it all happened in a place buzzing with activity or in a quiet corner. Let the Spirit guide you as you meditate.

We might pick one of the characters in the story and imagine the whole thing from that person's perspective. We could choose one of the apostles, or someone in the angry crowd, or the condemned woman herself. This particular story has some wonderful silences in it, while Jesus was drawing on the ground, or while the people were looking from one to another to see if someone would throw the first stone. What do you think those silences were like? How would we have experienced them, if we had been there?

We might even try to imagine what the situation felt like from Jesus' perspective. He knew that adultery was a terrible crime. It tears at the fabric of family life and causes no end of pain and suffering for its innocent victims. On the other hand, the situation thrust upon

Jesus was not really about adultery. If it had been, the leaders would have just taken the woman out of the town and stoned her. No, this confrontation was really about Jesus and the threat he represented to the established authorities. What do you think it was like for Jesus, knowing that if he said the wrong thing, the woman in front of him would be brutally killed? By allowing our sacred imagination to carry us back to that time, we will begin to know Jesus much better.

The gospels hold many such opportunities for us to have an encounter with the living Jesus. Probably, you already have certain favorite gospel passages that you can easily meditate upon in this way. It is spiritually healthful to do so.

Saint Paul also hints at another way that he got to know Jesus when he talks about "the sharing of his sufferings by being conformed to his death." Now we all have suffering in this life, of one form or another, and it is a good spiritual exercise to unite that suffering with the sufferings of Jesus in our prayer. But I think that Saint Paul is talking about a particular kind of suffering in this reading: one that comes directly from following in Christ's footsteps. Saint Paul's hard work in ministry brought him closer to Jesus, just as happens any time we share a difficult experience with a friend. It brings us closer together.

When I was younger I was active in the Boy Scouts, and sometimes our troop would go on long hikes together, ten or twenty miles with packs on our backs. It is amazing the way that exhausting experience would bring us closer as a group. I remember coming to a rest stop and leaning back against my pack all sweaty, sharing my canteen with a buddy. We didn't have to say a word; we knew what the other was feeling. The glow of that kind of testing experience can last for years. Saint Paul shared that kind of difficult experience with Jesus in carrying out his ministry and so can we.

When we try to be a peace maker in our family or in our workplace, and maybe things don't go very well with our attempts and both people end up angry at us, we can know just a little bit how Jesus felt in his life. We can grieve with Jesus over the lost opportunity for peace. When we stand up for someone who is weaker, and get shot down for our effrontery, we will know better what Jesus' life was like trying to help the poor and downtrodden of his time. When we come home tired at the end of the day, and our loved ones need us to do something for them, and we dig down and offer our last bit of energy for their needs, we will know what it felt like to Jesus when all the people kept coming to him day and night for healing. In those and so many other ways, as we walk in the way of Jesus, we will come to know him better and be conformed to his death, and likewise to his resurrection.

Next Sunday we begin the holiest week of the Church year. Come and sing Hosannas to Jesus on Palm Sunday. Sit with him in companionable silence on Holy Thursday. Grieve on Good Friday. Rejoice on Saturday at the Easter Vigil. Let us come to those liturgies ready to experience all their highs and lows, so that we too can come to know Jesus and the power of his resurrection.

KEEPING EASTER GOING

(Acts 5: 27–32. 40–41; Rev 5: 11–14; Jn 21: 1–19)

Well, here we are in the third Sunday of Easter already. Spring is flying by. I hope you had a wonderful Lent and Easter this year. I hope that your prayers and fasting and alms giving during Lent gave you a real encounter with holiness, and that the beautiful liturgies of Lent and Easter touched your heart. Maybe a particular reading or homily or hymn that you heard in this holy season shook you up, or calmed you down, or in some other way gave you the thing you needed in that moment.

I had an experience something like that at the Good Friday liturgy. Along with Deacon Jim, I was privileged to hold the cross while the community came forward in procession to reverence it. It is just a couple of boards nailed together, just an old wooden cross, but what a powerful symbol. So many different people came forward: Biker dudes in black leather and Wall-Street types in ties and pin stripes. Little kids who could only reach half way up the vertical bar, and older people who had trouble leaning over far enough to kiss the cross piece. Teenagers came forward leading their younger brothers and sisters by the hand. So many different people in different places in their lives, all unified in that very personal, and yet very public, display of love for Jesus. I realized in a special way at that moment that here is a community that really "gets it", that really understands the sacrifice of Jesus and that loves him mightily in return. That realization awoke in me an answering faith, and I thank you for sharing that sign of your deep love.

Many people can look back at their lives and find a treasured memory of a particular moment of renewed or revived faith. It is the sort of experience that brings us back to church each Sunday, and the contemplation of that sort of experience gives today's gospel a special relevance. Let's look closely at the account to see what it has to say to us today.

First, recall the context of the reading. John tells us that this is just the third time that the risen Jesus appeared to his disciples. The first time, by John's account, was on the day of the resurrection, when Jesus appeared to them in the safe house in Jerusalem where they had locked themselves away out of fear. In that meeting, Jesus breathed on them the Holy Spirit and gave them the authority to forgive sins. The second time they met was a week later in the same place, where the Apostles were still lying low. So far, they had yet to become the bold witnesses to the kingdom of God that we hear about in our reading from the Acts of the Apostles.

Then, as today's story begins, we find seven of the Apostles back in Galilee, in the sea-side town of Capernaum, the very place where Jesus first called them. The narrative doesn't say what they are doing there, but I picture them sitting around the kitchen table in Peter's house, looking at each other and wondering what was supposed to happen next. Being back in Capernaum again must have felt a little bit like waking up from a dream. It was a beautiful dream, but Jerusalem was a long way from Capernaum, and that dream must have seemed at odds with the unchanged realities of everyday life back at home.

So there they all are, and Peter tells the others that he is going to go fishing. Fishing? Excuse me, but whatever happened to Jesus' words: "Do not be afraid. I will make you a fisher of men?" It feels like the whole thing is in danger of unraveling at this point, but not to worry. Jesus is still firmly in charge, and in his appearance he continues their instruction in the faith. He challenges them to keep going and make something of the experiences that he shared with them. It is a challenge that the gospel extends to us as well. Are we going to make something of the good and holy experiences we have had this Lent and Easter, or are we going to go back to our lives of fishing, or banking or whatever is *our* life as usual?

To see what kind of response is appropriate for us, we have only to look at what Jesus asks of Peter. He doesn't ask Peter if he has worked out an organizational chart for the church yet. Nor does he seem particularly interested in knowing whether Peter has figured out the mystery of the Trinity or of transubstantiation in the Eucharist. No, three times he says "If you love me, tend my sheep." He says that to Peter and he says it to each one of us: "If you love me, tend my sheep."

Now I am sure that you are already tending some of the lambs of the Lord. Parents tend the little ones that gather around their table morning, noon, and night, for example. Loving couples tend to each other's needs. Younger people help out the family as they are able, and are true friends to others their own age. Older people share the joys and trials of growing older. Many people tend to neighbors or family members who need some extra help every once in a while. Such acts of kindness are very important ways in which we answer Jesus' call to feed his sheep.

When they are being lovable, it is a joy to tend to God's loved ones in this way, and other times, maybe not so much. But when the people we are trying to help are being particularly difficult, or for some reason we don't feel in a particularly helpful mood, it might help to remember today's reading and remind ourselves of the paramount importance Jesus places on this way of demonstrating our love for him.

Another thing that today's gospel invites us to consider is how we can extend that circle of people that we are actively trying to care for. For example, there's the person at work who always seems to go bananas as soon as the least little thing goes wrong. Maybe we can find a way to be a peaceful presence for that person in those situations. For we know that it's not always physical nourishment that people need, but emotional or spiritual nurturing. Many people simply yearn for someone who will listen to them sympathetically as they share their story.

Then too, in these difficult financial times, there are many people in our wider community who need help making ends meet. Many of you regularly bring canned goods on Sunday to share with local people who are in need; that is a wonderfully concrete way to help our neighbors. Soon we will have the opportunity to help out with the Loaves and Fishes program. Once a year, our parish provides a banquet at the cathedral in Trenton for people who are having a hard time of it.

Easter shows us that God loves us with a fierce and passionate love. The Bible describes God's love as "enduring" and "everlasting" and "full of mercy and kindness". His love is always looking for ways to be truly helpful to us. Our God doesn't do things by half measures. He shows the depth of his love in the person of Jesus. As we feel that love more strongly in our own lives, we are eager to find more and better ways to share in God's loving embrace of humanity.

As we continue with our worship this morning, let us cherish all the encounters we have had with the love of the Father this Spring and at all times. Let us be thankful for the opportunities we have to share that love with others, and resolve always to be on the look-out for other lost sheep that need a little bit more of the Father's tender loving care.

7th Sunday of Easter, May 16, 2010:
FORGIVENESS AS A VIRTUE

(Acts 7: 55–60; Rev 22: 12–14, 16–17, 20; Jn 17: 20–26)

When I was a young adult, I found out that when my mother was a child she had been treated very unkindly by a particular member of my extended family. Not just once or twice, but consistently over many years. Now, by the time I learned about all this, it was all long in the past and my mother had completely forgiven this person. In fact, when this person's health began to fail, my mother was the one who often took care of her. Once I learned the facts though, I could not forgive that person so easily. I did not want to be in the same room with her, and from that day to this, I have struggled to be as forgiving as my mother was. I am still praying for the grace to truly forgive.

And so it is with a lot of awe and a little bit of envy that I hear in today's first reading that Saint Stephen was able to forgive the angry crowd and ask God to forgive them, even while they were still in the midst of pounding him with stones. That was a tremendous demonstration of Christian virtue, and it shows us the depth of forgiveness that the human heart is capable of. Our readings today invite us to explore the dimensions of this important virtue, and its place in bringing about the unity that Jesus prays for in our gospel today. One reason my mother was ready to be so forgiving, as she told me, was for the sake of family unity.

That being said, one thing we need to be clear about, when we consider the Christian virtue of forgiving, is that this virtue is not supposed to leave us stuck in a position in which we are likely to be repeatedly hurt by someone. It is not God's will that we should ever be hurt by another person, either physically or emotionally. If we find ourselves in such a situation, it is just and right for us to take the necessary steps to protect ourselves, or to get whatever help we need to get out of the situation as soon as possible. We should not worry that we are destroying some ideal of unity by doing this. That unity was destroyed by the hurt we received. The virtue of forgiving is really about what happens after we are safe again. It is about how we deal with the memories of what came before. It is only when we feel safe and free to forgive that real reconciliation becomes possible.

Granting forgiveness for a serious hurt is not easy, but we have numerous modern examples of people behaving in this saintly way. Their witness shows the rest of us that solid Christian virtues are not just stories made up to praise people from long ago, but are living and present in our world today.

I recently saw an interview with a person who forgave a terrible deed, and found healing for himself in the process. His name is Bud Walsh, and his daughter was one of the people who died in the bombing of the Alfred P. Murrah Federal Building in Oklahoma City in 1995. She worked in the daycare center on the first floor and was killed instantly in the explosion. At first, Bud reacted as any of us might, with overwhelming grief and anger. He was a smoker, and soon he was up to three packs a day. He was a drinker, and soon he was spending all his time either drinking or hung over, and he says, sometimes it was both at the same time.

According to the interview, the thing that turned Bud around in his life occurred when he saw a television interview with the father of the man accused of the bombing. Just for one moment, Timothy McVeigh's father looked directly into the camera, and Bud saw in the eyes of the father of his daughter's murderer, the same terrible pain that he himself felt. That instant of deeper perception changed his life, and began a long process for him of learning to forgive, and even to being reconciled with the person who committed the crime.

Now it is likely that most of us do not have such a heavy burden of events in our life that are in need of our forgiveness, but all of us who have been around long enough have been hurt somewhere along the way and we can learn something important about forgiving from the example of experts in the virtue like Bud Walsh.

The first thing to notice is that initial reaction of shocked pain and righteous indignation when we are blindsided by some hurt. It is important to accept and acknowledge that reaction, without letting it take over our lives, as it did for a time with Bud Walsh. The hurt done to us was unjust and we deserve a time to just cry out in pain over it. However, we also need to recognize that holding onto that pain and anger for too long can hurt our health and damage our relationships with other people. Forgiveness can be a part of our way to move beyond that initial reaction and can lessen the damage.

A second important aspect of moving beyond our initial reaction of pain and anger is to recognize that we are not alone in our pain. When Bud Walsh saw the pain in Timothy McVeigh's father, he knew immediately that he needed to meet with him, to share the weight of pain between them. He also joined with the families of the other victims to share experiences. Finding a community in which one can share the burden of pain can make it easier to find the courage to forgive, and to accept the fact that it is impossible for anyone to undo what has been done to us. Our friends can't undo it, and neither can the perpetrator. The person who hurt us may not even desire to do that, but that hardly matters, because no one, not even with the best of intentions, can un-say what they said or un-do what they did.

Finally, one more hurdle to get over on our road to granting forgiveness is the idea we may have in the back of our minds that by forgiving the other person we are somehow discrediting or devaluing the hurt we received. But saying "it was nothing." is not the same thing as saying "I forgive you." Our forgiveness is not a way of saying that what was done to us was unimportant, or that what was done was excusable. Only inexcusable wrongs need our forgiveness in the first place. By forgiving these incidents in our own hearts, even if we never actually say so to the person who hurt us, we let the incidents go and allow them to recede into our past.

Bud Walsh, in finding his own path to forgiving, decided that he needed to speak out against the death penalty for Timothy McVeigh, his daughter's murderer. Even though he tried and failed to get that sentence reduced, he continues to speak out and work diligently against the death penalty in other cases. In doing this, he honors his loss and honors the best parts of his daughter's memory.

Like all the virtues, forgiving can be a difficult art to master. As we struggle with it, it may help to pray to saints, like Saint Stephen, who have demonstrated this virtue in their own lives, and can help us to obtain the grace to imitate their good example.

We should also remind ourselves that God does not call us to a virtuous life in order to give us a test that we must pass in order to get into heaven. God gives us the virtues to make our lives better right here and now. Bud Walsh found healing for himself on the path to forgiving. He gave up the drink and the smoking, and is a much happier person today. God wants us too to be free of all the burdens of the past. He wants us to be united with him in a place of light and hope and peace.

WITH JOY YOU WILL DRAW WATER

(Zech 12: 10-11, 13:1; Gal 3: 26-29; Lk 9: 18:24)

I would like to begin by wising everyone a happy Father's day. This holiday invites those of us who are fathers, whether biological or circumstantial, to rededicate ourselves to being good fathers, loving and supportive of those in our care, and it invites all of us to rededicate ourselves to being good sons and daughters, who cherish all the good things that our fathers give us, and pass them on to others.

Certainly, this is something that Jesus did in his life, and this thought gives us a partial answer to Jesus' question in today's gospel: "who do you say that I am?". Jesus was the true son of his Father in heaven. This is only a partial answer, though, because the real question is not "Who *was* Jesus?" The real question is "Who *is* Jesus for us today in Princeton at the beginning of the Summer of two thousand and ten?"

One way to respond to this question is to turn it into a meditation by a three-step process of, first, revisiting an important experience in our lives, and, second, reflecting on that experience in the light of Scripture, and finally, deciding what insights we can gain from that reflection about our life today.

When I was a young man, I worked at a camp during the summer, and one day when I was exploring one of the less-traveled corners of the camp, I came upon a spring at the edge of a meadow. In that shady hillside place, water was bubbling up out of the ground seemingly of its own accord. Someone, possibly a farmer who once used the meadow for his cows, had built a concrete bowl to capture the spring water, and in its abundance, the water filled up the bowl and poured over the lip and rushed downhill in a little stream. It was a lovely place to sit and think peaceful thoughts. Even now, forty years later, I can still re-experience the natural holiness of that place, and reconnect with the refreshment that I found there.

Now, a geologist would have an explanation for why that spring was there, and it would involve underground aquifers and hydrologic pressure, and the incompressibility of water as a fluid. And undoubtedly those explanations are all true as far as they go, but somehow they completely fail to capture the experience of that place. To me, the explanation that we get from Scripture for that spring being there is much more to the point: that spring was there because God meant it to be so.

Living in an arid country, the ancient Jews had a great respect for water, and they even had a special phrase to describe water that seems to be moving of its own accord, as my little spring was. They called such things "MAyim-chayYIM", literally "living waters", and they felt very strongly that such waters did not move of their own accord, but according to the will of God; they were on a mission from God to bring life and refreshment to the world. Such sources of water were greatly prized, and when possible, that was the kind of water that they would use for their washing rituals. Not that the water itself was magical in some way, but it was manifestly invested by God with the power to do what water does best: to refresh and cleanse. To make use of such water in a holy rite was to accept God's continuing care and participate in a very concrete way in a loving relationship with God.

Our reading today from the prophet Zechariah shows how this idea carries over into the spiritual realm. Zechariah says that on some great day in the future, "there shall be open to the house of David ... a fountain to purify from sin and uncleanness." Through it, God would "pour out on the inhabitants of Jerusalem a spirit of grace and petition". Later he adds that "On that day, living waters shall flow from Jerusalem, half to the Eastern Sea and half to the Western Sea, and it shall be so in summer and in winter." (which is to say, they will flow everywhere and forever.) Zech 14:8.

It is not quite clear what day in the future the prophet might have been looking forward to when he wrote these words, or if he had any specific event in mind at the time, but the Church has long applied these words to Jesus. As followers of Jesus, we come to know *him* as the true spring of living water. He is such a powerful source of life-giving water as to make my own experience in a meadow in the days of my youth pale by comparison. For each of us, Jesus dearly wants to be our true source of refreshment and cleansing and comfort this summer, and in all the seasons to follow.

Jesus can do this for us in big ways and in small ways. He refreshes us best of all through the sacraments. In the sacrament of reconciliation we meet the forgiving Jesus, and in the Eucharist we meet the Jesus who in his great love gives himself completely to us. In smaller ways too, Jesus can refresh us like a tall glass of cool water. When I am feeling down about something, I some times read, or just re-imagine for myself, one of Jesus' parables, like the parable of the Lost Sheep, or the parable of the Prodigal Son, and those bring me comfort.

It would be a good spiritual exercise to pick an experience of our own and meditate on it in this way. Let it be a concrete experience that we remember with joy. It might be an experience of water, or of light, or of bread or wine, or of friendship and fellowship and love. With Scripture to guide us, we might then ask ourselves "where is God in this experience?" and "how does this help me understand who Jesus is?"

Of course, not all of our vivid experiences are happy ones, and our scriptures today speak to this situation too. There is an undercurrent of sorrow in today's readings. These experiences too can help us to understand better who God is. If one of those sorts of experiences is uppermost in your mind today, it might help to contemplate the idea that Jesus once knew a similar experience. Jesus lost his dad when he was young. He was lonely at times, overworked at times, and felt abandoned, misunderstood and reviled by the ones who should have understood him best. He was betrayed by someone that he trusted and loved, and he suffered through a painful death. And the really amazing thing to contemplate in all of that, is that Jesus *chose* that life. Knowing just what would happen, he chose to come among us, casting off all the perfections of heaven, and taking on all of the pains and imperfections of this life. He did this purely for the greater good of entering into a closer union with all of us. When we know sorrow and pain, we know him all the better.

The final important step in our meditational experience would be to ask how does this new understanding impact my life today? What should I be doing, or doing differently, now that I have this insight? When I found that spring in the meadow, I was tempted to keep the knowledge of it to myself, to make that place my secret spot for meditation and refreshment. But in the end I found I could not do that, it was just too wonderful to keep to myself, and that summer I had the joy of sharing the experience of that place with fellow staff members and with campers. In their reactions, I re-experienced my own first encounter.

It is always this way with the gifts that we have from God. A fountain cannot be bottled up. By its very nature, it *must* spill out into the world, or it no longer is a true fountain. I think that this is one meaning we might take from the warning in today's gospel that whoever wishes to save his life will lose it. In contrast to a selfish, possessive attitude, whenever we share the gifts we receive from God, we fulfill the words of the prophet Isaiah: "With joy you will draw water at the fountain of salvation, and say on that day: 'give thanks to the Lord, acclaim his name; among the nations make known his deeds.'" (Is 12: 3)

16th Sunday in Ordinary Time, Jul. 18, 2010:

ONE CHURCH FOR THERESA OF CALCUTTA AND JULIAN OF NORWICH

(Gen 18: 1–10; Col 1: 24–28; Lk 10: 38–42)

The story of Martha and Mary is one of the most interesting psychological portraits we find anywhere in the Bible. We can really see their humanity in the practical domestic problem the two sisters face in today's gospel. Anyone who has ever lived with a roommate can probably sympathize with Mary, or with Martha, or maybe even with both of them at once. Through this little story, we can recognize them across the ages as our kindred spirits.

This is an important way to approach this story, but this personally very meaningful way of relating to gospel has not stopped some people from also seeing a metaphorical meaning in this reading. In this view, Mary and Martha represent two different kinds of spiritual life. Mary, who only desires to sit at Jesus' feet, becomes a symbol for contemplative spirituality, and Martha, who serves Jesus with food and the practical necessities of life, is seen as a symbol of a spirituality based on works of charity.

As we consider this difference, we might broaden the discussion a bit to include two other holy people that we know more about, and who were just as diverse in their response to the love of Jesus. Although at first these holy people may seem to approach life very differently, they also exhibit important similarities.

The first person to consider is Julian of Norwich. She lived in the fourteenth century in England and followed a Mary-like contemplative lifestyle. Julian was an Anchoress, which means that she lived a kind of hermit's life right in the middle of the city. For much of her adult life, Julian lived alone in a tiny room attached to the side of the cathedral in Norwich. After she decided that she was unalterably committed to this lifestyle, and the bishop concurred, the door to her cell was bricked-over so she could never leave again. There were just two little windows in her cell, one which opened into the church, so that she could participate in the Mass, and one which opened onto the street, so that people could pass in food and other necessities.

The only reason we know very much about Julian is that she wrote a book about a vision that she received from Jesus during a serious illness. As far as we know, this was the first book ever written by a woman in English. In her era, popular piety placed great emphasis on the horrors of hell and purgatory. This was a common topic for sermons and a recurring theme in a popular kind of entertainment, called "morality plays". The vision Julian received on her sick bed was completely at odds with this preoccupation with God's punishment of evil doers. Her vision was all about the greatness of God's mercy. She spent more than twenty years in meditation and contemplation on God's great mercy, as explained by Jesus in her visions. Her book is the fruit of all that time spent in prayer. I strongly recommend her book to anyone who wants reassurance of God's providential care.

A person who lived a more Martha kind of spirituality is Mother Teresa of Calcutta. As a young woman, she felt called to serve God in the missions, and she joined an order of nuns that taught school in India. Then, in September of 1946, while she was on a train ride into the Himalayan foothills, she received what she later referred to as "a call within a call", to serve the poor in a more direct way. Eventually, she left her order and formed the Sisters of Charity, to serve the poorest of the poor in the most menial and humble ways imaginable. At first, it was all they could do to provide the poor of the city with a dignified and peaceful place to die.

They tell the story of Mother Teresa, that once she was talking with a group of British diplomats trying to shake loose some money to support her work with those suffering from leprosy, and one of the diplomats with undiplomatic honesty said to her "I wouldn't touch one of those lepers for a thousand pounds!" Mother Teresa quickly replied "

Nor would I, but I would gladly bathe and tend to them for the love of Jesus."

So here we have these two different women, each inspired by the greatness of God's mercy and love. One lived in the twentieth century, and one in the fourteenth. One spent her adult life locked away from all human touch, and one spent hers cradling the human cast-offs of society. These two women responded to the call of Jesus in very different ways, but I can't help imagining that if they had ever met, they would have gotten along like sisters. I am sure each one would have appreciated the many gifts of the other, because really they were not that far apart.

Julian spent much time in solitary prayer all those years, but she was not completely disconnected from the town around her. She would talk with people who stopped by her window and offer them spiritual advice and counsel. Her book would have been a great achievement for anyone, but it is especially so for a woman of that era, and it was written not for herself, but as a gift to the people of her time, and of ours.

And although Mother Teresa spent much of her day tending to the poor, she did not neglect prayer and meditation. They say that once she was giving a lecture about the work of her order, and while explaining that her sisters spent a considerable amount of time in prayer and adoration, she remarked that everyone should spend at least an hour in prayer each day. After the lecture, a woman came up to her and complained that she couldn't possibly spend a whole hour in prayer each day, because she had far too much to do. She went on to list all her daily responsibilities. It was pretty long list, and Mother Teresa listened patiently and when the woman was finished, she nodded sagely and said "Yes I can see that you do have very much to do. Someone who is as busy as you are should spend *two* hours in prayer each day!" Mother Teresa understood very well that prayer is the engine that makes everything else possible.

And what about us? We are about half way through summer now, and maybe in this time when things slow down at least a little bit, we can use the opportunity to deepen our prayer life. There are lots of ways to do this. We could pick some well known prayer, like the rosary, and get into the habit of praying it before bed each night. We might even begin by just saying one decade. Or, we might go on-line each day and prayerfully read through the readings for daily Mass. The United States Conference of Catholic Bishops makes this easy to do. The readings are posted on their website, and you can even down-load them as a podcast! For something a bit lower-tech, we might stop by the parish library and get a book on one of the saints or on some other wholesome topic, and read that while we are on vacation. As you know, each Friday we have Eucharistic adoration in the chapel here. We might sign up for a half hour of quiet time with the Lord.

It would be a good thing to start such a program now, so that when September comes and things begin to speed up again, we will see just how much easier it is to face the many things we do each day with the power of prayer behind us. Like Mary and Martha, and Julian and Teresa, we all want to offer our hospitality to Jesus. The way we go about doing this will likely be different for each one of us, but for all of us, a strong prayer life will make great things possible.

WELCOMING THE HARVEST OF FAITH

(Rev 11: 19, 12: 1-6, 10; 1 Cor 15: 20-27; Lk 1: 39-56)

When I was young, my parents kept a vegetable garden. It seemed huge to me at the time, taking up about a quarter of our backyard, and around this time of year, the produce would come pouring out of it. Tomatoes and squash, radishes, beans and onions—we were often inundated with vegetables. And whenever one of their crops produced abundantly, my parents received it as a gift from heaven. They knew their share of crop failures, and they would greet an overflowing abundance with joy, and spring into action. They canned some things and froze others, and gave loads and loads away. Harvest time was a busy time at our house, but a very happy time as well. Even after they became relatively well off, and could easily afford to buy their summer vegetables at the local farm stand, they much preferred to do things this way.

Doubtless, many people here today have experienced a similar joy in an abundant harvest, either from a backyard garden or in some other aspect of life. This is a good thing, because that joyful emotion provides an excellent backdrop for considering the feast we celebrate today: the Assumption of Our Lady. It is wise of our liturgical calendar to put this feast day at the beginning of the harvest season, because the abundance of the physical harvest helps us to also appreciate the abundance of the spiritual harvest that God provides to our world.

The Assumption has been a feast day of the Roman Church celebrated on August the fifteenth since at least the Eighth Century, but the day acquired greater prominence in 1950 when Pope Pius XII solemnly declared it to be an undeniable truth of our faith that Mary was assumed body and soul into the glory of heaven at the end of her earthly life. The proclamation written by the Pope on this occasion is titled "The most-generous God." Here is the first paragraph of his pronouncement:

"The most generous God is almighty, and the plan of his providence rests upon wisdom and love. In the secret purpose of God's own mind, this plan tempers the sorrows of peoples and of individuals by means of joys that he interposes in their lives from time to time. By this means, under different conditions and in different ways, 'all things work together for good for those who love him'."

The truth of this comforting message is quite apparent in the life of Mary. She knew many sorrows: to live as a refugee in a foreign land far from family and friends; to lose her husband when her son was only half-grown; to hear abuse heaped on Jesus by neighbors and strangers alike; to stand by helplessly while he was being crucified. But these sorrows were surely tempered with many joys as well: to have a husband who was dependable and understanding; to raise up a son to be strong and wise and kind; to see the holiness of the people who were attracted to the Good News of Jesus; to receive the joyous news of the resurrection and spend the remainder of her life as a treasured member of the community that was true to Jesus' memory. And the final joy of her life, which we celebrate today, to enter body and soul into the glory of God's kingdom. In this way, she was privileged to be among the first fruits of the greatest harvest of all.

Pope Pius' message encompasses all of this, but it also includes more, because his message is also meant to apply to our lives. The Pope wrote his words at a bleak moment in human history. It was less than six months after the surprise invasion of North Korea into the south. Many people of that time, still recovering from the destruction of the Second World War, worried that we were then on the brink of a Third World War, a war in which nuclear weapons might play a far greater role.

These physical dangers are an unspoken part of the background of the Pope's message, and there is also direct reference in the letter to a more insidious threat. The post-World War II era was a time of increasing materialism: the idea that there is no external moral truth and all things are available as a means to our own ends. The Pope was not specific, but we can assume he was worried both about the consumerism being embraced by the West, and the Marxism being embraced in other corners of the world. The Pope worried that such intellectual trends were dangerous to the spiritual health of the world's people. He said that "the corruption of morals that follows from these teachings threatens to extinguish the light of virtue and to ruin the lives of men by exciting discord among them."

To counterbalance these powerful forces shaping the world in harmful ways, the Pope offered us the story of one plucky young Jewish girl from centuries ago, who never wrote a word that we know of, never invented anything, or led an army into battle, or did any of the things that might make a big media splash today. What she *did* do, was to say "yes" to God, and through that "yes" she became the means by which the world was forever changed. She had a hand in creating a great harvest of spiritual growth, which is still being reaped today.

The hope that the Pope expresses in his proclamation is that the story of that holy young woman might remind and convince all of us of "the value of a human life entirely devoted to carrying out the heavenly Father's will and to bringing good to others."

Our world too seems surrounded by dangers. Sixty years on, the Korean problem has changed, but has not completely gone away. We also face new and different dangers, that are just as scary in their own way. Many worry about the permanent degradation of the environment, or about violent extremism, or about an even worse financial crisis looming on the horizon.

And materialism is still with us. Although the current financial problems have caused some people to reconsider their attitudes toward material wealth, others still seem to live their lives by the motto "the one who dies with the most toys wins."

I think that the answer that the Pope would offer us in our worries and fears today is the same one that he gave the people of his time: the example of the young girl who said "yes", and created a great harvest for God. This image of Our Lady should be a comfort to us and also a challenge. It may be too late in the year for us to plant tomatoes and beans, but it is not too late for us to plant a kind word or a kind deed. It is not too late for us to imitate Mary and dedicate ourselves to doing good for others.

We might include random acts of kindness, like holding the door for a stranger, or being especially patient with a store clerk who is having a difficult day. We might also try some things that are more focused, like writing a letter to an old friend to remind him or her of some happy event in the past. We might make a commitment to take an elderly neighbor to the grocery store each week. We might concentrate on one of those world problems that especially disturb us, and become better informed about the issue, looking at it from all sides. Then we might pray to God through the intercession of Our Lady to show us how we can do something helpful for the situation, something which benefits all sides of the problem.

These are very small things, you might say, not at all on the same scale as the problems that we face as a society. That is true, but we need to remember that, by their nature, seeds *are* very small things. And we can be assured, that if we plant those seeds, then the most generous God will send his rains and they will grow, and they will add to the great harvest. And we have the promise of the Lord of the Harvest, that if we are diligent about it, in the end there will be enough for all.

BONE OF MY BONE AND
FLESH OF MY FLESH

(2 Sam 5: 1-3; Col 1: 12-20; Lk 23: 35-43)

One time when I was in the hospital, late at night my roommate and I were awakened by a piece of equipment in the room that was beeping insistently. We called for a nurse to fix the problem, but she was a long time coming, and lying there in the dark, the two of us began to talk. It was not about mundane stuff. We had already exchanged all the usual information about where we lived, and who our doctor was, and things like that. Now we talked about more important things. Who in our family were we most worried about? What were our hopes for the future? What were our fears? It was one of those special moments of intimacy when two strangers who have been thrown together by shared difficulties can see how much they have in common and end up talking honestly about things that really matter. It was a precious moment.

Such feelings of intimacy can arise in many different circumstances. In our first reading today, the people of Israel made David their king because they recognized him as a kindred spirit. They said "Here we are, your bone and your flesh." They were speaking about more than shared ancestry. After all, Saul, the king that David replaced, had plenty of family ties to the people, but he never became their kindred spirit. It was David who led the people out into battle and brought them back again. That shared experience "in the trenches," so to speak, was what gave them a special closeness. Notice how similar the people's words are to the words of Adam when he first saw Eve: "This one at last is bone of my bone and flesh of my flesh." *That* is the level of intimacy which their shared experiences gave to David and his people, and that is what led them to accept him as their king.

It is an amazing idea that people might be able to have that sort of feeling of intimacy with their king. We tend to think of kings as being shut away behind castle walls, with a "we are not amused" mentality toward their subjects. But that is not what David was like, nor is it what Jesus is like. Today we celebrate Jesus as our king, and truly he is a high and mighty king, far above anything in our experience. Our reading from the letter to the Colossians expresses this very well when it says that "in him all fullness was pleased to dwell." Maybe we don't feel that our lives are quite so full of every perfection, but Jesus also experienced all of the ordinary joys and sorrows that are common to humanity. We share those experiences with him, and so we can say to Jesus in all honesty "Here we are, your bone and your flesh."

Such an experience of intimacy is demonstrated in our gospel, in the interaction between Jesus and the good thief, who by tradition is named "Dysmas". They were very different people to begin with. Jesus, as we know, lived a life devoted to peace and reconciliation. Dysmas on the other hand is variously described in the gospels as a bandit or a criminal. Probably, he was more than just a petty thief. Remember that crucifixion was a punishment only for the most serious crimes. This was a time when serious armed resistance to the Roman occupation was just beginning, and Dysmas may have been a part of that movement. In any event, it is clear from the description that we have, that whatever his goals were, Dysmas often used violence to achieve them. But then came the encounter on the cross on that fateful Friday afternoon, and everything changed.

Notice the way Dysmas talks to Jesus. In most places in the gospels, when people have a request to make of Jesus, they use a respectful title like "lord" or "teacher". Very few times does anyone address Jesus using only his given name, as we hear Dysmas do today. His familiarity in his way of addressing Jesus underlines their intimacy. On the cross, there is no time or place anymore for the pretenses of polite society.

So what could have led Dysmas to say "Jesus, remember me when you come into your kingdom"? It is a strange thing to say to someone who is so obviously powerless and humiliated. Do you suppose it was desperate hope on his part? Dysmas was certainly in a hopeless situation himself, and he might have been trying the only possible avenue left to him. Or was it faith that made him speak as he did? Perhaps in his position of shared suffering, Dysmas could see the strength and kingly virtue that underlay Jesus' apparent weakness, and he realized that the sign above Jesus' head, which was meant to be ironic, was in fact telling the simple truth. Or maybe it was love. Father Richard Neuhaus wrote a book about the crucifixion called "Death on a Friday Afternoon", and in it he speculates that it might have been charity that led Dysmas to say those words. Dysmas might have assumed that Jesus was deluding himself in thinking that he was a king, but Dysmas knew that being stripped of that illusion would be worse even than dying on the cross, and so, out of kindness he played along with him.

In a sense it doesn't matter whether it was faith, hope or charity or some combination of the three that led Dysmas to say what he did. His motivations were probably complicated. Ours certainly are. And in any case, he could not really have understood what he was asking for, or the great gift that he would receive.

One thing that we might meditate about today in response to these readings is that we too can turn to Jesus in our own time of pain and suffering and find a new and deeper intimacy with our king. In John's gospel, after Jesus has been scourged, Pilate brings him out before the crowd, and says in Latin "Ecce homo" — Behold the man. We are offered that vision in our Mass today. Behold the man, our bone and our flesh. Behold our king.

When we feel betrayed or abandoned by someone that we trusted, we might say to Jesus "Oh, so *this* is what it felt like when your friend betrayed you with a kiss. Now I get it." Or when we are trying to do something really difficult, and we fail time and again, but quitting is not an option for us, we might say "Oh, so *this* is what it felt like when you were carrying the cross and you fell time after time." Or when we have a pain in some part of our body, and we can't do even the simplest things we used to do, we can say "Oh, so *this* is what it felt like to be nailed to the cross." Whatever we are suffering, ridicule or physical disability or shame, that experience can find its place in the cross of Jesus. We can invite Jesus to be with us in that moment, and his pain will become our pain and our pain become his.

What do you suppose it will be like for Jesus when we invite him into the deepest part of our humanity in that way? What words of comfort will our king have for us in that moment? Maybe it won't come across to us as words at all. Maybe it will feel like a hug or like shared tears. In some way or other though, Jesus will surely share with us a promise like the one he gave to Dysmas: "One day soon, you will be with me in paradise."

And it will be paradise for us when it comes. Not paradise because the streets are paved with gold, and not paradise because we can eat anything we want without gaining weight. It will be paradise because Jesus will be there. And that sweet feeling of intimacy which is so rare and fleeting in our world today will be everywhere and it will last forever.

Sing the refrain to the old spiritual:

> *Do Lord, oh do Lord, oh do remember me,*
> *Do Lord, oh do Lord, oh do remember me,*
> *Do Lord, oh do Lord, oh do remember me,*
> *Do Lord remember me.*

GOD WITH US ON OUR JOURNEY

(Sir 3: 2-6, 12-14; Col 3: 12-21; Mt 2: 13-15, 19-23)

Recently, my family took a vacation trip to far-off Bolivia. Mostly, it was a wonderful trip, but there were several difficult moments. For example, when we first got to the airport, we found out that we did not have all the necessary paperwork to get into Bolivia. Unbeknownst to us, the laws had changed since our last visit, and so we had just two hours to round up pictures of ourselves and fill out visa applications and get inoculated for Yellow Fever and get a letter of invitation *in Spanish* from someone living in Bolivia. When they told us what was needed, it seemed completely impossible. How could we get all of that in the middle of downtown Newark, a city that we rarely visited and knew little about? But, amazingly, with a lot of help and some twenty-first century technology, it all happened. God sent us just the right people and just the right help to make the impossible be possible. We made it back to the airport with all our paperwork just in time for a rescheduled flight.

That wasn't the only amazing thing that happened to us on that trip. A day or two before we were scheduled to return, we went on an overnight excursion up into the mountains. But when we were ready to come back to the big city, we were told that a town along the only road out of the mountains was staging a protest strike. They had blocked the road to protest something the government wanted to do and no cars or trucks could get through. They were allowing people to walk through their blockade, we learned, but that would mean an eight-mile hike under the hot summer sun. The TV predicted a long strike, and it seemed completely impossible for us to make it back to the city in time to catch our plane home. But somehow God made it all work. By the time we decided to go for it, and we actually got to the blockade, it was far shorter than we feared it would be, and transportation was available at both ends to make it all work. Again, God made the impossible possible.

Thinking about these difficulties gives me a new appreciation for our gospel reading today about the flight of the Holy Family into Egypt. That was surely a much more difficult trip than anything we faced. It is worth meditating on what must it have been like for Mary and Joseph to make such a trip in danger and uncertainty. It is true that they had a message from an angel telling them to go, and that must have been some comfort, but you have to admit that "take the child to Egypt" is a directive that is a little bit short on detail; *how* to go about that was something they had to figure out for themselves. And they were not world travelers, after all. It is unlikely that either one of them had ever been more than thirty miles from the place where they grew up. Initially not knowing the language or the customs, they lived in hiding in Egypt for years. As foreigners, they undoubtedly were subject to prejudice by locals.

Those kinds of difficulties and uncertainties must have put quite a strain on their family relationships. All those wonderful virtues acclaimed today by Saint Paul get much more difficult. I have to tell you that in the Kupin family, the milk of human kindness began to run a little thin as we got more and more tired and stressed-out by our adventures. And there they were, two newlyweds, with a tiny baby into the bargain, and fleeing to who knows where. As a new husband, Joseph surely felt a responsibility to be the protector and provider for his family, but in the circumstances too much was completely out of his control for that to be possible.

And yet, God made it all work for them. Undoubtedly he sent them the friends and the help they needed to make their impossible task be possible. For example, the gold from the Magi's gift probably came in pretty handy as they made their way along the road.

The good news for all of us to celebrate today is that God is ready and willing to give us that same kind of help in life. For we are, all of us, on a journey in this life, and sometimes we face situations that seem completely impossible. That is when we need the help of God to find a way.

Perhaps this year someone close to us will come down with a serious illness, and we will find our family fleeing for safety into the foreign land of emergency rooms and doctor's offices. We may find that the people there all seem to be speaking a foreign language full of words like "palliative care" and "neuropathy" and "insurance deductibles". It might be necessary to make important decisions in the absence of complete information. In those sorts of difficult situations, we need to remind ourselves that God will be there ahead of us, just as he went before Mary and Joseph on their trip into Egypt. We might not see how it is all going to work out, but if we ask him to do so, God will send us the people and the help we need to navigate that strange new land.

Or perhaps in this sputtering economy, we might find that our job has been pulled out from under us, and we flee into the strange realm of unemployment. Here too there are imponderable forms to fill out and strange and seemingly arbitrary rules that we have to learn to follow. If we invite him, God will be with us in that extremity too.

Or perhaps we have lost a loved one this year, and we are living for a while in the strange land of aloneness, trying to work our way through the myriad details of closing down a life. And we may be doing all that without the help of the person we have depended on for years. Here too, God is there before us, and if we can just keep putting one foot in front of the other, as Joseph and Mary did, God will help us to get through.

One place we can go to renew our trust that God will be there for us in new and difficult circumstances is to look back at our own lives, and try to see God's helping hand in our past difficulties. Maybe he didn't give us exactly the help we would have wanted or expected, but if we take the long view, and look with eyes of faith we will see God's helping hand. I mean, I would have much preferred it if God would have just sent me an angel two months ago to tell me about the new visa requirements. But he didn't do that—or if he did I wasn't listening. But what he did do, was make the whole thing work out in the end.

Only it was on his schedule, and in his own ever-surprising way. If you look back at your life you may see the same sort of thing.

To conclude, here is a prayer from the Mass that has something important to say on this topic. It is a short prayer that the priest prays on our behalf right after we say the Lord's prayer together. The Lord's prayer ends with the words "deliver us from evil", and right after that the priest says this:

> *"Deliver us, Lord, from every evil. Grant us*
> *peace in our day. In your mercy, keep us free*
> *from all sin and protect us from all anxiety as we*
> *wait in joyful hope for the coming of our savior*
> *Jesus Christ."*

That is a prayer worth meditating on. You might even want to memorize it so you can repeat it when needed. I don't know about you, but "protect us from all anxiety as we wait in joyful hope" sounds pretty good to me. That is the gift that God wants to give us this Christmas season. Let us accept that gift, and continue with our worship confident that God will be with us, wherever our journey may take us.

CALLED BY GOD FOR SOMETHING GREAT

(Is 49: 3, 5-6; 1 Cor 1: 1-3; Jn 1: 29-34)

When I was in grammar school, we had a safety patrol. That was a team of kids from the upper grades (mostly boys) who, when they were on duty, wore a nifty white strap that wound around their waist and over one shoulder, and who were supposed to keep order on the school buses and make sure that everyone crossed the street safely when they got to their stop. Our safety patrol was run by Sister Julius Marie. I found her a bit intimidating. That nun could really hit a baseball, for one thing—out of the park almost every time she came to bat. But also, she had the unenviable task of trying to teach me long division. For that alone she deserves a place in heaven.

Anyway, when I was in the sixth grade, one day as I was leaving math class, Sister Julius asked me to stay behind for a moment, and she told me that she wanted me to join the safety patrol. Now I was a shy little guy, and I mostly survived grammar school by keeping my head down, but here she was asking me to take a leadership role. It was a strange idea to me, and as I considered it, I found myself pleased that she thought I was capable of doing such an important job, but I also felt unsure that I could really do it. Much later I realized that probably what was in the back of her mind was that by enlisting into the safety patrol one of the people who was most likely to absentmindedly step out in front of truck, she was actually solving several problems at the same time. But I didn't think of that at the time, and after consulting with my parents, I accepted the position and I took the responsibilities of being a safety patrol member very seriously.

Perhaps you have had similar experiences in your life, when someone in charge looked around and picked you out of the crowd, and said "Come here, I have just the job for you." It might have been a teacher or a coach, or a parent. Maybe you felt pleased or intimidated or annoyed. But however the event played out, such a moment is an important opportunity for growth. That experience is also part of what we bring with us as we listen to today's readings, because they are all about being "called" and "chosen".

In our first reading we listen in on the thoughts of God as he chooses the person who is going to be his Messiah, his anointed one who will save his people Israel. It is clear that God had great plans for this person. And even thought these words were written more than 600 years before the birth of Jesus of Nazareth, we believe they apply to him. He is the person God was speaking to when God said that he had formed him as his servant while he was still in the womb of his mother, and told him "you will be a light to the nations, that my salvation might reach to the ends of the earth." How do you think Jesus, in his humanity, felt when he read the book of Isaiah and it dawned on him that those words might apply to him? Kind of pleased and eager? Maybe reassured and maybe at the same time a bit intimidated?

In our gospel we have the example of John the Baptist, telling of his own calling and his experiences, how he witnessed the descent of the Holy Spirit on Jesus the Messiah. His own calling was intertwined with the great calling of the Messiah that we heard from the book of Isaiah

Finally, we come to today's epistle, in which the verb "to call" appears three times in the first sentence. This reading is the very beginning of Saint Paul's first letter to the Corinthians. Saint Paul originally founded the Christian community at Corinth, but then went off on other missionary journeys. He loved the people of Corinth, but when he wrote this letter to them, he was none too pleased with what he was hearing about how they were behaving. We will be hearing much more from this letter over the coming weeks, but right here at the beginning, in his words of greeting, Saint Paul is setting the context for what he wants to say to them. First, he reminds them that he, Paul, was called by God for the ministry that he was working in. Like John the Baptist, Paul had a call from God that was bound up with the Messiah's calling.

Then, Saint Paul takes this idea one step further. He reminds the people of Corinth that they too have a calling that comes from their association with Jesus. They are called to be a holy people. Notice how Paul says it. They are called to be holy along with "all those everywhere who call upon the name of our Lord Jesus Christ." That group includes us. Just like the people of Corinth, we are called to lead the kind of holy life that will give strong witness to our faith in Jesus.

How does that call sit with you on this mid-winters day? Are you pleased and eager? Maybe reassured, or maybe a bit apprehensive? One thing that might seem difficult about our call to holiness is that we might feel that to answer this call, we have to pretend to be someone that we are not. We might imagine trying to become some sort of a plaster statue of a saint, without earthly cares or strong emotions. That is not what the call to holiness is all about. God loves who we are as individuals, after all he made us. We don't have to pretend to be someone else, but to really answer God's call we will have to stretch our muscles a bit: physically, mentally and spiritually.

Father James Martin has some important things to say in this regard concerning the great saints of history in his book "My Life with the Saints". Father Martin makes two important points. First, he remarks on how different the great saints all were as individuals. Think of the concern for nature of Francis of Assisi, and the scholarship of Thomas Aquinas and the compassion of Mother Theresa of Calcutta. Those saints had very different personalities, and each one followed his or her unique path to sainthood. That should give us encouragement as we struggle to find our special path to sainthood. Paradoxically, when the saints of history were most stretching themselves to follow the way of Jesus, they also were being most fully themselves.

The second important point that Father Martin makes is that in general, the saints found joy in their efforts. Being a saint does not usually lead to a life of ease and physical comfort, but it does regularly lead to a life of joy. Perhaps my old friend Sister Julius Marie dreaded the hours she spent helping us struggle with our long division problems, I don't know, but when she was in the batter's box on the playground, it was obvious that she loved her vocation. And in both situations, I am sure she was doing something holy and she was exactly where God wanted her to be.

This week it might be good to think about how God is calling us to stretch ourselves to greater holiness in the new year. Maybe he wants us to stretch ourselves physically and do more for others. For example, our bulletin sometimes runs requests for rides to church. We should make an effort to respond to such requests and so build up the web of relationships that is our community of faith. Or maybe we are being called to stretch ourselves mentally. Bible study will be starting up soon, and that could be a way to respond to this call. Also our parish library has lots of good books that could help us to learn more about our faith and our Catholic traditions. Or maybe we are being called to stretch ourselves spiritually, to deepen our prayer life or practice more fully a particular virtue that has been on our mind recently.

Our liturgy today invites us to take Saint Paul's words seriously and seek diligently and joyfully for the unique path to holiness that is our calling from God. As we do so we can also take comfort in the words he offers in benediction: "Grace to you, and peace from God the Father and our Lord Jesus Christ!"

7th Sunday in Ordinary Time, Feb. 20, 2011:

AN ACHIEVABLE KIND OF PERFECTION

(Lev 19: 1-2, 17-18; 1 Cor 3: 16-23; Mt 5: 38-48)

For the past several weeks, our gospels have been presenting some very challenging demands to us. And then, at the end of today's gospel, Jesus tops it all off with "So be perfect, just as your heavenly Father is perfect." It is important to understand both what Jesus is *not* trying to say with these words, and what he *is* trying to say to us.

First, what he is not trying to say. He is *not* saying "Never make a mistake; never fail at what you do." It's important for us to recognize that and remember it, because otherwise we might be tempted to give up as followers of Jesus. We know we are never going to get to a place where we don't make mistakes. In fact, only trying to avoid failure might not even be such a good thing. There was a coach in my high school who frequently told us "If you are not failing some of the time, you are not trying hard enough." We know that it is not good to play a sport in a league in which you win every game. When an individual or a team finds itself in that situation, the sensible thing to do is to move up into a stronger league where there is more competition. Similarly, when we find ourselves succeeding too easily in the spiritual practices we have set for ourselves, that is a sign that is time for us to move on to something a bit more challenging.

So what *does* Jesus mean for us to take away from this verse? One way to come to grips with that meaning is by looking at its Old Testament background. There is an Old Testament source for the verse, just as there are for so many others in Matthew's gospel. It appears to be a blending of two verses, in fact. The first is in the book of Deuteronomy in a section which talks about how terrible it is to offer sacrifices to false gods, and then says "You, however, must be whole-hearted before the Lord your God." (18:13). That is, be perfect in the sense of having undivided loyalty. We hear the other source in our reading from the book of Leviticus today which says "Be holy, for I, the Lord, your God, am holy" (19, 2). What follows in Leviticus is a list of rules for living that implement that call to holiness, including those we hear today and many others. We can well imagine that Jesus was trying to recall such wholesome advice to his listeners and expand upon it.

The call to be whole-hearted and holy in all that we do fits together very nicely with the beginning of our epistle today in which Saint Paul reminds us that we are a holy temple of God. This is a reality that we express very concretely every Sunday when we come together at the Lord's table. One thing that Jesus is trying to tell us today is that being a holy temple of God is not a part-time occupation. It is not something we *do* on Sunday morning; it is something that we *are* all week long. All our doing should flow from that way of being. I would like to examine two of the many ways in which we are challenged by Jesus to take the holiness we find here and extend it all through our lives.

Today we hear "If someone presses you into service for one mile, go with him for two miles." This is an allusion to a principle of law in the ancient world, called *angaria* in Latin, which said that a government official had the power to require unpaid assistance from a private individual in a matter involving the common good. For example, when Simon of Cyrene was forced to carry the cross for Jesus, that is described in the gospels as a case of angaria. Now, in principle, it is a very good idea for people to support the common good, but we can imagine how this rule of law was open to abuse. And yet, Jesus, for reasons that are variously explained, tells people that they should cooperate with angaria, and even to do so generously, doing more than the minimum required.

And what about us? Angaria does not play an important part in U.S. law, but we do have some regulations that require people to do unpaid work to support the common good. Some examples are being called to jury duty, or the requirement to shovel the sidewalks in front of our house after a snow storm, or the requirement to sort items for recycling. Perhaps Jesus today is calling on us to see how well we support the common good. We might work harder to fulfill the spirit of such laws, and not just do the bare minimum required. It is not easy or convenient, but it is an aspect of holiness to generously support the common good, and who knows if we might not be privileged at some point to carry the cross of Jesus when we do so.

Here is a second example. Today Jesus tells us to love our enemies. That's pretty hard to do, and surely it is a sign of true holiness. Maybe we can begin with the people who sometimes annoy us. Imagine you are on your way home and make a quick stop at the supermarket. You grab a few things and head for the 5-items-only lane. In front you is an elderly lady who is moving very slowly. She laboriously counts out her money while your ice cream slowly melts as it sits on the conveyor belt.

What does it mean to be a holy temple of God in that situation? Maybe it means stepping back from our hurriedness and setting aside the worries about what we need to do when we get home, and really being present to the person in line in front of us. Not feeling pity for her, but feeling empathy with her—imagining what it must be like to be her. That elderly woman in the frayed sweater once wore a beautiful royal-blue crinoline prom-dress. The person having trouble counting out seven one-dollar bills used to get A's on all her math tests. All that history is still a part of her and just in those few moments standing in line, we are given the opportunity to notice her and honor her. We can treat her as we would wish that other people would treat our own mother in a similar situation. Not easy to do, but Oh so very holy to try.

It is doing simple things like these in all parts of our life that falls under the call of Jesus to be perfect as his Father is perfect. Not so much that we succeed in everything we try, but that we always try as best we can to do the right thing.

Some of you may know that I help out with the Hispanic community that is a part of our parish. Well, doing that has required learning some Spanish, of course, and I'm trying to do so. I'm still not very good at it, but at the beginning I'm sure I was pretty bad. I remember one of the first times I tried to proclaim the Gospel in Spanish. After Mass, one of the good ladies in the community came up to me and thanked me for reading and said "And you read so well! You did mess up a few words. Left out a syllable in this word and mispronounced that word", and so on. Then she gave me a big smile and said "but aside from that, it was perfect!" That, to me, is a lovely definition for "perfect", which fits very well with our gospel today. It is a definition that can bring us hope. The same sort of sentiment is expressed very well in the first letter of John, which has this to say:

> *"God is love, and whoever remains in love,*
> *remains in God, and God in him. In this, love*
> *is brought to perfection among us. The result is*
> *that we have confidence in the day of judgment*
> *because as he is, so we are in this world. There is*
> *no fear in love, but perfect love drives out fear, be-*
> *cause fear has to do with punishment, and so the*
> *one who fears is not yet perfect in love. We love*
> *because he loved us first." (4,16b-19)*

This short passage talks movingly about the goal of having perfect love. We are called by Jesus to the perfect love that drives out fear. This week we might want to read slowly through this part of Matthew's gospel, and ask in what ways we are being challenged to try harder for that perfect love of others. Surely, if we try for it, we will fail sometimes, but that's OK. If we keep trying, and take full advantage of the graces available to us in the sacraments of Eucharist and Reconciliation, then when we get to heaven, we can expect God to greet us with words similar to those of that kind Hispanic lady: "You did so well! You messed up here, and here, and here, but aside from that you were perfect!"

2nd Sunday of Lent, Mar. 20, 2011:
WHAT BLOCKS OUR RESPONSE TO GOD'S CALL?

(Gen 12: 1-4; 2 Tm 1: 8-10; Mt 17: 1-9)

Today as we gather in prayer, we remember the people of Japan, and all those who have been so deeply affected by the recent natural disasters there. Our heart goes out to them, and to the people of Libya and Bahrain, who are facing terrible man-made disasters. It is important for us to take note of the feelings of empathy we have when we hear or read about such situations and it is important to respond to those feelings, either in prayer or in action of some kind, or both. This is important because those feelings are one way God has of calling us out of ourselves and into a new relationship with him.

In today's readings, we see a number of different people who are invited by God to go with him on a new journey of faith. The reading from the book of Genesis gives us the beginning of the story of Abraham and Sarah. Abraham is called "our father in faith", in part at least for his willingness to leave behind his comfortable surroundings at God's direction and begin something new and different. In the process, he and Sarah became God's special friends.

Peter, James and John were invited to climb mount Tabor with Jesus, and there they met two of the greatest heroes of their tradition: Moses and Elijah. That must have been an exhilarating and slightly uncomfortable experience. Probably, they would have wanted to comb their hair and wear better clothes, if they had known about it ahead of time. Imagine what it would be like to meet George Washington, or Babe Ruth, and multiply that by about a thousand. And then they heard the voice of God. No wonder Jesus needed to reassure them and tell them not to be afraid.

And then finally, we have the letter to Timothy. For many years, Timothy was a friend and companion to Saint Paul, but now he was being asked to strike out on his own and do something new: to be a "bishop" or "overseer" of a Christian community. At the time, nobody really knew what that job entailed. It was still being invented under the guidance of the Holy Spirit. We can see in his letter how Saint Paul was trying to reassure him, and give him strength for the new journey he was on.

In Lent, we too are being called by God to enter into a journey of faith where we can have an encounter with him. Just like climbing a mountain, or going off to a strange new country, or taking a new job that we need to design as we go along, answering God's invitation will take us on an unpredictable adventure. And it must be said that adventures are sometimes difficult and uncomfortable things. "They make you late for dinner", as someone once said.

In his writings, Saint Augustine has much to say about human nature and how that affects the way in which we respond to God's call, and so in the spirit of the season, I would like to yield the floor to him so that he can present us with three uncomfortable questions about how we are balancing the competing demands of our lives. These question are not presented so that we can beat up on ourselves, but so that we might see our lives honestly and decide what we need to do to respond to God's invitation.

The first question concerns our natural desire to please our senses. Now, our senses are a gift from God and a very good thing. Pleasing our senses helps us distinguish good food from bad, and it helps us to appreciate the many beautiful things there are in God's creation. But working too hard to please our senses can also lead us astray. Pleasing our senses means an endless quest for novelty, for one thing. For example, I usually have a sandwich for my lunch. If one day I have pickles on my sandwich, that can be an enjoyable thing. But when I have pickles every day, the pleasure quickly wears off. Now I want potato chips, or hot sauce or something else new and different. And if I usually have five potato chips with my lunch each day, pretty soon I need ten chips to feel a special pleasure. That is the way our senses work; they respond to novelty. And of course the same applies to much more serious issues than pickles and potato chips. There is alcohol and the kinds of pictures we can find so easily on the internet, and whatever else it is that draws our fancy. Pursuing such things can lead us where we do not really want to go.

So, the question Saint Augustine would have us ask is "this past year, have we been following our desire to please our senses at the expense of following Jesus?" When we follow Jesus, we concern ourselves more with pleasing others. For example, to cook a meal and enjoy it is a good thing, but to cook a good meal and share it with someone who is hungry, is a pleasure of a different order, and much more in keeping with Jesus' message of love for one another. It is also a pleasure that does not wear off so easily.

Saint Augustine's second question concerns our natural desire to acquire things. Here too, the desire itself is a good thing in moderation. In this climate we need a warm coat in the winter, and in the spring we need shoes that don't leak, and so forth. But for many of us our tendency to acquire stuff goes way beyond these simple needs. Our culture doesn't help us much with this one. If you ask most people how much money they really need to get by, they would probably respond "more than I have now." One gets the feeling that that would always be the answer. Recently I heard a news commentator bemoaning the fact that the U.S. was falling way behind in the number of billionaires we produce each year. Apparently, right now India and China are doing much better at this. Somehow, I don't think that is the biggest problem we have as a nation.

Saint Augustine would ask us "in this past year have we been following our desire to acquire stuff at the expense of following Jesus?" When we follow Jesus, we have more trust that God will provide us with what we need when we need it, and so are more willing to share what we have now with other people who have much less.

Saint Augustine's final question has to do with our natural desire to be in control. The desire itself is a good thing. For our health, we need to have a feeling of being in control of our body and our personal space. But often our desire to be in control of things can go way beyond what is healthy. We might want to control every detail of the world around us, so that we can be completely safe and never face any nasty surprises. Or we might try to act on that deep feeling we have that if everyone would just do what we say, the world would be a much better place.

Saint Augustine would ask us, "in the past year have we been following our desire to be in control of things at the expense of following Jesus?" When we follow Jesus we are open to the promptings of the Holy Spirit. We stop trying to make God follow our will, and seriously try to determine what God's will is for our lives and cooperate with that.

Lent is an invitation from God to strike out from our place of comfort and go on an adventure with him. Though there may be many difficulties along the way, our gospel hints at the endpoint of that adventure; it ends in glory. Yes, we may miss a few meals. We may end up leaving behind things that we once thought precious. We may end up in some situations that are completely beyond our control. But what a trip it will be, with Jesus as our guide and the Holy Spirit our companion and God the Father our final rest. Today God himself tells us how to take the next step when he says: "This is my beloved son... Listen to him."

CHECK OUT THE END OF THE STORY—IT'S GOOD!

(Reading for children's stations: Jn 14: 1-3, 25-27)

When I was young, and I had just learned to read well enough to read chapter-books, I enjoyed checking a book out of the library and reading it at home. In the first couple of chapters, I would get to know the characters in the story, and begin to care about them, but then, in the third chapter maybe, something really bad would happen to one of the characters, like a war or a flood or an illness. When that would happen, I wouldn't want to finish the book. But sometimes, if I really liked the book, I would turn to the last chapter to see whether the book had a happy ending, and if it did, that would give me the courage to go back and read the hard parts in the middle. —All right, I'll be honest, I still sometimes do that with the books that I read today.

Wouldn't it be nice if we could do the same thing with the story of our own lives? Because we do sometimes face really hard chapters in our life. Maybe we find out that our family is going to move to some other city or state, and that will mean a new house or a new school where we don't know anyone, and maybe the house or the school doesn't seem as nice as our old ones, and the people aren't as friendly, but we have to do it anyway. Or maybe someone we love very much gets sick and goes into the hospital. And we are really worried about them, and our home gets all upset and sometimes there is no clean laundry, because nobody has had time to do the washing, or there is not much in the fridge, because nobody has had time to do the shopping. Or maybe, there comes a time when there is a lot of arguing going on in our house. Mom and Dad don't seem to get along any more and they are fighting all the time, and we worry that they might be thinking about a divorce, but there is nothing we can do to fix the problem.

When one of those bad things happens to a good friend of ours or to us, it would be great to be able to just turn to the end of the story and see how it is all going to come out. We can't really do that, but we almost can. We can't learn how this particular chapter in our life is going to turn out, but we do know that we have a God who loves us, and who is going to make very sure that the last chapter in our life story ends happily. And that can be a comfort and give us the strength we need to keep going.

That is one of the things we can learn from our prayer this evening. Tonight we are going to pray about some terrible things that happened to Jesus. We don't do that because we think it was good that all that stuff happened to him. No, we and all of Jesus' friends wish that none of that had ever happened to him. But it did. It really did. It is not just a story. And the thing for us to keep in mind as we pray is that even when we get to the last stations, and Jesus dies and his body is laid in the tomb, that is not the end of the story of Jesus' life. There is still one more chapter to go. That is the Easter chapter, when Jesus returns from the dead and visits with his friends again. His life is changed; it is different from what it was before, but his new life is good and he is happy.

A thing for us to remember, is that the same God who loved Jesus and took care of him, also loves us and will be with us when we are in trouble. In our gospel today Jesus asks us to remember this good news and have faith in God and have faith in him. It may happen that some of the things we are most worried about in our life this evening are not going to turn out as we hope they might, no matter how much we pray about them and how good we try to be. But God has promised us that however bad it gets in the middle chapters of our life story, there will be a happy ending to the story. Whatever bad thing happens to us, somehow new life will come out of it and eventually it will be for our good and the good of those we love. And the very last chapter—that will be very, very good. So, this evening as we pray the stations together, maybe we can make an act of faith in Jesus, and say:

- Even if someday I am accused of something I didn't do, and I am condemned for it, I will believe that that is not going to be the end of my story.

- Even if I fall under the control of bullies who make fun of me and hurt me, I will stay faithful, because my Easter is coming.

- Even if I need to do something really difficult, that I don't want to do, and I fail and have to start again. And then I fail again and have to start over, and even if I fail a third time and have to start over, even then I will believe that God is with me and cares about me and I will believe in my Easter.

- Even if someone I love should die, and I see the big stone over their grave, and I know I will never talk to that person again until I get to heaven, even then I will believe that that is not the end of the story for that person or for me. I will keep believing in Easter

Thank you, Jesus for coming to be with us, and enduring all the difficult things that happened in your life to show us the Father's love, and to show us the real end of the story.

Thank you, God our Father, for loving us so much that you sent your son to show us the way to you, and for making sure that the end of our story will be a happy one.

Be with us, Holy Spirit of God. Always be our comforter and remind us of what we see and hear tonight, so that we can have the courage to be faithful through all the hard chapters in our life story, and so get to the last chapter, the really happy chapter, the Easter chapter, when we will be with God forever.

4th Sunday of Easter, May 15, 2011:
AFTER THE RESURRECTION, THEN WHAT?

(Acts 2: 14, 36-41; 1 Pt 2: 20-25; Jn 10: 1-10)

For the last three Sundays we have been having beautiful gospel readings that bear on an important question that must have been of concern to many in the early Church. The question is, "Now that Jesus has died, risen and ascended into heaven, how will the community be able to get along without his continuing physical presence?" The readings over these last three Sundays provide a comforting answer by illustrating a number of important ways in which Jesus continues to be an active presence within the Church right down to this very day.

Two weeks ago, on Divine Mercy Sunday, we heard the story of the risen Jesus entering the locked upper room on the evening of the resurrection breathing onto the Apostles the Holy Spirit, and empowering them to forgive sins. The continuation of this gift within the Church is an important way in which the love of Jesus still guides the Church. This is true on a grand scale in the sacrament of Reconciliation, and also on a more intimate scale within our own lives. The experience of forgiveness, either as the forgiver or the forgiven, is a true experience of the risen Christ present among us.

Then, last week we had the reading from Luke about the two disciples on the road to Emmaus. Walking along listening to Jesus but not recognizing him for who he was, the two disciples felt their hearts burning within them as their minds were opened to a fuller meaning in the Scriptures. This is also an experience that we can continue to have, as we explore the depths of Scripture and try to apply the lessons we find there to our lives.

The Emmaus reading also highlights the bread and wine of the Eucharist as an experience of the presence of Jesus in our lives. The two disciples were energized by their recognition of Jesus in the breaking of the bread, so much so that they retraced their steps for miles and miles, going back to Jerusalem to share the story with the other disciples. In the Mass we have our modern equivalent of this Emmaus experience. Here we find our bread for the journey and the fire in the heart that keeps us going.

And then, finally, we have today's reading which emphasizes the way in which good leadership within the community communicates to us the experience of the risen Jesus. Our gospel says that the leaders who enter by way of Jesus are recognized by the community. The sheep hear the voice of the shepherd and follow. The gospel story itself is set during the earthly ministry of Christ, and the examples it places before us are somewhat negative, but we can provide many positive examples from our own experience. Our parish has been blessed with a succession of good priests who have led the community well, and we can be sure that this will continue to be true as our parish makes a transition in leadership over the next few months.

It is also true that having heard the voice of Jesus in this way within the Church, sensitizes us and allows us to hear his voice in other situations in which leadership is important. When I was a boy, I was a member of a troop of boy scouts, and we had many fine scout masters. My all-time favorite was a man we called Uncle Herman. He was retired, and his own son had long since grown up and left the troop, but Uncle Herman stayed on. He had a special gentleness and compassion for the youngest scouts who were just entering the troop. I can still picture him sitting with the group around the campfire in the evening. In Uncle Herman, I could hear the voice of Jesus singing. Many of the songs we sang were loud or funny, but the ones Uncle Herman loved best had a spiritual theme. One of his particular favorites was "We are climbing Jacob's ladder." He guided many a boy through their confusing teen-age years with little more than his gentle smile, a dog-eared scout handbook and all those songs.

Maybe sometime you have been in a similar situation of being part of a group that depended on a guide to lead you through unfamiliar and possibly confusing territory. The guide may have been imperfect, as we all are, but when the relationship is working as it should, we can hear in it the voice of Jesus calling our name and leading us with care.

One important time for us to remember to listen for the voice of Jesus is when we are fretting over a decision. When this happens to me, I tend to ask my friends and loved ones for advice, and they are usually quite happy to offer their opinions. And that's good, but taken all together, their advice can seem contradictory, and I usually find myself agreeing with the last person I've spoken to. It is at a time like that when it might be helpful to ask ourselves the question "In which of these voices can I hear the echo of the voice of Jesus?" Our gospel promises that we will be able to discern his voice when we hear it, and then we will know what to do. If we don't hear that from our friends, it may be time to look further afield for our advice.

We might even carry this meditation one step further, and think about the times when we are called to act as a guide for others. This might come about in a formal way through our position in the workplace or in the family, or it might arise in a more informal way, when we have the opportunity to offer advice or sympathy to a friend or loved one. When that happens we might pause and think about the Jesus that we have met here in the sacraments of reconciliation and the Eucharist, and the comfort we have found in our reading of Scripture. Starting from that solid foundation, we can ask ourselves, "What would the Jesus that I have come to know want to say to this person in front of me?" Maybe he would want us to offer words of encouragement, or words of challenge, or words of consolation. It may slow us down to consider such a ponderous question, but it might not be such a bad thing for us to think a bit more before we speak, and to work harder to put some of the gentleness of the Good Shepherd into our conversations.

So we can take comfort in the many ways that Jesus continues to guide and watch over the community through his gifts of the sacraments of reconciliation and Eucharist, in the Scriptures and in the leaders he sends to guide us. This week we might meditate on the particular ways in which we have most deeply experienced the guiding hand of the Good Shepherd in our lives. We can wrap that up with a prayer of thanksgiving and praise.

Meditating in this way will be good preparation for the last step of our life's journey, when we enter the heavenly banquet. When I imagine the heavenly banquet, I see us all gathered round the table sharing the stories of our journey through life. Some of the stories will be happy ones, and some sad. There will be stories of being lost and being found. There will be stories of being hungry and being fed. There will be stories of surprise encounters with beauty and grace. They will certainly be stories full of life. For our guide promises us that much at the end of today's gospel when he says "I have come that they may have life and have it more abundantly." That is a promise about the end times, true enough, but it is also a promise about the life we share now, in this place and time.

THE TRINITY AS A DANCE OF LOVE

(Ex 34: 4-6. 8-9; 2 Cor 13: 11-13; Jn 3: 16-18)

Today is Father's Day, and I want to begin by congratulating all fathers. Whether you are a biological father, or a volunteer in that role, whether you are a god-father, a father-in-law or an expectant father, you play a very important role in someone's life, and that is a great responsibility.

It is a day for all of us to think about all we have learned from our fathers, and show our appreciation. I learned many practical things from my father, like how to saw a straight line, but even more importantly he left me with a lot of happy images, for example, him crabbing on the Chesapeake bay or working in his garden. But far and away, the image that seems most relevant to today's celebration is that of him and my mother dancing. My dad was a shy man, and about the only time I ever saw him really cut loose was when we would go to a family wedding or some other big celebration, and there would be a dance band, and he and my mother would try to dance every dance. And if they played a polka, well, there was no holding them back. What a joy that was to see.

Even today, when I search for a mental image of what it means for "two to become one flesh", I see my parents out there on the dance floor, twirling about their common center of gravity and having a grand old time. It was clear that they lost nothing of their individuality by entering the dance. They were still themselves, but by giving themselves over to the other in the dance, they became something more. Perhaps you have had a similar experience.

This same image of the dance can be a fruitful way for us to think about the nature of the Holy Trinity, whose feast we celebrate today. In the Eastern church, one way they have of trying to understand how it could be that there are three persons in one God, is that they describe it as a "perichorea" a Greek word meaning literally "a dancing around". And I can almost see it. Father, Son and Holy Spirit, together dancing the great dance of creation. Holding hands and spinning around their common center of gravity; dancing the world into being and laughing as they spin.

It's a beautiful image —not a perfect one perhaps —but we will never have an image that perfectly captures this great mystery. All we can do is keep delving and meditating and discovering riches as we go. It is also an image that might make us reflect a bit on our own lives. For we have been created in the image and likeness of God. And just as God is inherently a community of love, so we too flourish best when we join the dance of a living, loving community.

In a response to today's feast day we might think about all the different communities we are a part of and treasure each one. On Father's Day we can't do better than to begin with our nuclear family. That is where many people get a solid foundation in being loved. I hope your family experience was or is just like that. Many families are, but then some aren't. Those of us who have had a difficult family life must find their circle of love in some other setting.

And be it good or bad, all of us are eventually called beyond the nuclear family to something larger. There are so many possibilities. There is our extended family, and our parish, our school, workplace and neighborhood. In any one of these places we might be surprised and pleased to discover a dynamic community of love that we can be a part of.

Of course, even the best of these communities will only be a pale shadow of the indivisible love of the Trinity. We do remain human, after all. Saint Paul in our epistle today shows a clear understanding that sometimes our communities of love can be pretty far from the ideal. Saint Paul was writing to the Corinthians. That was a community he had founded, and now as he went on further missionary journeys, he was hearing things he didn't like about the way the community was celebrating the Eucharist, and generally about the way they were living. In this letter, he is being pretty stiff with them, but here at the end of the letter, Saint Paul tries to look on the bright side. He tells them to rejoice first of all, and also to pull up their socks and start behaving more appropriately. Here is what we heard him say "mend your ways, encourage one another, agree with one another, live in peace and the God of love and peace will be with you." That is the thing they should focus on and rejoice over. And we should too, for that promise applies to us as well.

But we do have to be careful exactly how we hear that sentence of Saint Paul. It almost sounds like an "if...then" sentence. *IF* you do all those hard things, *THEN* God will come and be with you. That would be pushing the words too far. The situation is more complicated than that, as our other readings show us.

In today's gospel, it says "God did not send his son into the world to condemn the world, but that it might be saved through him." God comes to us while we are still in our sins, while we are still part of communities where people are not in a harmonious dance together, but rather everyone seems to be jumping up and down and tromping on people's toes. It is not the case that we have to become perfect, and then God will consent to come and be with us, it is rather that God's coming among us gives us the spark we need to change those dead and broken communities into living and loving ones. That is a very different take on things, and certainly something that we might rejoice about.

Our first reading today, from the book of Exodus extends this theme. Let me set the scene for you. Just one month earlier, God had led the Israelites out of their slavery in Egypt. He crushed the armies of Pharaoh that threatened them, and gave them food and water in the desert. Now, they are camped at the base of Mount Sinai, and Moses has gone up to receive the Ten Commandments. While Moses is delayed on the mountain the people begin to be worried about being abandoned and they build the golden calf to worship instead of God.

So there is Moses on the top of the mountain with God, and Moses asks God to overlook all the sins and failings of his stiff-necked people and come and be their God anyway. This is an invitation with the virtues of honesty and humility, but it sure doesn't seem very inviting. I don't think Moses has much of a future as a party planner. But the amazing thing, the thing worth celebrating, is that God said "yes". He did go along with them through the desert experience and eventually led their children into the Promised Land.

So, I want to leave you today with a question. What do you suppose would happen if we were to make a similar invitation to God? If we were to pick one of the communities that we are a part of, one that is not functioning very well right now, and we were to ask God to come to be with that community and help his stiff-necked people to dance more harmoniously together? I don't think he would be slow to answer. I'm sure he would not. He might come as Father, Son or Holy Spirit, depending on whether we need a Father's advice, or a Brother's help, or a spirit of wisdom to tell us when to speak and when to be silent. He will show us what we need to do. For, as the book of Exodus says, our God is "a merciful God, slow to anger and rich in kindness and fidelity."

16th Sunday in Ordinary Time, Jul. 17, 2011:

THE GARDEN OF OUR SOUL

(Wis 12: 13,16-19; Rom 8: 26-27; Mt 13: 24-43)

It is a very happy accident that we read the beautiful agricultural parables we have in this place in Matthew's gospel in the season of high summer, when our local farms and backyard gardens are yielding up their fruits and vegetables. This delicious bounty can allow the parables to take on new and deeper meaning for us, more like what they must have been like for Jesus' first listeners, many of whom were subsistence farmers.

My family used to keep a backyard garden when our children were little, but about the only thing that is left from that time is one hearty asparagus plant. It has been with us for many years, and is like an old friend that we greet anew every Spring. From it we can usually get about one meal's worth of asparagus, but only if we are watchful. We need to be watchful because we have a very narrow time window in which we can harvest the vegetable. Typically, we watch the spot day after day in the Springtime, and see nothing breaking the soil, and then we will get distracted for a day or two, and suddenly all the asparagus fronds are five feet high and peeking in the sunroom window! The speed with which that old plant grows in the Spring is a wonder to behold.

This sense of wonder at the surprising power of plant growth is an important starting place for the second parable we hear today —the one about the mustard seed. Jesus tells us that the kingdom of heaven is like a tiny little mustard seed, which when planted, quickly grows to be a great plant. And we can see the truth of this parable in history.

The Church began as a tiny band of rag-tag disciples, without any political power, and it has grown into a world-spanning organization, overseeing many beautiful places dedicated to God's worship. It has many places that we, like the birds of the air, can find our rest.

That is a wonderful thing to consider, but this hopeful message of growth also applies to us on a much more intimate scale. When we receive the sacrament of Baptism we can view that as a tiny seed of faith being planted in the garden of our souls. What a very simple beginning that is for our faith. A few words, some drops of water and the whole thing is over in a half hour. For a long time we may not see any particular effects of our baptism, but as our faith grows and matures, it can quickly become an important and beautiful part of our life.

This morning I would like to extend the mustard seed analogy to our faith life and see what implications it has for the ways in which we approach our faith. The first thing that might be pointed out, is that our faith, like a young plant, needs to be cultivated. If it is to grow to its full potential, it needs to be tended and cared for.

For one thing, our faith needs to be able to spread its roots out all through the garden of our lives. It needs room to grow, and if we try to keep it hemmed in the little corner of our life where we keep all things religious, it won't be able to grow as strong and tall as it otherwise might.

The roots of our faith need to stretch out, and if there is a corner of our life that is toxic, our faith will not be able to grow there. For example, there might be a corner in the garden of our life where we store up all the wrongs that people have done to us —wrongs that we are unwilling or unable to forgive. That toxic corner of our garden is not going to do our faith any good. If we want our faith to grow, we need to make an active effort at emptying the toxins out of that hidden corner of our life.

In addition to an adequate place to grow, a plant also needs exposure to light and water. Last week, we had a beautiful reading from the prophet Isaiah, which described how rain comes down from God to do his will and does not return to him until it has achieved the purpose he has set for it: to promote life and growth in the world. Isaiah then says that God's word behaves in a similar way. God sends his word to his people in order to promote the growth of our spiritual lives. To continue the analogy we have been following here, God's word is the water and the sunshine that makes the mustard seed of our faith sprout and grow and blossom in a thousand ways.

So how can we get this sunshine and living water? One good way is the experience we are having this morning, coming to Mass. Here we do truly find the word of God, and that is a very good thing. Participating regularly in Sunday Mass will certainly keep our faith alive. But it is not clear that just coming to Mass on Sunday is really enough to make our faith prosper and grow as well as it is capable of doing. Now, I know that many of you will remind me that a deacon's homily is often full of the best organic fertilizer, but even with that, Sunday worship may not be enough all on it own.

What we really need to make our faith grow is to feed it the word of God all week long. Surely we would not put a tomato plant out into the sunshine for one day a week and expect much to come of it! There are many ways we might feed our faith every day of the week. One is to improve our prayer habits. Doing this doesn't have to be a complicated burden. There are many prayer books we might work from, or we can just take a few moments each day to talk with God, as we would to a loving father. In the morning when we rise, we might pause to ask God's help in the new day, and dedicate our day to his glory. Before bed at night, we might pause to recall all the surprising good things that came our way during the day, and thank God for each one. We might also ask forgiveness for the times we slipped up and were not quite as good a person as we wanted to be. Making simple prayers like those throughout the day allows us to bask our faith in the sunshine of God's presence all day long.

We might also consider doing a bit of spiritual reading each day. Many of us are thinking about vacation, and it would be a great idea to stop in first in our parish library and pick out a good book to read at the beach.

It may seem like a bit of hard work to cultivate our faith in these ways, but we have the great promise of God that if we do cultivate our faith, the results will be astounding. Our faith will grow like a sturdy and dependable tree. And then, when we face the heat of temptation, as we all do sometimes, our faith will give a cool and shady place to escape to. And when the winds of change come blowing though our lives one day, as happens to most of us sooner or later, our faith will be a steady fixed point in our lives, even while everything else seems to be dancing in the wind. And finally, when we get hungry in our souls, as we all do get hungry sometimes, our faith will produce fruits for us of surpassing sweetness, that will give us the strength we need to go on.

This is a wonderful promise from God our Father. And the really, really good news is that even if we haven't been particularly careful in the past to cultivate our faith, it is not to late to begin now. Like that faithful and long-suffering asparagus plant in my backyard, the little mustard seed of our faith is right there waiting for us, ready to spring into new growth and blossom as soon as we give it some loving care, and provide it with the light and the living water of God's word.

21st Sunday in Ordinary Time, Aug. 21, 2011:
SEEING JESUS AS BOTH GOD AND MAN

(Is 22: 19–23; Rom 11: 33-36; Mt 16: 13–20)

About a year ago, through the magic of the internet, an old friend got in touch with me whom I had not spoken to for more than forty years, not since we were both teenagers. As we exchanged e-mails I was impressed to learn that he had done very well for himself. He had had a distinguished career as a fighter pilot in the Air Force, and then after retiring from that work, he found a place high up in the Washington bureaucracy. Now as it happens, I sometimes interact with people in the government as part of my work, but usually I talk with people just a few steps up from the bottom of the government ladder, but here he was, was just a few steps down from the top. It was a little strange for me to contemplate being chummy with someone who works at that level.

As I learned all this about my one-time friend, I found myself a little bit reluctant to renew our friendship. It seemed that we had had very different lives, and I wondered what I could say to a person who was used to flying million-dollar aircraft at 600 miles an hour. But something told me to keep going, and last spring, we finally got together for dinner. It was a little bit awkward at first, but we quickly got down to discussing the people we had once known and our families and we found that we still had a lot in common. It turned out to be a very pleasant evening. I am so glad that I did not let the titles and honors and labels that my old friend had acquired get in the way of our renewed friendship. It is sad to think I almost missed the opportunity to reconnect with him.

I bring this situation up today, because it is situations like that that help me to understand today's gospel a little better, and why Jesus seems to say at the end of the gospel "Don't tell anyone who I really am". Let's look a little more closely at the gospel to see how this all fits together.

Jesus began by asking "Who do the people say that I am?" This seems a very human, very vulnerable, question. It's not the sort of question that one would expect from the Lord of the Creation. It is the kind of question I might ask one of my coworkers, after I give a presentation about something. None of us can see ourselves the way others see us, and Jesus, in his humanity, really did not know how he was coming across to the people. He needed the disciples to give him that feedback.

Then Jesus has his follow-up question: "How am I coming across to you guys, who have been with me for a while?" and good old Peter shares his growing conviction that Jesus is not an ordinary preacher or even a prophet of old come back to life, he is the Son of the Living God, the long-awaited savior of the world. Good answer, Peter!

But then comes the odd bit, when Jesus says not to tell anyone else about this. An impressive amount of ink has been spilled in scholarly literature ruminating about why Jesus might have said such a thing. One possible answer to this riddle is that having the labels "Son of the living God" and "Messiah" would have gotten in the way of people getting to know Jesus as he wanted them to do, a little bit as my friend's job title and honors almost kept me away from getting to know him better.

After all, if Jesus had wanted to begin his earthly ministry as the "King of Kings" and "Lord of Lords" he could have done so. That could have been accomplished without a birth in Bethlehem or spending his teenage years kicking around Nazareth. He could have come in on the clouds with a few legions of angels around him, and nobody would have had the slightest doubt about who was now running the show. But God, in his ever-surprising ways, chose not to do things that way. Jesus appeared on the public scene as a wandering preacher and the son of a common laborer. He let the people get to know him that way first, before they came to their own realization that he was the Son of God and their long awaited Messiah. And we shouldn't minimize the leap of faith that was required to see Jesus that way. It was difficult for many people of his time to see beyond Jesus' humanity, but those who learned to see him with the eyes of faith, finally understood Jesus for who he truly was.

In many ways, we have the opposite problem from Jesus' first disciples. Most of us encounter Jesus first as Lord and savior. Right here in our sanctuary, for example, we have a beautiful eight-foot tall statue of Jesus pictured in the moment of his greatest self-sacrifice, when he could say to his Father "It is finished; I have given everything; I have done all that was right for me to do." With images like that to contemplate, we have little trouble getting to know the eight-foot tall Jesus. And there is nothing wrong with that. The titles and honors that we give to Jesus are an important part of who he is. Contemplating them teaches us much about him. But what we don't want to do, is to let those labels get in the way of a closer relationship with the human side of Jesus, the man of Galilee, who was maybe five-foot tall in his natural life and who walked the dusty roads and knew the human pleasure of putting his feet up at the end of a long hard day. *That* Jesus we need to work a little harder to get to know, but it is well worth doing so.

One way for us to get closer to the human side of Jesus' nature is to read the gospels looking specifically for those aspects of Jesus' character. The gospel of Mark is a good place to begin this search. We can read each story about Jesus and try to imagine what it must have been like to be in that situation. We can let our holy imagination take us to that place.

To get started, we might go through each of the five senses and ask ourselves "what would I have seen in that place?" what kind of houses and plants. "What would I have heard?" perhaps the sounds of children at play. "What would I have felt?" maybe warm sunshine or a cool breeze. Imagine experiencing all those things along with Jesus.

One benefit of this exercise in getting to know the human side of Jesus is that it can enrich our prayer life. For me, there are times when I am praying and I really want to talk to the Jesus who calmed the seas with a word, or the Jesus who healed people with a touch, or the Jesus who is the justice of God come down from heaven to put all things right. When I or someone I love is in some kind of difficulty or I feel hurt or afraid, it is a great comfort to know we can pray to Jesus with confidence in his power and his love.

There are other times, though, when that kind of prayer is not quite what I need. For example, when I am feeling tired, and still have three things that I really need to do that day, or when I am trying to do something good, and I am misinterpreted, or it's just not working the way I hoped—in those times I desire the companionship of the Jesus who walked the dusty roads of Palestine, the Jesus who only ever wanted to do good things for people, but they wouldn't listen to him. I want to talk to the Jesus who laughed and who cried and knew all the emotions that make up the human condition. And the wonderful thing is, by the grace and mercy of God, we also have access to that side of Jesus in our prayer as well. That privileged access can bring great comfort.

These multiple paths to prayer are a gift and a mystery that are well worth contemplating and celebrating today. They give us a fuller answer to Jesus' question "who do you say that I am?" They lead us more deeply into the joy and wonder of Saint Paul's words: "Oh, the depths of the riches and the wisdom and knowledge of God!"

BEING AND DOING

(Is 55: 6–9; Phil 1: 20–24, 27; Mt 20: 1-16)

When I was a child, one of my jobs around the house was taking out the trash. It was not a job I liked very much. I was a squeamish child, and the job was smelly and messy. Emptying the wastebasket from my sisters' room was particularly noxious to me—worse even than the one from the bathroom. Now, if you had asked me why I was doing that job, I am sure my reasons would have changed over time. At first, I probably would have responded that I would get into trouble if I didn't do it, or perhaps I would have said that I would be rewarded in some way if it did my job well. At times, my parents used both the carrot and the stick to try and get me moving.

Then as I got a bit older, and punishments and rewards were less of an issue in my life, I became conscious of this task as my responsibility within the family. I was taught that we all had jobs to do in the family, and this was mine. I received from the labor of others, and so it was only right that I do my part. There even began to be a bit of pride in it for me. I remember one summer, I got so good at it that I could hear the trash truck down at the end of our street, and I could whip through the house gathering all the wastebaskets and get all the trash out to the curb before the truck got there, without one Kleenex spilled along the way. *Children: do not try this at home.* Many times I'm sure I almost gave my mother a heart-attack as I raced around the house.

As I grew older still, my view of family chores changed again, and I began to see my job as a gift I could give to the family—even to my sisters. I don't remember now exactly when this happy transformation in my thinking happened. It must have been some time in high school, and I think that one of my religion teachers at the time had a lot to do with changing my world view. Thank you, Brother Don!

Today, on Catechetical Sunday, we remember and honor all those who have helped us to see the sacred aspects of life, including the meaning of the things we do in service to others. Such instructors include our parents, and our teachers in school, and those who have mentored us or given us good example in less formal settings. Today, we thank God for the presence of all of them in our life, and honor those who continue this noble tradition in our parish today.

When you think about it, we are all called to be teachers of religion in some way or another, and we have an important and difficult job. Now don't get me wrong, I know that no amount of inspired teaching or good examples will make our five-year-olds do their chores out of a sense of pure altruistic love. That's part of the difficulty of the work; we need to interact in age-appropriate ways with those given into our care. Probably we have to begin with some system of rewards and punishments, but what begins as an act of obedience, can, over time, come to be seen as a kind of mutual assistance, and that can be trans-formed over time into an act of love. Our children are not going to be able to work all this out for themselves, though. They need our help through word and example.

If we *are* to be good examples, we might have to take a hard look at the things we do for others, and ask where *they* fall on the continuum from obedience to mutual aid to love. And this applies even to the things we do for God. For example, we might feel exasperated with the owner of the vineyard in the parable in today's gospel, and ask, if that is going to be how the game is played, why would anyone ever want to work all day in the Lord's vineyard? A related question is: what would it take to make me content to labor there? These big questions are not all that far from the question "why do I have to be the one to take out the trash?"

In its place in Matthew's gospel, today's parable makes its point even more clearly. It sits sandwiched between two stories about Jesus that bring these important questions to a sharp point. Matthew loves this kind of structure with one story sandwiched in between two other related stories. It is one subtle way he has of focusing our attention on what is important in the gospel message.

Just before today's reading there is the story of a man who came to Jesus with an important question: "what must I do to inherit eternal life?" First, Jesus told him to obey the commandments, but when the person persisted, wanting to do even more, Jesus looked on him lovingly and told him to go sell all he had and give to the poor, and come and follow him. The man went away sad, because he was very wealthy. This story might make us wonder whether the man was asking quite the right question. Is getting into heaven really a matter of what we have to do, or is it about who we have to be? Is it about doing particular things for God, or being in a certain relationship with God?

Then, right after today's parable, comes the story about two brothers who were both apostles coming to Jesus with a request. These two wanted the places of greatest honor in heaven, the chairs to left and his right of Jesus' heavenly throne. Jesus asks if they can drink from the cup that he will drink—a reference to his painful death. They say they are ready to do that, but Jesus responds that even so, he can't promise that they will have those favored seats. Then he adds that he can promise that they will drink from the same bitter cup as he will. This story might make us ask whether we are doing things for God in order to accumulate rewards or honors for ourselves, or are we doing things in order to be closer to Jesus?

In all three of these readings, we might feel a bit sorry for the participants: the all-day workers and the rich man and the two apostles. We might have the vague feeling that something about God's reward system seems not quite fair. If that's the way we are feeling today, maybe Jesus is asking us to grow a little in our view of our relationship with God, and reconsider why exactly we are doing what we do.

It is no accident that one of the most powerful images that we have for the relationship between God and his people is that of a husband and wife. This image appears prominently in the writings of prophets such as Hosea, and in the letters of Paul. Now, in a good married relationship, there is no talk about contractual duties and benefits, or about rewards and punishments. It is all about the gifts that we bring to one another. A married relationship is built on trust and we try not to count the cost of what we do for our spouse; we would do anything necessary, because of our love.

God feels the same way about us, and he invites us into that sort of relationship with him. This relationship needs to be acted out in practical ways, of course; it is not something that is just in our hearts or up in our heads. We act on it when we fulfill the commandments and when we praise him with joy, and, it must be added, when we do humble things like taking out the trash.

As our gospel indicates, our God is a loving and generous God. If we enter into a relationship with him, it is true that we may have to leave some things behind, and we'll find lots of hard work to do in his vineyard, and we'll surely have the occasional bitter cup to drink, but we will also receive his most generous gifts. As Jesus tells us in Luke's gospel, "Give and it will be given to you. A good measure, tamped down and shaken together, running over, will be put into your lap. For the measure you measure with will be measured out to you." (Lk 6:38).

WORKS OF FAITH, LABORS OF LOVE, AND ENDURANCE IN HOPE

(Is 45: 1. 4-6; 1 Thes 1: 1-5; Mt 22: 15-21)

When my wife and I were first married, we were determined to share equally in all our burdens, including the household chores. You might say we were obsessive about it. For example, in the beginning, we took turns cooking our meals, and whoever didn't cook, cleaned up the kitchen. This worked for a while, but somehow it didn't make either one of us very happy. Jane is a competent cook, but aside from baking, cooking is not something that brings her pleasure, whereas I think its fun to grab spices off the shelf and attack a helpless bit of chicken. And while I would not say that I am incompetent as a cleaner-upper, I do remember more than once catching Jane re-washing a perfectly clean plate after I had gotten done with it.

Well, it didn't take too many instances of "Oh, can I help you with that?" or "Would you like me to do that for you?" before the situation around our house was radically changed. I was doing most of the cooking, and Jane was keeping the kitchen neat and clean. Our basic plan to share equally in the household chores hadn't changed, but how we implemented that plan was very different from our first expectations. And, as our work schedules have changed over the years, the details of who is doing the cooking around our house have changed as well. We always know we've got the balance right because it brings *both* of us joy.

This idea of having an unchanging guiding plan for life and also having flexibility in the details of how it will be carried out can help us to appreciate today's gospel. Today we are presented with one in a series of incidents from Matthew's gospel in which Jesus has a confrontation with the authorities. This time, they really think they've got him cornered. If he says not to pay taxes, he will be in trouble with the Romans, and if he says to pay taxes, he will be in trouble with his more nationalistic followers. However, Jesus cleverly side-steps their trap and gives them an answer that no one could possibly argue with: give Caesar what is Caesar's and give God what is God's.

In these few words, Jesus is contributing an important idea to the guiding plan for our lives. God knows that we have to live in the world, and that the world makes demands on us that are difficult to ignore. God wants us to find a balance between what the world demands, and what we owe to him. It is our job to work out the details of how to set that balance, but it isn't always easy to do. Wouldn't it be lovely if everything in life came with a picture on it? This thing has Caesar's picture on it, so we give that to him, and this other thing has God's picture on it, so we give that to him. Problem solved.

Unfortunately, life doesn't come to us in such neat packages. We may feel that in our lives today all too often we are being forced by circumstances to choose between worldly goals and spiritual goals. Perhaps we would like to read the Bible more or meditate more, but there is usually some pressing practical problem that gets in the way, some fire that needs to be put out immediately. Jesus' clever words today can begin a conversation about how we want to use our time, talents and treasure each day.

Although Jesus does not give us an explicit answer to the difficult practical questions that the world presents to us, in a real sense he doesn't need to, because his whole life is the answer we need. We should study his example, and try to get in sync with his way of living, in order to truly render to God what is God's.

One person who studied the example of Jesus and thought hard about its implications for our lives is Saint Paul, and in today's reading from the letter to the Thessalonians, he gives us the benefit of his thinking. It is clear from our reading how much Saint Paul loved and admired the community at Thessalonica. He says today that he prays for them continually, fondly remembering their "work of faith, and labor of love and endurance in hope of our Lord Jesus Christ."

Faith, hope and love are a triple of virtues that Saint Paul groups together often in his writings. This threesome has come down to us through the tradition of the Church as the "theological virtues", because they are such a simple and clear description of our relationship to God. If we are really looking for something with God's picture on it in this life, it would be those three virtues. Whenever we act on the basis of those virtues, we render to God what is God's. How exactly we do that is likely to change as our lives change, but we will know when we've got it right, because it will bring us joy.

One season where we face many practical decisions of these sorts is coming up very soon now, Christmas. I saw a cartoon recently in which one young child asks another "What is Halloween?" and the other answers "Oh, that's the first day of Christmas." Truth from the mouths of babes!

The Advent and Christmas seasons have an important religious component for us, of course, but like it or not, they also have a really big secular component. There is the Christmas tree in Rockefeller Center, the television specials, the inflatable snowmen on the front lawn, and all the rest. That secular stuff isn't bad in itself, (well, maybe putting a waving Santa and eight reindeer with blinking noses up on the roof is going overboard), but in moderation it's not bad. However it does make us work a bit harder to keep the balance we are striving for.

A question we might start thinking about *now* is how we can make the coming Christmas season be more of a work of faith and a labor of hope and love. In order to do that, it is probably going to be necessary to open up some space for action by simplifying the secular aspects of our celebration. Perhaps if we cut back a bit on the present giving and all the hours we spend shopping for the prefect gift for everybody on our list, we will have more mental energy left for other things. It is not something that Caesar wants us to think about, but it is possible to show our love for someone without giving them a present, even at Christmas. With the recovered time we could participate more deeply in our Advent celebrations around the church, and read and think about the daily readings in our Advent meditation booklets. We might spend more time doing things with our family or elderly relatives. If we ask, the Spirit will guide us in ways to give to God what is God's in the coming season, and every other season.

Now you may think I am rushing things to harp away about Christmas when we are still in October, but rebalancing our Christmas season is a difficult thing to do single-handedly. To be a thing of joy, we need to do it cooperatively, with friends or family or other relatives. And if we want to start a conversation about doing such a thing, *now* is the time to do it, before Christmas fever sets in.

It has been a hard year for many people, and that might encourage our rebalancing of our celebration this year, but we should not do it just because we cannot feed Caesar the way he wants to be fed. It would be better to begin with the positive motivation of making room in our celebration for things that speak very directly to our faith and our hope and our love this year.

Keeping at this won't be easy; even talking about it is upsetting to some people. But we can get help along the way, and not the least from our parish's patron saint. It might be helpful to imagine Saint Paul writing a letter to us from heaven, a letter to the Princetonians, which he joyfully begins: "We give thanks to God always for all of you, remembering you in our prayers, unceasingly calling to mind your work of faith, and labor of love, and endurance in hope of our Lord Jesus Christ. Grace and Peace be with you."

JESUS AS A COACH FOR OUR LIVES

(Ez 34: 11–12, 15–17; 1 Cor 15: 20–26, 28; Mt 25: 31–46)

I don't know if you have been following the news coming out of Penn State these last few weeks, but it has not been pretty. An assistant coach there is accused of child abuse, and maybe there was a cover-up, or a willful failure to see what was going on by a number of other people. It is a depressingly familiar story —one that is especially sad for the damage already done to so many lives and reputations.

Today, I don't want to dwell on legal or moral ramifications of that situation, because the facts aren't really known yet, and in any event those are problems for others to work out. It will be more useful for us to focus on our own spiritual lives, and consider how this story impinges on those. We may be hurting a bit too, feeling our trust shaken. One of the reasons that this story has shocked and disturbed so many people is that it involves high-profile athletic coaches, and coaching is an institution that we hold in great esteem in this country.

Players and those who follow the game tend to treat a successful coach with great honor and respect. During a game, the coach's word is law, and even during periods of training the players obey him or her, because they trust that the coach knows the game and that everything is being done to draw out players' best performance. So, at the end of a practice if the coach says "give me five laps", the players make the effort to run the laps, no matter how tired they are. We don't have kings in our country, but within their sport, coaches would seem to be the next best thing.

Many, many coaches live up to the great trust we place in them. Perhaps you have known one or two personally. Today we might give thanks for all the experiences we have had of good coaching, either in athletics or some other field of endeavor, and in our prayer, we might extrapolate from those experiences to what it would be like to have the perfect coach. The good news of today is that Jesus is willing to fill that role in our lives if we will allow it.

Today we celebrate the feast day of Christ the King, and in our reading from Matthew's gospel we see Jesus at the end of time judging all humanity. But today's gospel should not leave us with the impression that Jesus has gone far away, leaving us with some unpleasant jobs to do, and that he will come back sometime in the distant future to judge our performance. Really, Jesus is much more like a good coach who is always right there on the sidelines as we try our best out on the field. If we listen, he will give us all the guidance and support we need to succeed.

 Personally, I did not play sports in high-school, so I had very limited contact with the various coaches around the school. About the only time I saw them was when I went to gym class, which I dreaded. But I do have one very positive memory for those times, and it makes up for all the rest.

My golden moment happened when we were having a unit on gymnastics, and as part of that unit we were supposed to swing up onto a bar that was about six feet off the ground and while sitting on the bar, we were to do sort of a backward summersault to dismount. Right. Well, my problem was, that I don't like heights. I mean, this ambo is OK, but this is about as high as I like to go even today. I was much worse about heights back when I was in high school, and that bar looked awfully high. So the last thing in the world I wanted to do was try that crazy maneuver, but I was too embarrassed to just say no.

When my turn came, I took a deep breath, and somehow I got myself up to be sitting on the bar, but then I froze. I grabbed onto the bar with both hands and was too afraid to move a muscle. No way was I going to spin around backwards. Well, the coach had wandered off by this time, but my spotters realized I was in trouble and called him over. Coach Mullis was a big guy with a gruff manner, but when he came over to me, he responded to the situation with all the gentleness of a horse-whisperer, and talked me down off the bar. He said "Feel my hand on your back. What you need to do is to relax into it, and then when I tell you to, let go of the bar." Somehow, I found myself trusting those words and with the coach's help, I made it back to *terra firma* in one piece. Good thing too, or I might be sitting up there still!

What Mr. Mullis did for me that day in gym class, is what Jesus is willing to do for any of us in our real lives. All of us find ourselves in scary situations occasionally. Difficult things come along like an illness, or job-loss, or starting over after a long-term relationship ends, or learning to trust again someone who has hurt us. But God does not just leave us alone to deal with those hard things. If we listen, we will hear him saying "I have my hand on your back. Relax into it, and when I tell you to, let go of the bar." That last bit might be the hardest part. Sometimes we need to let go of the thing that we are holding onto as our security, but which is really the thing that is holding us back. It might be money or our pride in our reputation, or maybe it is a chemical helper. We need to let go of that and put our trust in Jesus instead.

The next time we get stuck in such a difficult place we might listen for encouraging and comforting words from Jesus. If we are having trouble hearing those words or trusting them, we might turn to the Bible, and specifically to the psalms, where God's help is a recurring theme. For example: "My help is in the name of the Lord/who made heaven and earth." from Psalm 122, or "I sought the Lord, who answered me/ and delivered me from all my fears." from Psalm 34.

There are many other psalms we might equally well choose from. The gospel writers even tell us that there was a psalm on the lips of Jesus while he hung on the cross, though in the gospel we only have the first words of the psalm: "my God, my God, why have you abandoned me", and not the psalm's happy ending. I'm sure Jesus prayed that psalm right through to the end on that day, and that he found comfort there of a sort that we too can share in.

Our gospel today is really presenting to us a picture something like a "trophy day" at the end of a long sports season. We should keep that day in mind, certainly, but that vision of the end times will help us best if it feeds back and helps us to try harder in the challenge we face today, which, as the gospel explains, is to see the face of Jesus in each person we interact with, and then act accordingly. In the end, working hard to do that each day is what will make us happiest with ourselves when trophy day comes along.

In that regard, I want to end with a few verses from the second letter of Peter that remind us of the attitude that we should have. The context of the verses is that, at first, people thought Jesus was going to return very soon. But then time went on and on, and still he didn't come back. There began to be persecutions, and people began to worry and wonder. These verses were intended to reassure everyone and encourage an attitude of watchful waiting. May they also do the same for us!

"What we await are new heavens and a new earth, where according to his promise, the justice of God will reside. So, beloved, while waiting for this, make every effort to be found without stain or defilement, and at peace in his sight. Consider that our Lord's patience is directed toward salvation." 2 Pet 3:13-15a.

4th Sunday of Advent, Dec. 18, 2011:

COPING WITH COURSE
CORRECTIONS IN LIFE

(2 Sam 7: 1-5, 8-12, 14, 16; Rom 16: 25-27; Lk 1: 26-38)

This is the time of year when many high school seniors are deeply involved in the college application process. Some may be anxiously awaiting early decisions letters and others may still be working on applications to be decided on later in the spring. For all of you, teens and parents alike, who are caught up in this process and feel in a state of suspension and uncertainty, we sympathize and pray that everything will work out for the best for you.

I remember when our older daughter was going through this process. She had decided in high school that she wanted to be a veterinarian, and she applied to Cornell University, both because it has an excellent veterinary school, and because some good friends were alumni. Well, she didn't get into Cornell, and that was a great disappointment to her, but she did get into a very good school which also had a pre-vet program. And then, after being there for a while, she got interested in other things and veterinary medicine was no longer her dream. As it ended up, her minor in child development finally led her into a career choice, and now she is one of the happiest, most contented people I know. Would the same thing have happened if she had gotten into Cornell? Perhaps, but this side of heaven we'll never know for sure.

This sort of semi-controlled course correction in life happens to many people at all stages of life. If we look at such experiences with the eyes of faith, we can see how our lives are a complicated mixture of things we control, and events that are beyond our control, and somehow in the mystery of all that, we believe that God's plan for our lives is made real. We do what we can, and God does the rest, and in the end, as Julian of Norwich has said, "all will be well, and all will be exceedingly well."

I think something similar is going on in Mary's life in today's gospel. There she was, a young woman perhaps 15 or 16 years of age, and she was asked to take on the responsibility of parenting a very special baby. She had choices in her life, and she also was presented with a unique opportunity she could not have foreseen. I don't know what Mary worried about as she mulled over the angel's words, but she may have had many practical questions on her mind: how to deal with her new husband (what would he think about all this?) and a new baby (what would it be like to live with a baby who someday would be called the "the Son of the Most High"?) How would her friends and the other townspeople react to this news? A million questions must have leapt to mind, but she answered them all with her deep trust in God, and said the simple "yes" to God that rings down the ages.

All of our readings today show us that God has a plan for humanity, and within that big plan, he has a plan for each one of us, which stretches from here to eternity. The existence of such a plan in the mind of God should not lead us to passivity, however. We have choices to make and a part to play. We should always be working to find the good in our lives, but we should do so in a way that is open to God's wishes for us, saying in our prayer "This is what I want, Lord. If it be your will, help me make it happen." We should also trust that if we are forced by circumstances into some situation that is clearly not good for us, and can't be God's will, that even in that place, God's plan can still rescue us and lead us home to him.

We might feel that we could trust God's plan for our life more, if only we understood it better, say, for example, if an angel were to come to us and explain all our options and their consequences. But I'm not so sure that is true. It may be out of kindness that God withholds certain details of his plan from us. Notice that the angel did not fill in all the details for Mary, either. In particular, he seems to have left out any mention of the crucifixion that Jesus would someday suffer. Surely, that omission was made as a mercy to Mary. How could she have possibly raised her child with the foreknowledge of that day in her heart?

The things that she was told were difficult enough to deal with. She was asked to believe that she would soon become pregnant without any of the normal physical necessities, entirely through the power of the Holy Spirit. Furthermore, her child would someday become a universal king, even though he would be born into a working-class family with a noble lineage but no political power. Now, someone who was sophisticated in the ways of the world would surely have laughed off such possibilities, but even a young girl whose early education focused mostly on hearth and home must have had questions in her heart that made her "yes" more difficult to say.

The same seems to have been true of the Apostles. In the gospel of John, when the Apostles are seated with Jesus at the Last Supper, Jesus tells them that he is about to leave them, and they begin to get worried. They must have felt they were loosing their guidance in life, and they want some security about the future. Attempting to reassure them, Jesus tells them that they know the way to go to follow him, and that is when they get really confused. They don't know where he is going, how can they possibly know how to follow him? Finally, after trying to calm them and saying several times that he will send them the Holy Spirit to guide them, he says "I have much more to tell you, but you cannot bear it now." (Jn 16:12). We might get into something of the same state if God were to try to tell us more of the details of his plan for us. It would be a classic case of TMI—too much information.

But like the Apostles, we do know some things about the plan. We know the endpoint, for one thing: God's plan for each of us is that we get to heaven to be with him. And we also know in a general way the part that we are expected to play in God's plan for our life. It is pretty simple to state, even though it is not always so simple to carry out. At the Last Supper, Jesus repeats it several times: our part in God's plan is to love each other as Jesus has loved us. That's all there is to it, good guidance for every occasion. I am reminded of Mother Theresa's advice when someone asked her what she should do with her life. Mother Theresa said "Do what's in front of you." Wise words. We should always be on the lookout for the person God is placing in front of us this day who needs an expression of love that we can provide. That is our part in the plan. The rest, that part that is beyond our direct control, is in God's capable hands.

Now, it might seem nearly impossible for us to follow the good example of Mary and trust so deeply in a plan that we know so little about, but in fact we are not being asked to trust in the plan exactly, but rather we are being asked to trust in the one who makes the plan: our Father in Heaven. Our trust comes from knowing that God is a loving Father to each one of us. He knows what needs to be done to make his plan work, and he will do it. We can strengthen our hope and faith by getting to know God better. Part of that process can be looking back at our own lives with the eyes of faith, and noticing how God has helped us on our way, sending us the people and experiences we needed at each turning point in life, to help us to mature into a more loving person.

As we continue with our worship this morning, let us ask God to send us the Holy Spirit to be our counselor and lead us step by step though his plan for our lives. In our prayer, let us recall that God is our loving Father and let that be the strength we need to follow Mary in saying "I am the servant of the Lord, may be it done to me according to your word!"

WHY SHOULD WE GO TO CHURCH?

(1 Sm 3: 3–10,19; 1 Cor 6: 13–15,17–20; Jn 1: 35-42)

Several months ago, I participated in the retreat that our confirmation candidates had just before their confirmation. It was a pleasure to be with them in that important moment in their lives. One of the best parts was when we broke up into small groups and had very wide-ranging discussion of our faith. I have to tell you, I was impressed. You parents out there are doing a great job of bringing up young people who are inquisitive and engaged and serious about their faith. You and they are to be commended.

An interesting question that came up in one of the discussions was "Why do we have to go to church; why can't we just be good people on our own?" It was a sincere question, though not one I was expecting, and we had a good discussion about it. The question has stuck in my mind since then, and it wasn't until I was preparing my homily, that I realized that today's readings provide three interesting perspectives on this important question. I'd like to walk through those readings with you and let them speak to us about the benefits of coming together regularly as a faith community.

The first reading is about the boy Samuel, who grew up to be a great prophet in Israel. In the reading, God is trying to speak to Samuel, but Samuel doesn't understand what is happening. It is only through his interaction with the elderly priest Eli that he learns that it is God who is calling him by name and he learns how to respond.

The same thing is still true today. God calls to us, but the call is subtle and easy to misinterpret. God speaks to us through Scripture and liturgy and prayer and possibly in many other ways. Personally, I don't hear God talking to me in my dreams, unless he is still worried about my forgetting to prepare for my history exams, which I somehow doubt. However, when I am worried about something, I bring it into my prayer, and I sometimes find when I go back to consider my problem, that something has moved. My attitude, or some feature of the problem is different from the way that I saw it before, and suddenly I can see my way to the next step, or maybe I find a new peace in the realization that this one is not going to change. I don't often see the hand of the mover in my life, but I do see things moved.

Well, that's pretty subtle, and many other ways God interacts with us are just as subtle. It would be very hard for us to work out all of that on our own. We need to be taught to distinguish the voice of God from all the noise around us, and be reminded of how to respond. Happily, we can draw on the accumulated experiences of many generations of saints who tried with all their heart to hear God's call, and succeeded. That is a rich body of experience that comes to us through the community of faith.

Furthermore, the attitude of listening that Eli recommends is hard for us to maintain on our own. It gets easier when we gather together on a regular basis and practice it all together. Together we learn to say "Speak, Lord, for your servant is listening," and say it with feeling.

Our gospel provides an additional insight. The main characters in the little drama are Saint Andrew, brother to Saint Peter, and an unnamed person. Scholars have a lot of ideas about who that other person might be, but the absence of a name is convenient for us because it means we can each think of ourselves as being that other person. First the two seek out John the Baptist, but he tells them to follow Jesus, and the two do literally pursue Jesus down the road. When they finally catch up with him, Jesus asks them that wonderful question: "What are you looking for?" It is not a sarcastic question "What ARE you looking for?" Nor an aggressive one "What are YOU looking for?" It is an open-ended offer from Jesus for them to name their heart's desire. It is significant that Jesus would begin the conversation this way, with this particular question, because the deep desire God has placed in our heart is also his deepest wish for us.

Getting a good handle on this aspect of our life is also kind of subtle: it is not always easy for us to get in touch with our deepest desire in life and distinguish that from momentary distractions. Some of you know that I was in the hospital two weeks ago, in an ongoing effort to deal with my long-term illness. Everything came out OK in that procedure, and I thank you for all your thoughts and prayers. There were some anxious moments along the way, and they remind me that when I am feeling worried or upset about something, I very often find that I no longer know what my deepest desire is. I don't know what I need, only that it is "not this".

In such a situation I like to come here and be with you people and share these holy rites with you. Because whether I need peace, or hope, or joy, I can find them here. Often, it is only after the need is satisfied that I know what it was. The increased ability to get in touch with the deepest desires in our lives is a great benefit to being part of this community of faith. This too improves with practice.

OK, if the first two readings that we have talked about carried a subtle point, the section from the letter to the Corinthians seems anything but. In no uncertain terms, Saint Paul is laying down the law. One important thing for us to keep in mind, though, as we listen to this reading is that Saint Paul really loved the Corinthians. They welcomed him when he was a stranger, and he founded their faith community and lived with them for a time. He also knew they were living in a precarious situation. Corinth was a port town, and many people there seemed to have the an attitude toward life that said "What's the harm in a little fun?" Well, says Saint Paul, it depends what your deepest desire in life is.

He knows that if we don't live a life that is consistent with our deepest desires, we are bound to be frustrated and unhappy. If our desire is to live a life that is full of the gifts of Holy Spirit: wisdom and understanding, right judgment and courage, knowledge, piety and awe, then that is within our grasp by the power of the resurrection, but we still have to live a life that makes those good things possible. So, there may be quite a bit of harm to be found in a little fun if it is taken with the wrong person or at the wrong time or at someone else's expense.

This is the argument that Saint Paul is trying to get across to his beloved Corinthians, and to us. In our society it is all too easy to avoid hearing such inconvenient truths, but if we come here regularly we will do so. We should look forward to such occasions the way we would seek out the criticism of a good coach. As psalm 141 says, if a good person rebukes me, it is a kindness.

Additionally, it's not always easy to apply Saint Paul's advice to particular situations. We will find good people here who can give us more personalized help. Having a regular confessor is one good way to do this. We also have people in our parish trained in spiritual direction who can help us to reflect on the action of God in our lives. And generally, we might cultivate friendships with people here who seem a few steps ahead of us on the spiritual path. Here, we can each find a Saint Andrew to walk with.

So, those are three things available from this community: a better attitude of listening to God, and getting in touch better with our deep desires, and help in living a life that is consistent with those desires. There are other benefits as well. This week we might meditate on all the goodness of God that flows into our lives through our presence here, and let our gratitude for that inspire a renewed prayer for an open heart: "Speak, Lord, for your servant is listening."

7th Sunday in Ordinary Time, Feb. 19, 2012:

CHRIST HAS NO BODY NOW BUT YOURS

(Is 43: 18-19, 21-22, 24-25; 2 Cor 1:18-22; Mk 2: 1-12)

For several Sundays now we have been presented with wonderful stories of Jesus healing people. Two weeks ago it was Peter's mother-in-law and many townsfolk of Capernaum, last week it was the leper who approached Jesus in the wilderness, and this week we have the paralyzed man with such audacious friends. The concrete and homey content of these accounts give us a good opportunity for meditation. We can take the perspective of the different participants in the story and let the whole scene play out in our sacred imagination and so more deeply experience the power of the Good News. To get us started, I'd like to go through today's story with you now, looking at it from the perspective of each of its participants in turn.

These days, I find it easiest to connect with the paralyzed man. Some of you know that I have been in and out of the hospital over the past few years, and in so many ways I feel like I have been lifted up and brought before Jesus by friends and relatives. Many people, including many in this community, made offers of help. "I'll do your yard work." "I'll make you soup." "I'll drive you home from the hospital." The offers have been ingenious in their variety, and have been much appreciated by me and my family.

I do have to admit, though, that I have sometimes felt a certain reluctance to take people up on their kind offers. I think this is an attitude that I have absorbed from our culture, but it is not a very healthy attitude. We are taught to strive to be independent and to avoid being indebted to other people. As children we are taught "Neither a borrower nor a lender be."

Self-reliance can be a strength, but it is easy to go overboard with it. Sometimes it seems like we are trying to build a society in which no one has to share anything with anyone else. Not having to depend on other people's kindness might sound good at first, but when we think more carefully about this idea, we realize that this is not a state to be desired. Another name for this state is "separation" and "isolation." A more Christian motto for us to follow would be "both a borrower and a lender be." That would certainly be closer to the attitude we see in today's gospel. There was no way for the paralyzed man to repay his friends for their help, but there was no thought of indebtedness, only shared need and shared response. The paralyzed man had the strength to admit "I could really use your help," and we can too.

Now let's take another perspective, and try to see this story from Jesus' angle. Jesus came to teach us about the Kingdom of God, and we might imagine he would get upset when his teaching was interrupted by a hole in the roof and a descending body. The interesting thing is that he didn't get upset, even though those four friends were doing something completely outrageous. True, roofs in that time and place were not the tight and solid constructions that we think of today, but still, those friends went completely over-the-top in their urgency to help their friend. And in this way, they were showing themselves to be true children of their loving Father in heaven, because God too is outrageously generous and goes completely over-the-top in his compassion for us.

God's overflowing love for us is evident in all of creation. There are so many beautiful things out there for us to experience: a sunset, a starry night, and the fall foliage, to pick just a few random examples. None of those things needed to be beautiful for creation to function properly; their beauty is simply an extra gift to us from our loving God. At all scales, from the microscopic to the cosmic, God has crammed the world full of untold beauty, and he has kindly given us the senses to perceive it.

When humanity sinned and separated itself from God, God gave the very greatest sign of his over-the-top love for us. He sent his only son into the world to save us. As the Easter liturgy sings to God: "to ransom a slave, you gave away your son." That's quite a thought. Jesus put off the mantle of his glory and emptied himself of all the infinitudes of Godhood and entered our world as one of us to save us and to teach us how to live. What an astounding act of mercy and love that was!

Jesus recognized a kindred spirit of compassion in the bold action of the four friends, and quickly wove the event into his lesson, making of it a concrete example of his theme, which was God's abiding love and forgiveness.

A third perspective on the story comes from the friends of the paralyzed man. Their action certainly benefited the paralyzed man, but notice that it benefited them as well. I can just imagine them five or ten years after the event, sitting around together in the evening shadows, when the cool breezes begin to blow, having some wine and maybe some humus and pita bread, when one of them says to the others: "Do you remember the day? Do you remember the day when we took old Joe on the stretcher to visit Jesus? Remember how crowded it was, and we wanted so badly to get him in there, and finally we thought of going in through the roof. How some guy came out and said 'What are you doing?', and we said 'Don't worry, we'll fix it.' And then we moved all the tiles and the people inside said 'Whoa! What is going on here?' But we lowered him down, and Jesus smiled up at us and came over and took him by the hand and lifted him up, and he was cured! That was a good day. That was the best day ever."

Good people that you are, you probably already have a memory or two that you can look back on with that kind of joy. Such memories are a lasting treasure. And the thing for us to notice today is that if we hope five or ten years from now to have more good memories like those to keep us warm, now is the time to take action. Now is the time to be on the lookout for someone in our family or in our parish or our workplace that would benefit from being lifted up in some very practical and concrete way.

So we have looked at the healing event from the perspective of the paralyzed man, and Jesus, and the man's friends. I want end by look at it from the perspective of those gathered in the house. I am sure that at first, they experienced the events as a disruption of their connection with Jesus. They all had their places and were seated happily on the inside. They wanted to listen to what Jesus had to say, which was a good thing, but then the roof opened and everything changed. It is important for them and for us to recognize that God's love can be a disruptive event in our lives. It often overturns the accepted order. We shouldn't expect to know what it's going to look like, or how it is going to pour over us next. If we are going to participate in that love, and show ourselves to be true sons and daughters of our loving father in heaven, we should be prepared to miss dinner sometimes, or be put out in other ways.

This week, as we begin the Lenten season, maybe we could pray to be open to that kind of disruptive love. Let's think about what kind of over-the-top loving deeds we can be a part of this Lent. Here in our parish, and in our homes, and in our workplaces we can build a caring community in which such deeds are commonplace.

Saint Paul tells us today that Jesus is the "yes" to all the promises of God. As followers of Jesus we have become a part of that great "yes". I would like to leave you with part of a poem from St. Theresa of Avila which emphasizes our critical role in the continuing story of God's outrageously generous love:

> *Christ has no body now but yours,*
> *No hands, no feet on earth but yours,*
> *Yours are the eyes with which he looks compassion*
> *on this world.*
> *Christ has no body now on earth but yours.*

ACTING AS TRUE CHILDREN OF GOD

(year A readings: 1 Sam 16:1, 6-7, 10-13; Eph 5:8-14; Jn 9:1-41)

When I first went to grad school I lived in student housing on campus. I was intensely involved in my studies at the time, but I did make a number of friends over dinner in the cafeteria. One young woman in particular I remember as pleasant to talk with. She was studying mediaeval literature, and, amazingly, she was able to make the subject an interesting topic for dinner conversation. Well, after several months of this life, around the beginning of December, the young woman reminded me that the grad dorm was throwing a party that night, and asked if I was going. I allowed as how I might, but then I got involved in my work, and by the time I looked up at the clock, I was sure the party would be over. Unlike many undergraduate parties, graduate-student parties tend to fizzle out early.

Next morning, I found tied to the handle of my door a bunch of balloons which looked suspiciously like the party decorations from downstairs. Only then did I remember my conversation with the young woman. I realized that she must be the culprit, and that she must like me more than just a little bit, to have made this gesture. Right on the heels of that thought came the realization that I had strong feelings for her as well. That was an eye-opening moment for me. Standing there, toothbrush in hand, looking at my dorm room door, it was as if I had been blind, but now, joyfully, my eyes were opened and I could see the world in a new way. To make a long story short, eventually we married, that good woman and I, and nearly forty years later, we are still together, and life continues to be a wonderful adventure for us both.

Remembering that eye-opening experience as a young man gives me a tiny hint of the joy that must have come with having one's blindness healed by Jesus. Today is Laetare Sunday, and "Laetare" is Latin for "rejoice". In this Mass we recall with joy that the salvation we will celebrate in a special way on Easter Sunday is already ours. Our gospel reminds us today that God wants to heal us of all the different ways we are blind in our life, and when he does so, it is a joyful and world-changing experience. For it is not just physical blindness that is the topic of the gospel message today. Spiritual blindness is the real focus of our reading, and two particular kinds are emphasized.

The first kind of spiritual blindness is illustrated by the religious leaders who were told about the healing Jesus performed and found something to dislike in it. Jesus performed his miracle on a Sabbath, and that was a significant problem for them, because mixing up that teaspoon-full of paste and rubbing it on the man's eyes was a kind of work, and work was prohibited on the Sabbath. In the minds of the religious leaders, doing even such a tiny amount of work betrayed a fundamental disrespect for God's law. They must have reasoned that a truly good person could have waited for a day and healed the man then. After all, the man had been blind since birth, surely one more day couldn't matter that much. But Jesus saw the situation differently. The man had been blind far too long already. So, no, Jesus could not wait one more day to heal him, not even one more hour. God's great love would not allow any such delay.

For the religious leaders, Jesus was shown to be a sinner by his actions that day, and thus they were blind to all the good that we see in him. I wonder if sometimes we aren't afflicted by a similar sort of blindness. When someone disagrees with us about some serious matter, it is often very difficult to recognize any good in that person. Our first reaction might be to write such people off as liberal snobs, or stick-in-the-mud conservatives or whatever other labels we care to pin on them.

Today's gospel invites us to be healed of that kind of blindness and see some goodness in the people that we disagree with. I'm pretty sure that most people we disagree with are not the anti-Christ, nor even the spawn of the devil. We will be much happier in this life if we can learn to see the people that we disagree with as children of God, and speak to the goodness in their souls when we talk to them. Think how that would transform our difficult discussions, if we could begin our conversations with that vision of the other person. Today, Jesus offers us that gift of sight.

The second kind of blindness in today's gospel is illustrated by the townspeople. Remember what happened when the blind man went away to the pool of Siloam, and then came back able to see? Very few people were able to recognize him. I think that is because, when he was just the blind guy who sat by the city gate, no one really looked at him. They had the same kind of selective blindness that many of us know how to adopt when we do not want to be bothered by someone else's need.

That blindness can be a kind of self-protection. It is certainly true that we cannot help everyone. We face too many calls for help to answer every one. Sometimes we may not have the skills or the resources to help a particular person, and we have to pray and trust to God that they will get the help they need elsewhere. But the thing we should try to avoid is that narrowing of vision that does not allow us to even see the needs of the people around us, be they financial, or emotional or spiritual. For it is a great joy to be able to see a need in someone and be able to respond effectively.

Jesus had some pretty stiff things to say about this kind of selective blindness. Remember in Matthew's gospel when Jesus talks about the son of Man coming at the end of time and telling some people they were not welcome in heaven, because they never gave him food to eat or clothes to wear when he needed them. The people say "Lord, when did we ever see you hungry or in need and not help you?" And remember Jesus' response "whatever you did to the least of these my brethren, you did it to me." Ignorance and blindness will be no excuse, but Jesus offers us an escape from that fate by opening our eyes to those in need around us. If we let those five words "you did it to me" become part of our prayer life, they can be a real eye-opener.

Our first reading today tells us "not as man sees does God see." And really in being asked to be healed of our spiritual blindness, we are asking to see the world as God sees it. That is the vision that will last, and by God's grace it can be ours. There was a Christian rock singer back in the eighties named Amy Grant, who had a song that fits right in with these ideas. In the song she asks herself what she would like people to say about her after she dies. Answering this question in her song, she sings that she wants people to say this:

> *She had her father's eyes, her father's eyes*
>
> *Eyes that found the good in things, when good was not around,*
>
> *Eyes that found the source of help, when help could not be found,*
>
> *Eyes full of compassion, seeing every pain,*
>
> *Knowin' what you're goin' through and feelin' just the same.*
>
> *Just like my father's eyes, my father's eyes. ("Her Father's Eyes" second refrain)*

May God grant us that same grace: to be his true children, children who show our family resemblance to our Father in heaven, in all that we see and do. Laetare! Let us rejoice!

2nd Sunday of Easter (Divine Mercy), Apr. 15, 2012:
GOD'S MERCIFUL PATIENCE

(Acts 4: 32-35; 1 Jn 5: 1-6; Jn 20: 19-31)

When I was in college, I took a course in small-boat sailing, and by the end of the course, I fancied myself quite a sailor. So, when summer came, and I had a chance to show off my skills by taking a friend out for a sail, I was happy for the opportunity. We rented a small boat and had a pleasant couple of hours out on the water, right up to the time when we began to get close to home.

You see, the dock where we had rented the boat was at the end of a long narrow inlet, and unfortunately, the wind was blowing from that exact direction. This was a problem, because the one thing a sailboat cannot do is sail directly into the wind. If you point a sailboat into the wind, the wind spills out of the sail and the boat stops moving. It is called being "in irons". I knew all that. I knew that to sail up-wind, you have to zigzag toward your goal. But I must have missed something important in that class, because I had a lot of trouble with the required maneuver. Every time I tried to turn, the boat got locked in irons. It must have taken us about an hour to finish the last hundred yards to the dock. After a while, the guy who had rented us the boat took pity on us, and tried to help by calling out instructions: "Pull the tiller to the left. Push the sail to the right." When I followed his directions, the boat would start moving again, that is, until I needed to do another zig or a zag, when, as often as not, we would end up right back in irons. We did get back to shore eventually, but it made for a long afternoon.

What I remember best from that day, aside from the ribbing I got from my friend, was the incredible patience of the guy on the dock. He just kept explaining what I had to do next, no matter how many times I got myself stuck.

That patience is now one of my most potent images of God's patient love for us. No matter how many times we get ourselves into trouble in this life, God continues to treat us with mercy and love. As many times as we may end up with our boat pointed in exactly the wrong direction, God continues to send us the help we need to get moving again. Today, on divine mercy Sunday, we celebrate God's loving kindness and accept it with humility and joy.

Our gospel today offers us three examples of how we can get ourselves stuck in this life, and how God continually sends us the help we need to get unstuck. One example of this is in the words of Jesus today: "whose sins you forgive are forgiven them, and whose sins you retain are retained." Now, the Church has long taken this as a indication of the Church's power and responsibility to transmit God's forgiveness to us, but these words also apply to us on a more personal level, when it comes to us forgiving the sins of those who have hurt us. Older translations talk of sins being "held bound" and I think that is a powerful metaphor for what goes on in our hearts when we do not forgive others. The sins are held bound and we are as well. When we find it hard to forgive some wrong that was done to us, we can waste a lot of energy on that old hurt, thinking about what that person did and what we should have done or said in response. It is as if our boat has gotten locked in irons and we cannot move on.

God helps us by sending us the Holy Spirit. Jesus says today: "Receive the Holy Spirit. Whose sins you forgive are forgiven them." With the guidance of the Holy Spirit, we *can* learn to forgive old hurts. One of the symbols for the Holy Spirit is the rushing wind, and that wind can blow away those tired old thoughts, refill our sails and help us move on. What a joy it is to be moving again and no longer bound by the past.

A second example from today's gospel is in the story of the apostle Thomas. He gave God an ultimatum. Unless he saw this and touched that, he would not believe. I think that sometimes we can get stuck in that sort of trap in our prayer. This happens particularly when there is something important that we are hoping for and we pray for it most fervently. After some time of this, if we don't get what we desire, our prayer can get all turned around until it seems to say "God, I won't believe that you love me unless you give me this thing that I really need." That is a dead-end kind of prayer, because God in all his wisdom and mercy for us, may have every good reason not to give us the particular thing we desire, and unless we can widen our focus and contemplate the whole course of our life, we may miss other evidence of God's love.

The Easter mysteries that we continue to celebrate together can help us to get back to that wider context. When we begin to wonder if God cares for us any more, or if he still remembers us and loves us, we have Jesus to look to. He says to us, "You want to know if God loves you? Here touch my hands. Put your finger into my side and do not be unbelieving but believe." Whenever we get stuck in a kind of prayer that is not going anywhere, we should turn back to Jesus and his cross and recognize that we have already witnessed the full measure of God's love. With that thought in our hearts we can find the courage to pray with Jesus "Lord, not my will but your will be done."

A third way we can get stuck in this life is hinted at by the first words Jesus says to the Apostles in the upper room. He says "peace be with you." The Apostles really needed those words of peace. In their fear and confusion, they had locked themselves away from the world. It seemed to them that the whole thing with Jesus had gone very seriously wrong, and they might soon be arrested and sent to the cross.

Sometimes, we may also get worried by an uncertain future. Maybe not in quite so dramatic a way, but we may have serious concerns about how things are going to turn out for us. Maybe we hear news reports that convince us that the world is going from bad to worse, with no end in sight. Or perhaps something we have depended on for a long time, like our paycheck or our good health or the companionship of a good friend, is taken away, or begins to look dangerously uncertain.

In those sorts of situations we might become perturbed and not know what to do or what to pray for. Here again, we have the Easter mysteries to meditate on. If God could bring good out of the cruel death of his son, he can surely bring good out of the things that are worrying us today. Trusting in that truth can make us bold.

As we think about the different ways that God helps us in this life, it becomes clear that our situation is even better than my situation was with the guy on the dock. It is as if the guy on the dock were not content to just stand there and call out advice and encouragement. Instead he turns to his son and says "get into a boat and go out there and help those guys. Show them how it's done." In his loving kindness, God sent Jesus to show us how to live a holy life, and the Holy Spirit remains with us to remind us of those lessons. Such is the depth of God's love for us.

So, as we continue with our worship this morning, let us joyfully give thanks to God for his merciful love, and let us resolve always to listen to the promptings of the Holy Spirit. Let us be ready to forgive others, and to make our prayers with an openness to God's will, and to trust in God's providential care, and to do whatever else may be necessary to keep our boat moving forward in this life. Until one day we too reach our safe harbor, and enter the welcoming embrace of our loving God.

7th Sunday of Easter, May 20, 2012:

BEING PREPARED SPIRITUALLY

(Acts 15:15-17,20-26; 1 Jn 4: 11-16; Jn 17: 11-19)

As Monsignor said at the beginning of Mass, we are blessed and honored to have many of the Cub Scouts and Girl Scouts from our parish here celebrating with us today. I was involved in scouting for a number of years, and among the many life-lessons that I learned through that experience is the importance of being prepared for the unexpected. You may know that the Boy Scout motto is "Be Prepared".

This motto is good advice for us in our material life, and also in our spiritual life. Our readings today show us how the early church tried to be prepared for what life was going to be like after Jesus returned to heaven. In our first reading, the Apostles have decided that they needed to replace Judas Iscariot, who had betrayed Jesus and then committed suicide. They wanted to bring the number of disciples back to the full force of twelve. This is an event of more than historical significance to us, since we take our connection to the Apostles very seriously. In our creed we say that the Church is "one, holy, catholic and apostolic." That last word is an important part of who we are. One of the jobs of Pope Benedict XVI and our bishop John is to keep us true to our apostolic traditions.

At the end of Mass this morning we will be giving out some awards to some of the scouts who are present here today. These are specifically for their work in learning more about our faith. These awards show that they and their parents and leaders take their connection to the apostolic tradition very seriously.

Those of us who may be a bit too old to work on scout badges also have many opportunities to reconnect with our traditions. One wonderful way that I have just learned about this spring, is a set of DVD's called, simply enough, "Catholicism". They are available for purchase on-line. Just Google for "Catholicism series", and we have been airing them here in the parish during Lent and Easter. Soon they will be available to borrow though our parish library. The videos are beautifully produced, with wonderful views of the best of religious art, and they present a very thoughtful and approachable introduction to what we believe as Catholics. We all know that our Church has been through some difficult times and gotten a lot of bad press in the last few years, but I guarantee you if you watch these videos you will happy and proud to call yourself a Catholic. Reconnecting to that rich heritage is one important way that we can "be prepared" for what life throws at us.

Another important way that we can be spiritually prepared for life is evident when we look a little bit closer at our first reading. The first thing Saint Peter did when he spoke to the assembly was to quote from Scripture—one of the psalms. Notice that it is not that Saint Peter had this problem, what to do about Judas, and then went to Scripture to try to figure out what to do, rather his whole life was spent in conversation with Scripture. Like good Jews of the time, he prayed five times daily, often reciting memorized psalms. In that context, when he found that he had a problem, the relevant verses just came bubbling up for him.

We too would do well to be a little closer to Scripture. It is not so hard to get started. This is the year when we are reading from the gospel of Saint Mark. We might decide to read one chapter from Mark's gospel each night before going to bed, It will take about 10 minutes to read it through slowly. We will want to have a version with footnotes, in case there is something confusing, but I am not suggesting we use this time as a kind of Bible study. This is a time to be in conversation with the word of God. Let it talk to you, and you talk to it.

DANCING IN THE GRAVEYARD

(Ezek 17:22-24; 2 Cor 5:6-10; Mk 4:26-34)

Jesus came among us to usher in the Kingdom of God, a reign of "justice and peace and the true joy that comes from the Holy Spirit" (Rom 14:17). And in one sense, all that is with us now. If we so choose, we can live in God's kingdom today. And yet in another sense, God's kingdom is something that will only come to us in its fullness at the end of time. This somewhat ambiguous status can make the kingdom of God a complicated idea for us to get our heads around, and in many places in the gospels, as in today's reading, Jesus goes to great lengths to try to explain what it is all about. Today we see Jesus as the good teacher of the kingdom of God.

This is an appropriate image for us to consider today for two reasons. First, because we are just completing the academic year and saying goodbye to the teachers we have had contact with this year. We give thanks for all their efforts at instilling wisdom and virtue in us or our children. The second reason that the teaching Jesus is an appropriate image for us to contemplate this weekend is that Sunday/today is Father's Day, and one of the important roles of a father is to be a teacher. We also give thanks today for all the things we have been taught by our natural fathers, and by others who have served in a fatherly role in our lives.

Before we look more deeply into the teachings of Jesus about the kingdom of God, I would like to explore a bit more about the particular way in which he taught. As we see today, Jesus frequently taught using parables. The word 'parable' means to 'put one thing beside another', that is, to make a comparison. This was a traditional method of teaching in Jesus' time, and he was a real artist at it. He used little stories from daily life, concerning things we understand very well, to help us to reach beyond that, to things we want to know better.

Parables can be an effective teaching tool because they require some effort on our part. We may have to struggle to understand how the kingdom of God could possibly be like a farmer, or like a mustard plant. Those are surprising comparisons to make and the more whimsical or farfetched they seem, the more they invite us to dig deeper and see the point that Jesus is trying to make. In this way, our contemplation makes the parable our own.

Sometimes I think we make too much of the last verse of today's gospel which says that Jesus taught the apostles in private about the meaning of the parables he used. We might conclude from that that Jesus was giving the apostles the good stuff, and only giving the rest of us hints about the truth, but that's not quite the right way to look at it. What Jesus gave the apostles in private was the understanding they needed to fulfill their calling in that time and place. But the parables themselves aim higher than that. Every time we contemplate one of the parables of Jesus, we may find a new and different insight into how we can live more fully in the kingdom of God. This makes the parables timeless. They can be every bit as meaningful to us today as they were to his first listeners.

Now let's look again at the parable of the farmer. Jesus points out that a farmer has a particular relationship to the land and his crops. He has an important role to play in preparing the ground and planting and harvesting the crops, but in a very real sense, the farmer does not make the crop grow. He may not even understand all that goes on inside the growing plant. That is what Jesus means by the blade and the ear of the plant, how it moves from one phase of growth to another. The farmer can neither hurry those steps along nor slow them down. It all unfolds naturally before his eyes, and through it all, his job is to keep a watchful eye so that when the time for harvest comes, he can rush out and gather it in at its prime.

Jesus is telling us that the kingdom of God has some of those same aspects as it develops in our world. We have an important part to play in that development. We plant the seeds of the gospel in our communities through our loving words and our kindly deeds, and we have to ready to help with the harvest of good works. But there is also a lot we don't understand about the inner workings of that process. We don't know how our kind words or friendly deeds for others will work themselves out for good. We may never see the ramifications of a kindness done for a stranger, but we have confidence in God's ability to make something wonderful grow from such tiny beginnings.

So, that's a bit of the meaning I find in this parable today. As you consider it, you may find something different, and that's great. Such variety is a gift of the Holy Spirit. And that is one good reason we should all be studying the parables of Jesus and sharing our insights. Another reason is that the gospels are not the only place we will find such parables. If we are on the lookout for them, we will find that God is giving us little acted-out parables all through our daily lives. Here's an example of what I mean.

This past weekend I went away on retreat. It was a time to get away from the daily routine and look at life a different way. The retreat had a lot of time for personal meditation, and on Saturday morning I was out on the grounds looking for a quiet place to meditate, and ended up taking a walk through a large and well-kept cemetery very near the retreat house. I found a bench under a tree, and set there and tried to empty my mind of all thoughts and cares and really experience the beautiful morning. After a while, I noticed that there were some children playing hide-and-seek among the graves. Shrill voices and laughter were echoing off the stones as they ran around. So, were they being irreverent? Well, maybe a little bit, but their unexpected presence was a comfort to me.

You see I had been thinking about some medical things that I have coming up, and was weighed down by thoughts about the brevity of our lives—pretty heavy thoughts, but right there in the middle of what could have been a scary or a sorrowful place, God was showing me that it is possible to find life and laughter and joy. Later, I reflected on the verse in Matthew's gospel in which Jesus welcomed some little children saying that "the kingdom of God belongs to such as these." (19:14).

It was not a deep or unique insight, perhaps, and I don't think it means we should all go out after Mass today and dance around in the graveyard, but I do believe that God was giving me this parable to consider as a sign of the peace and joy that comes with living in the kingdom of God. The thing for us to rejoice in today is that God offers all of us such signs of consolation frequently, and studying the parables recorded in the gospels is one way to prime ourselves to recognize them better.

Today we are wearing green vestments as a sign of hope. We should look at the green color and remember the growing things that Jesus talks about in his parables. That enduring sense of hope is the real touchstone for God's message to us. When we wonder if we have taken the right meaning from a parable we should ask ourselves "Does this make me love better and hope more?" There are so many things in our lives we don't understand or have much control over, but like the farmer in today's parable, we trust in God's ability to make his kingdom continue to grow in our hearts and in our world. In the end, it is he who makes all things grow while we stand by and watch in awe: "first the blade, and then the ear, and then the fullness of grain within the ear."

29th Sunday in Ordinary Time, Oct. 21, 2012:

TRUE FAITH, CERTAIN HOPE AND PERFECT CHARITY

(Is 53:10-11; Heb 4:14-16; Mk 10:35-45)

When I was a sophomore in high school I was very fortunate to have a great teacher named Brother Don for several of my classes. Now, Brother Don was not an imposing figure in the classroom. He was quite short, for one thing, shorter than most of us students, and he was somewhat overweight and balding. But those things were not what one noticed first when meeting Brother Don. What one noticed was his lively manner. Here was a person that was truly alive. He was interested in everyone and everything, and he found joy in many unlikely places. Classes with him were full of light and good cheer. I may have learned more facts and figures in some of my other classes in high school, but when I think about where I learned the most about Jesus and what it means to live in the kingdom of God, my classes with Brother Don are at the top of the list.

Brother Don has been much on my mind over the last several weeks, because our gospel readings for the last month and more have all been about that very important question: what does it mean to live in the Kingdom of God today? Remember two weeks ago. In our gospel that week, Jesus taught us about fidelity in marriage and our other personal commitments and our need to welcome the kingdom of God into our lives with the innocence and joy of little children. Then last week, Jesus taught us that riches and all the baggage we acquire in our lives can make it very difficult for us to follow Jesus into God's kingdom. And in this week's gospel, the focus is on leadership in the kingdom of God. What is required of those called to be leaders in God's kingdom?

This leadership question is important for us to think about, but unfortunately, what may leap to mind first when we ask ourselves this question are examples of bad leadership. Not in this parish, certainly, but in the parish you were in before this one, you might have had some bad experiences with those to whom we look for leadership.

Perhaps your pastor then was Father Noski, who responded to every suggestion about parish life with three reasons why what you wanted to do was completely impossible. Or perhaps you were in a parish with Deacon Frownmeister, who filled his homilies with so much criticism that you were sure no one could possibly live up to his standard of holiness. Many of us have those sorts of bad examples of leadership lurking in our past, but we need to get beyond them to consider the good examples we have experienced, people like Brother Don. We want to think back to people who were able to draw out the best in us and fill us with the desire to follow Jesus ever more closely in our lives.

It is important for us to do this, because we all are called to be leaders in the kingdom of God, and we need those good examples to imitate. Leadership in God's kingdom is not just for those called to the clergy or to religious life; leadership roles come in all shapes in and sizes. In our work or in our ministries in the church, or in our other activities we have many opportunities to be leaders. Sometimes we may have been given a formal leadership role, but even if we don't have any formal role, we are still often called to be informal leaders. Whenever someone admires us for something that we have done, or asks our opinion about some important question, we are being thrust into a position of leadership, and we should think carefully about how we respond.

Our best example of leadership in the kingdom of God, is, of course, Jesus himself. Notice the great humility of Jesus. Last week, a rich man ran up to Jesus and knelt before him and said "Good teacher, what must I do to inherit everlasting life?" And what was Jesus' immediate response? He asked "Why do you call me good?" We can imagine that as he said this, he was lifting the man up off his knees and welcoming him as an equal. In responding in this way, Jesus was not saying that he did not deserve respect, but only that he did not want to be put up on a pedestal and made larger than life. Jesus knew that allowing such a thing would distract attention from the one God who is the true source of all goodness. We too, in our own lives, should be equally careful how we respond to complements and the approval of those around us. When we allow such attention to puff us up and make us big in our own eyes, then we are probably getting too big to be good leaders in the kingdom of God. We should always recall where we got the good qualities that other people admire, and admit that it all comes from God, and give glory to him alone.

The other important part of the leadership of Jesus is his emphasis on service. As leaders in the kingdom of God, it is very tempting to see our role as ones who pass judgment on others. To take a somewhat simple example, if we are admired for our pie-baking ability, we might come to feel that it is our duty to criticize every pie that comes our way, to point out how in great and small ways it fails to live up to the standards for pies that we set for ourselves. Such a response is not life-giving, and it is not the kind of leadership that Jesus expects of us. Rather as servant-leaders we would use our praise and encouragement to help move those around us in better directions and open up the possibility of being better pie bakers to all those we interact with. As it goes with pies, so it goes with all other aspects of life. As servant leaders we always want to be supportive and encouraging of the attempts of others to follow their deepest desires for more holiness in their lives.

Being humble servant-leaders in this way is not easy. Often it requires us to set aside our own needs and desires and to focus on the needs of others. It requires a deep commitment to self-emptying love. No one understands this fact better than Jesus himself, and in today's gospel he challenges James and John and all of us to make such a commitment when he asks "Can you drink the cup that I will drink?"

Now, if we had to face that hard question on our own, I don't know where we would find the courage to answer "yes"; certainly I would have great difficulty doing so. But we don't face that question alone. We are part of a community that takes that commitment very seriously. Today we can find encouragement in the example of people around us and in the people in our past who have modeled good leadership in our lives. We can also find encouragement by considering the lives of the saints. As James Martin points out in his excellent book "My Life with the Saints", the saints were people just like us who struggled to answer "yes" to the call of Jesus, and we can allow them be our companions in our own struggles. I would like to leave you with a prayer of Saint Francis, one of my personal favorites. Try to hear this prayer as a prayer of aspiration. It is the prayer of someone who is trying to follow Jesus, but who knows that he is not quite there yet. In that sense, Francis is very much like the rest of us. Here is his "prayer before a crucifix":

> *Most high and glorious God, enlighten the darkness of my heart, and give me true faith, certain hope and perfect charity, sense and knowledge, Lord —that I may carry out your holy and true command.*

"True faith, certain hope and perfect charity" are virtues that will make us true leaders in the kingdom of God. They would be wonderful gifts for us to pray for as we kneel before the crucifix today.

Our Lord Jesus Christ the King, Nov. 25, 2012:

FINDING FREEDOM IN TIMES OF TRIAL

(Dan 7:13-14; Rev 1:5-8; Jn 18:33-37)

Today we are celebrating one of the great feasts of our church. It is the last Sunday of the church year, and with joy in our hearts we acknowledge Jesus as the king of the universe, and the king that reigns in our hearts. Long live the king!

In today's gospel, we see Jesus talking with Pontius Pilate, a person who was very different from Jesus. In this conversation, it appears that one person is a prisoner, while the other is free, but, as we know, appearances can be deceiving. Pilate was the highest representative of the Roman government in a large part of the homeland of the Jewish people. And throughout that country, the word of Pilate was law. It might seem that he would be the freest person in all of that country, but John's gospel shows us that, in fact, Pilate was not free when it came to doing one particular act of justice.

Saint John tells us that the leaders in Jerusalem brought Jesus to Pilate for judgment, but they did not want to go into his palace, because they wanted to remain pure for the festival of Passover, which was about to begin. The law of Moses did not permit Jews to enter into the buildings of pagans. For this reason they remained outside with a large crowd of the people of the city. Now Pilate wanted to interrogate Jesus in his throne room in the palace, so that's what he did. However, the more he asked questions of Jesus, the more questions he had for the Jewish leaders who were outside, and so he had to go back and forth numerous times, first asking Jesus a question and then asking the same question of those outside. In this way, Saint John pokes fun at Pilate and shows us that all his powers were useless in this situation. He was afraid of the angry crowd outside his walls, and that made him a prisoner to their opinions.

The situation was very different for Jesus. True, he was under the custody of the Roman soldiers, and his hands were bound, and he was standing before the throne of Pilate, but Saint John shows us that Pilate only had questions in his soul, while Jesus had the truth. Pilate did not really understand what was going on, but Jesus, of his own accord, had decided to be where he was, and he knew exactly what was going to happen. Jesus was the one who was free in this situation, because he had the inner strength to follow the road which his Father had chosen for him.

Saint John invites us to consider "what is true freedom?" and "what are the things in my life that make me more free, or make me more bound?" The desire of our Father in heaven is that we be truly free. That is our inheritance as his children, but it does require our cooperation for us to be able to take up that inheritance.

Right from the outset, we need to recognize that even though we may have many responsibilities in this life, that does not necessarily make us any less free. Parents are responsible for their children, those who are married have responsibilities toward their spouse, friends have responsibilities to their friends. None of these relationships built upon love should make us less free, rather they give us opportunities to express our freedom in what we do for our loved ones.

I remember a time many years ago when my younger daughter was just a baby. At first my wife stayed home with our daughter, but then after six months of maternity leave, my wife had to return to her job. So, we looked for a daycare that we could trust with our precious bundle of joy. Finally we found one that we liked that had an opening, and my wife went back to work. Things did not work out so well, however, because soon after we began, our daughter repeatedly came down with colds. After many trips to the doctor's office, we decided that the daycare was just too dangerous for her health and we needed to find some other arrangement. But what could we do? I was working full time, and so was my wife. Well, for the next three months, I worked part days and my wife worked the other part, and we kept our daughter at home. In many senses, this was a difficult time for our family. It seemed like we never had time for anything, and sometimes we felt trapped by the situation. But in another sense it was a very good time for our family. Although my boss was not very happy most of the time, I remember very fondly the hours I had at home with my young child. In the end we found a neighbor who was able to help us out and watch our daughter during the day, and our work schedules soon settled down to something like normal.

Of course there are many families who have to face similar times of difficulty, and many whose difficulties are much greater, but in all cases when we can approach our shared difficulties in a spirit of love, they do not impose restrictions on our freedom. Rather they become opportunities for us to express our freedom. That is the example of Jesus as he stands before Pilate.

But it must also be remembered that there are things that can get in the way of our freedoms. Anything that does not allow us to complete our obligations or fulfill important promises we have made, is something that puts us into prison. In addition to the obvious examples of alcohol or drug abuse, there are other, perhaps more subtle, things that can get in the way of our freedom to act out of love. For example we should ask ourselves if sometimes we spend too much time watching TV or surfing the internet. Also, sometimes we might be behaving a little bit like Pilate, and worrying too much about the opinions of the crowd. We might listen too much to people at work or in our school, and ignore the voice of our conscience about what would be the just thing to do in certain situations.

Other times, we might feel too worried about life, or just too tired, and begin to believe that it is impossible for us to follow through on all the promises we have made. In that sort of a situation, we might want to pray that the Holy Spirit might fill us with his power, so that we can fulfill our promises. We might want to pray the psalm from today's Mass, Psalm 93, which will remind us of Jesus and what he did to save us and how he reigns now as the king of our hearts. We might also want to pray Psalm 91, which is a beautiful song of trust in God. Undoubtedly, Jesus knew this psalm well and prayed it often. The psalm begins:

> *You who dwell in the shelter of the Lord,*
> *And reside in the shadow of the Almighty,*
> *Say to the Lord: "my shelter, my refuge,*
> *My rock in whom I trust."*

This psalm can be a fountain of peace and hope in difficult times.

Next Sunday is the first Sunday of Advent, and Advent is a time of preparation. If we look back at the year that is just ending, and we see that we have not always embraced the freedom of the children of God as well as we might have liked, this Advent might be a time to examine our lives more closely and try to get rid of things that are keeping us from being truly free. This will make us better able to live up to all of our responsibilities with love in our hearts, and also allow us to fulfill all the promises that we have made to those around us. In this way we will be showing ourselves to be true citizens of the kingdom of our lord and savior, Jesus. Long live the king!

4th Sunday of Advent, Dec. 23, 2012:

ZECHARIAH'S GIFT OF SILENCE

(Mic 5:1-4; Heb 10:5-10; Lk 1:39-45)

I don't know about you, but around this point in the holiday season my expectations for the holidays often begin to gallop out of control. Naturally, when we plan something special like a meal or a party, that involves a healthy dose of imagining how things are going to turn out, but the kind of expectations I'm talking about here go way beyond that. I set my heart on certain foods or activities, and if they don't come off just right, the season doesn't feel right. For example, when I'm in this sort of a mood, I might feel a sudden need to go out and buy something exotic, like smoked salmon imported from Scotland to have for breakfast on Christmas morning.

Perhaps you have had similar over-the-top expectations for the holidays in the last few days. If so, maybe you've also experienced some of the same problems, too. One problem with having such grand expectations is that we can set ourselves up for disappointment, when something we decide we need isn't available, or we get it and it just doesn't measure up to the hopes we placed in it. Another problem is that when we cling to our own expectations for the season, we are not leaving room for other people's strong desires, and such conflicts can be difficult to resolve—everyone involved can end up feeling like they are the aggrieved party.

This little pre-Christmas reality check fits into the broader context of considering carefully the way that we sometimes, with all the best of intentions, try to force our own expectations onto the world, and how that can often lead to sorrow. Luke's gospel offers us a Christian perspective on this broader question. It invites us to widen our view of our lives and to take into consideration God's hopes and desires for us and our world. It counsels us to place our plans in the proper place within God's plan. And I'm not sure, but I think that probably won't involve much in the way of imported smoked salmon.

In our gospel today we see the meeting between Elizabeth, pregnant with John, who will someday be known as "the Baptist", and Mary, pregnant with Jesus, who will someday be known as "the Christ". Now, it is too much to imagine that either one of the women could have really understood what their child would someday do, or the impact he would someday have on the world. The normal expectation of the society that they were living in was that a son was a bit like an insurance policy. A critically important duty of a son was to care for his parents in their old age. This was especially important for the mother because a woman living alone had few honorable ways to survive. However, one sees no trace of this expectation in Elizabeth and Mary. One gets the real sense that they are both open to whatever God wanted to make out of their lives and that of their children. They are coming to the birthing of their sons without any expectations, except that everything that happens will redound to the glory of God.

In that regard, Luke's gospel sets up an instructive contrast between Zechariah, the father of John, and Mary, the mother of Jesus. As chapter one of the gospel unfolds, each of these people knows that it is impossible for them to have a child at the current moment—Zechariah, because he and Elizabeth are too old, and Mary, because she had not yet left her father's house to go and live with her husband. And each of them receives a visit from an angel who tells them that, nonetheless, a child is on the way for them. Mary reacts with a question that expresses her surprise, and then with acceptance. Her best line in the gospels is "Behold the handmaiden of the Lord. Be it done unto me according to your will."

Zechariah, who receives his vision while he is serving as a priest at the temple in Jerusalem, similarly responds to the angel's announcement with a question, but the angel must have sensed some doubt or reluctance in the Zechariah's heart, because the angel's response to his question is quite different. Loosely translated, the angel's response goes something like this: "You want proof that this is going to happen?

I'll give you proof! You will be perfectly silent from this moment until the day the baby is born. Maybe then you will come to understand that I have come from God and this is all going to happen according to his will." That was surely a bit of a slap-down for a learned priest of God. We get the strong feeling that Zechariah should have known better and responded differently.

So how can we be sure that we will recognize God's actions in our lives? Probably it will be offered to us in more subtle ways than an interview with an angel. For us, it will probably be more like it was for Elizabeth, who could feel the natural event of the baby moving within her womb, and give it the correct spiritual interpretation. One way we can learn to do this better is to dial down our own expectations for the future, so that we can be on the lookout for evidence of the will of God in the way that events conspire to move us in certain directions. We will need to watch carefully, because one thing that the Bible shows us is that our God is a God of surprises.

I remember a time in my family when an unexpected snow storm turned a New Year's Eve party into a sleep-over at my sister's house. The sleeping arrangements were pretty rough, because nobody had planned to spend the night, but we had such a good time being together that we decided to turn the event into an annual tradition. Even after the family expanded into the next generation, for many years my sisters and our families got together to greet the New Year and spend the night in the same house. It got pretty crowded, but the cousins in particular remember those days with joy. Here it seems God was leading us to a better place through a snow storm.

Perhaps for you it will be some other unexpected, and possibly uncomfortable, event. So, if some of our plans get spoiled this Christmas, say if a package doesn't arrive in time, or a roast gets burned, or someone in the family has a melt-down in an inconvenient time and place, we should look around to see where God is trying to lead us in that situation. I grant you, that's not always easy to discern. Often the implications of such an event are best understood after the fact, when we 'see it in the rear-view mirror', so to speak. Also, having a quiet time to reflect about it can help a lot. Maybe when things get really crazy we can find a way to step aside mentally for just a moment to take a deep breath and to ask "OK, God, where are we going with this?" And then before doing anything about our problem, we look to see which direction Love is pointing us to.

Contemplating such a moment of prayerful silence brings us back to the example of Zechariah and the "proof" that the angel gave to him. Maybe the silence of Zechariah wasn't so much of a slap-down after all, but rather a well-placed gift from God: some quiet time for thinking rather than speaking. If so, the gift worked because after the baby was born and Zechariah gave him the name that the angel had foretold, Zechariah's voice was restored and what came out of his mouth next was one of the most beautiful passages in all of Luke's gospel. These particular verses go by the name "Zechariah's canticle" and all clergy and vowed religious recite them every day when they pray the Divine Office. We pray Zechariah's canticle at dawn, and Mary's canticle at sunset. Zechariah's canticle ends like this:

> *In the tender compassion of our God,*
> *The dawn from on high will break upon us,*
> *To shine on those who dwell in darkness and the*
> *shadow of death,*
> *And to guide our feet into the way of peace.*

That is the prayer I have for all of us on this final Sunday of Advent, that when we need it most this Christmas season we will be able to experience the prayerful silence of Zechariah, and in that silence we will be able to open ourselves to the unexpected actions of our surprising God, and he will guide our feet into the way of peace.

2nd Sunday in Ordinary Time, Jan. 20, 2013:
KNOWLEDGE AND WISDOM

(Is 62: 1–5; 1 Cor 12: 4–11; Jn 2: 1–11)

We are back in our green vestments today. Green is the color of hope. When we see the first green buds on the trees, we know that winter will soon be over. Now it's not easy to maintain hope with all we hear on the news these days, but our readings today can be that hint of spring green that reminds us of God's promise of what is to come.

When I hear today's reading from the letter to the Corinthians, I can't help but think about the day when I first entered training for the diaconate and met the 17 other men who would be in my class. One of the first things we did was to go around the group introducing ourselves, and as we were going around, I couldn't help thinking to myself, "Oh my, what a motley crew God has assembled for this work." We came from all different kinds of backgrounds. One man was a car salesman, another was an electrical engineer. There was a lawyer, and a retired electrician and a retired teacher who worked part time in a liquor store. And I'm sure my new friends were thinking the same thing about me: Where did they get him? It was only after I got to know them all much better that I understood that, as different as our backgrounds were, we were all animated by the same spirit. We were all there because we wanted to help the people of God in whatever way God wanted. Over our four years together it was with awe and joy in my heart that I saw each person's initial calling blossom into useful ministries.

I have the impression that Saint Paul felt that same sense of awe when he contemplated the list of gifts he gives us today. Remember that

Saint Paul originally founded the Christian community at Corinth. When he first came to the city, nobody knew anything about Jesus or the gifts of the Holy Spirit. But then, as the people he met and taught grew strong in their faith, the gifts of the Holy Spirit blossomed among them. I am sure that Saint Paul had particular people in mind as he listed gifts like wisdom and faith and healing powers. Mentally, he must have had their faces before him as he made his litany, praising God for the pure wonder of a weaver becoming a preacher or a farmer becoming a healer. Surely only the Holy Spirit could work such miracles out of such a motley crew of individuals as Saint Paul found when he first got to Corinth. Saint Paul wanted to share that sense of awe with the community, and remind them of how it all began.

Saint Paul also had some other goals in mind for this part of the letter. One was to remind the good people of Corinth that the gifts the Holy Spirit brings are meant to work together for the common good. "Every gift is given for some purpose" he reminds them. The gifts of the Holy Spirit are all about service, they are not a matter of personal pride. Furthermore, no gift stands alone, and hence no gift is more important than any other. After Saint Paul left Corinth, he apparently heard some disturbing news about the way his little community was functioning, or I should say, the way it was *not* functioning, and that was one reason he was moved to write this letter. He goes out of his way to list some gifts that need to work together to be effective.

Consider for a moment the first two gifts he mentions. He says "to one is given through the Spirit the expression of wisdom, and to another the expression of knowledge through the same Spirit." That is an interesting pair to lead off with. Knowledge and wisdom are not opposites, by any means, but then when you think about it, they are not quite the same thing either. I guess that most of us know a person or two who has a lot of knowledge in some particular area, but also doesn't have enough sense to come in out of the rain. Such people can be both a help and a danger to any project they get involved in. Often, they do much better when teamed up with someone who has less knowledge and more wisdom.

The person who is always spouting wisdom can sometimes be a problem too. One can get lost in the "on the one hand" and "on the other hand" of pure reason. For example, in the book of Proverbs in the

Bible, there are two verses right next to each other that seem to give contrary advice. Proverbs 26:4 counsels "Do not answer a fool in his folly, lest you become like him yourself." But then the very next verse says "Answer a fool in his folly, lest he think himself wise" Wisdom can say both "yes" and "no" to every question and it takes knowledge about the current situation to properly decide which bit of wisdom to apply to today's problem. So wisdom and knowledge work best when paired together, but unfortunately, the two don't always get along. That was something that Saint Paul heard was happening with the gifts that were found among his beloved Corinthians.

Thinking about the many gifts of the Holy Spirit can lead us to reflect on our own lives to acknowledge the gifts the Holy Spirit has given to us that are meant to support the common good. These gifts arise out of our varied backgrounds and they are present in our lives for us to share with our spouses, our family, our community, our workplace and our church. In our humility, we might not think of ourselves as gifted, but any of us who have been around for awhile have had experiences that have given us a special perspective of life, and have given us skills that can be of assistance to others. It is a matter for rejoicing when we recognize that a gift we have might be useful to someone else.

At the same time, we should also reflect on the gifts that others bring, which are meant in God's great plan to balance our gifts and keep them in their proper place. Giving thanks for the gifts of others can sometimes be a little harder. It may take a bit more meditation and personal insight to do so, because when we are in the middle of some difficult situation to which we feel we have the solution, that other person's gift can begin to feel more like a problem to be solved, rather than a gift to be appreciated.

It can be difficult to appreciate other people's gifts in this way, but it can also be a good spiritual exercise. I know for myself, when I am trying to get someplace quickly, I feel a bit put out if I get stuck behind a person who has the gift of driving slowly. I find I can react in one of two ways. One is life giving, and the other, not so much.

One way to react is to get upset and let my blood pressure rise. I start concentrating on the places I need to get to, and I obsess about being two minutes late. Then I start looking for any opportunity to pass the other person, even if that might not be an entirely safe thing to do. I find that reacting in that way is a warning sign of having too much on my mind and too much to do.

There is a different way to react to this situation that is better for our stomach linings and better for our souls. It is a transformative idea to imagine that the Holy Spirit is offering us this situation as an opportunity to slow down for a moment. It is true that there are many times I have said to myself I need to stop rushing around so much, and that it would be better to be a few minutes late than to do something dangerous. So, I should be thankful for that gift. It is an uncomfortable truth that sometimes the gifts of the Spirit come to us through other people at a time when we least expect them and don't even find them to be particularly convenient, but by the same token, that may be the time when we need them most.

So, as we continue with our worship this morning, let us resolve to share our gifts with this community that God loves so well, and to give thanks to God for the gifts of others. Let us pray that we always recognize them whenever they come to us and that we can always value them for the way that they keep our gifts in their proper place, for the greater glory of God.

The Conversion of Saint Paul, Jan. 27, 2013:

WORKING TOGETHER FOR THE LORD

(Neh 8:2-4,5-6,8-10; 1 Cor 12:12-30; Lk 1:1-4,14-21)

Possibly, some of you know that over the last several years I have been having problems with my health. Through many conversations with doctors, I have learned a lot more about the body than I ever knew before, including the different functions of the liver, and the activities of smaller parts like the spleen, and others whose names are not to be found in my small Spanish dictionary. Truly, in health or in disease, the body is a marvelous thing, composed of many complicated parts. But normally, each part does its job calmly and quietly without our knowledge or help.

Today we understand a lot more about the functions of the parts of the body than Saint Paul ever did, but that knowledge only increases our awe at the miracle of the human body. It is with that kind of awe in his heart that Saint Paul compares the Christian community to a well-functioning body. And he does not just say that we are like a single body, he says that we are the very body of Christ. Such is our honor, and such our responsibility. The different ministries within the Church complement each other and together accomplish greater things than anyone could accomplish alone.

Many people first experience this sort of cooperation in the family of their birth. In God's plan, the parents of a family are one flesh. They work together for the good of the family, and the children help more and more as they grow older. Possibly, grandparents and aunts and uncles or cousins are also part of the mix. Each does what he or she can, and each receives what he or she needs. At least that is the idea. We know that sometimes things do not end up going according to the best of plans, but even those who do not find cooperation and love in the family of their birth, can still find those elements in the Christian family.

The Church should be like a large family. Many times in his writings, Saint Paul addresses the people he is writing to as "brothers and sisters". This is more than just a manner of speaking; it is, or can be, a reality. Here in the Church we find acceptance and understanding. As we heard in the readings last week, in the Church there are many diverse ministries, but one Spirit. If we ask, that same Spirit will teach us how to cooperate well with each other.

I have seen in Bolivia a few grand church buildings that have shown me what is possible when the people of God work together in community. These buildings were built out in the countryside in the eastern part of what is now Bolivia, far from the large cities. They were built in the 17th century. When they were built, much of the countryside was still a jungle. At this time the Jesuits arrived in the area and taught the people about Jesus and the Christian faith, and together with the people they constructed large and beautiful church buildings. The largest of these is in a town called Concepcion. Today, that church serves as a cathedral. The construction of that church required the wood of two thousand trees, and today three thousand people can come to the church and participate in the Mass there. Possibly, these churches are not as tall as the famous cathedrals of Europe, but they are surely their equal in beauty.

We can be sure that the Jesuits could not have built such temples in the Jungle alone. For one thing, there were too few of them, and also the methods of construction that they brought with them from dry Spain did not work in the wet jungle. In the same way, before the coming of the Jesuits, the people were not building large building of this sort. But together they discovered new ways of building, and built beautiful churches and great schools for the greater glory of God. In this way, they acted as the true body of Christ. The church buildings which we can see there today, now three centuries old, are a testimony to what can be accomplished when everyone believes and truly feels that we are one body with different members and all are equally important in carrying out our specific functions.

And what are our works? Here in Princeton, we already have a large and beautiful church building. We already have a Catholic school. But still, our works are many. First and foremost, we should fill this building with praise. We should learn the hymns and sing them with joy. God desires a living temple, not a mute one.

And there is more. If we truly wish to be the body of Christ, then we must do what Christ would do if he were here among us in the flesh, as is each one of us. Surely this includes the words of the prophet Isaiah: to bring glad tidings to the poor, to announce liberation to prisoners and healing to the blind, to bring liberty to captives. In today's gospel, Christ tells us to take this Good News to the whole world. Each person that we interact with should feel that they have been touched by the love of Jesus. We should accept strangers warmly. This is our great honor, and equally our great responsibility.

Some days I feel this honor very strongly in my heart. Other days the responsibility is a weight hard to carry. But whether because of the honor or the responsibility, we must keep going. I have seen some of the good works that you have accomplished, and I know that you are already doing many of the things I have spoken of this evening. But our example in service is Jesus, and the love of God continually invites us to do more. I very much like the beautiful words of Saint Theresa Of Avila:

> *Christ has no body now but yours,*
> *And does not have any hands except for yours.*
> *His only feet are yours,*
> *And yours the eyes with which Christ looks com-*
> *passion on the world.*
> *Yours the feet with which he walks about to do good,*
> *Yours the hands with which now he blesses us.*

Let as follow along then, building the community that Jesus desires, using well the charisms he has given us with the result that as Saint Theresa says, our eyes and hands and hearts might be the hands and eyes and heart of Jesus. Amen.

STEPPING OUTSIDE THE DAY-TO-DAY

(Dt 26:4-10; Rom 10:8-13; Lk 4:1-13)

One of the most memorable camping trips I ever went on happened in the summer after my sophomore year of college when a boyhood friend and I went hiking in a park in the Pacific North West. We hiked a long way along the rugged and nearly deserted shoreline. The ranger had warned us to keep a careful eye on the tides, and sure enough, by the time we were setting up camp, there was water on three sides of us and a high cliff behind us, but we had chosen a good spot and stayed dry (we were both Eagle scouts, after all).

This was long before there were cell phones, so that night we felt completely cut off from humanity and on our own in the immensity of nature. My friend and I were both very quiet that evening, lost in our own thoughts. It seemed to be a perfect time for meditating on really big questions, like "Who am I, when I'm away from all my contacts in the civilized world?" and "Where am I trying to get to in this life?" At that point in my faith journey, I did not look for a spiritual side in daily events, but now in my memory, that time on the beach seems a holy time in a sacred place, and I am sure there were angels on the spot, waiting to see how two young men from Maryland would respond to those eternal questions.

I don't know what it was like for Jesus to go out into the desert for forty days, but I wonder if his experience wasn't similar, leaving behind society and entering into the immensity of nature to face some important questions about his life. The gospel says that the Holy Spirit led him out into the desert, and he must have needed that time to prepare for the outpouring of self in his ministry and his ultimate sacrifice. The basic question that Jesus faced was "Can I do all that the Father expects of me?"

In his divine nature, Jesus may have had all the answers, but Jesus had a human nature as well, and the human heart is naturally full of questions. Our gospel today describes Jesus' time in the desert as a struggle with the devil, but in our terminology today it would also be fair to describe it as Jesus having an internal struggle —a struggle to understand and commit himself to his Father's will in his life —a very human struggle against taking the easy way out. Taken together, that is what the recorded temptations seem to add up to.

It is important for each of us at some point in our faith journey to take time to face the big questions of life directly. Many people find that much easier to do that when they are out of range of the larger society. Society has so many different ways of defining us. Am I an "A" student or a "D" student? Am I seven years old, or 17 or 37 or 67? Am I an investment banker or a dish washer? Am I single, married, widowed or divorced? Am I politically conservative or liberal? A good credit risk or bad? The world constantly tries to slot us into simple categories with definite expectations.

The good thing about going out into the desert or being surrounded by high tide, is that we can shrug off those definitions for a time and see ourselves for a moment as God sees us. Remember the words of God that we heard just a few weeks ago directed toward Jeremiah the prophet: "Before I formed you in the womb, I knew you. Before you were born, I dedicated you." Can you hear the loving care in those words? I hope so, because that love is directed equally well to each one of us. And it is much easier to hear that message if nobody is yelling at us about an overdue report or puffing up our egos with praise for completing some minor task. Hearing that loving message is the starting point for knowing who we truly are.

Lent offers us the opportunity to step outside our normal lives and see our life in a new way. Now, it would be wonderful if we could all make a forty day retreat in the desert and really sort though all the issues of our life, but probably most of us have commitments that make that impossible. We should try to think big, though. It might be possible to spare a few days or a weekend for a little spiritual refreshment. This would be a great gift to offer to your spouse. You watch the kids and house while he or she spends some quiet time with God in a place of natural beauty. Or maybe the two of you can get away together, and let the grandparents have some quality time with the kids. If not a weekend, how about at least a long afternoon? Even that can be hard to manage, as I know well. But, even if that sort of a mini-retreat isn't possible, there are some things we can do to make some time for quiet Lenten reflection.

For example, every time we close our bedroom door when we retire for the night, that can be a time when we symbolically shut out the world's influences and turn our thoughts to higher things. That time of reflection is precious, so we should not fill it with remorseful thoughts about days long gone or fearful imaginings about the future. Those things are in God's hands. If any of those thoughts come into our heads we should just let them pass on through and be gone. A better use of our time is to reflect on the day that is ending and the one will come with the dawn. We could reflect on the good things God gave us today and try to see if there were opportunities for good that we missed through our selfishness or inattentiveness. After giving thanks and asking for forgiveness for today we can then ask what God wants us to do tomorrow. That will of course be different for each one of us, but it will surely involve living a life of virtue.

Today, as we honor and celebrate the scout troops who are here with us, we might pause and consider the Scout Law and the wholesome virtues it holds up for our consideration. We honor all those scouts who commit themselves to following the law, and we greatly thank the leaders who give so much of their time to make this program possible. The Boy Scout Law consists of just 15 words, "a scout is" followed by twelve adjectives. The Girl Scout Law is very similar, but today I'll repeat the Boy Scout one, because I know that one better. I am going to read through those twelve adjectives slowly and ask you to consider each one. If you feel a bit of a quiver inside as you hear one particular adjective, that may mean that God is offering it to you for your special consideration this Lenten season.

A scout is
Trustworthy, Loyal, Helpful,
Friendly, Courteous, Kind,
Obedient, Cheerful, Thrifty,
Brave, Clean and Reverent.

If one of those adjectives seemed to leap out at you as I read them aloud (or some other one that comes to mind), maybe that quality is something you need as your special companion this Lent. To accept the invitation of companionship, we need only keep an eye out for the occurrence of that virtue in the people around us, and meditate on its beauty, and try to practice it more fully in our day-to-day life. Doing so will make for a great Lenten season, and once we get to know the beauty of that virtue, we will want it to be a permanent part of our life. We can always use more beauty in our lives.

So as we continue with our worship this morning, let us ask God to show us the virtue we most need in our lives this spring, and to guide us all through a good Lent to a glorious Easter.

5th Sunday of Lent, Mar. 17, 2013:

I'LL HAVE WHAT HE'S HAVING

(Is 43:16-21; Phil 3:8-14; Jn 8:1-11)

I've never been in prison, as an inmate, I mean, but I have seen enough old movies that I'm pretty sure I wouldn't much care for the experience. And when it comes to prisons of the ancient world, I have no doubts at all; unless you had someone on the outside to look out for you, a prison sentence in the ancient Near East could be a pretty grim affair. In such a prison, it would be very natural to have a great longing for all the creature comforts that are lacking, like a decent bed and clean water for drinking and washing, and wholesome food. So it is with great astonishment that we read today's epistle which shows that Saint Paul reacted to his time in prison in a completely different way.

The letter to the Philippians, which we read from today, was written by Saint Paul from prison, and in it he says that he counts all the things he has given up to be so much rubbish. Actually, the Greek word he uses, *skubalon*, is even stronger than our translation makes out. That Greek word could be used to describe sewage. Saint Paul tells us that if the choice is going to be between being in prison because of Jesus or having all the honors and comforts and privileges that the world can give but not knowing Jesus, then he would choose prison and Jesus. Now one might imagine a well-meaning person saying such a thing while sitting in an easy chair with a warm cup of tea close at hand, and we can even grant that such a person might be sincere in saying it. But to say such a thing while in prison? That is astounding, and it deserves further study.

As we ponder this witness of Saint Paul, it is also important to note that this letter has a strong undercurrent of joy in it. Saint Paul uses the words "joy", "glad" and "rejoice" a dozen times in the letter. As we read it, we might feel a bit like a person going into a restaurant feeling a bit worn out and tired, who upon sitting down, notices that the people at another table are all laughing boisterously and eating their meals with gusto. When the waiter comes to take his order the person waves away the menu and says "I'll have whatever they're having!" That's what I want to say when I read the letter to the Philippians: "Please, God, I'll have what he's having."

My brothers and sisters, the Good News of Lent and Easter is that this wonderful experience is just as available to us as it was to Saint Paul. No matter what our problems are this spring, we can be as joyfully free in our own lives as Saint Paul was in his prison cell, by coming to know Jesus as well as Saint Paul knew him. We too can obtain what Saint Paul calls "the supreme goodness of knowing Jesus and the power of his resurrection." Now you might think Saint Paul must have had an advantage over us, living when he did, but that's really not true. Just like us, Saint Paul never met Jesus in his physical person. Saint Paul only knew the resurrected Jesus. He mostly learned about him from the stories told to him by the apostles, and we can do the same.

Today's gospel is a perfect opportunity. To use this beautiful short story to get to know Jesus better, we have to engage our sacred imagination as we read. We will make the situation more real for ourselves by imagining what it must have been like to be there on that day. Perhaps it was sunny and hot that morning, or perhaps a cool breeze was blowing in from the west. Maybe it all happened on a street corner buzzing with activity or in a quiet garden. Let the Spirit guide you as you meditate.

We might pick one of the characters in the story and imagine the whole thing from that person's perspective. We could choose one of the followers of Jesus, or someone in the angry crowd, or the condemned woman herself. This particular story has some wonderful silences in it, while Jesus is drawing on the ground, or while the people are looking from one to another to see if someone would throw the first stone. What do you think those silences were like? How would we have experienced them, if we had been there?

We might even try to imagine what the situation felt like from Jesus' perspective. He knew that adultery is a terrible sin. It tears at the fabric of family life and causes no end of pain and suffering for all concerned. On the other hand, the situation thrust upon Jesus was not really about adultery. If it had been, the leaders would have just taken the woman out of the town and stoned her. No, this confrontation was really about Jesus and the threat he represented to the established authorities. What do you think it was like for Jesus, knowing that if he said the wrong thing, the woman in front of him would be brutally killed? By allowing our sacred imagination to carry us back to that time, we will begin to know Jesus much better.

The gospels hold many such opportunities for us to have an encounter with the living Jesus. Probably, you already have certain favorite gospel passages that you can meditate upon in this way. It is spiritually healthful to do so. It is also helpful to share this sort of thing with others, and if you want the opportunity to do so, you might want to join our Bible study group, or the *Lectio Divina* group that meets each Tuesday evening in the spiritual center to ponder the Sunday scriptures, or perhaps you would prefer the men's prayer group that also discusses the Sunday scriptures and meets on Thursdays.

Saint Paul also hints at another way that he got to know Jesus when he talks about "the sharing of his sufferings by being conformed to his death." Now we all have suffering in this life, and it is a good spiritual exercise to unite that suffering with the sufferings of Jesus in our prayer. But I think that Saint Paul is talking about a particular kind of suffering in this reading: one that comes directly from following in Christ's footsteps.

When we try to be a peace maker in our family or in our workplace, and maybe things don't go very well with our attempts and both people end up angry at us, we can know just a little bit how Jesus felt in his life. We can say "Dear Jesus, now I get it. This is what it must have felt like for you." Or when we stand up for someone who is weaker, and get shot down for our boldness, we will know better what Jesus' life was like, trying to help the poor and downtrodden of his time. When we come home tired at the end of the day, and our loved ones need us to do something for them, and we dig down and offer up our last bit of energy for their needs, we will know what it felt like to Jesus when all the people kept coming to him day and night for healing. In those and so many other ways, as we walk in the way of Jesus, we will come to know him better and be conformed to his death, and likewise to his resurrection.

Next Sunday we begin Holy Week. On Thursday, Friday and Saturday, we will walk together through the final hours of Jesus' earthly life. This is a wonderful opportunity to come to know Jesus better. Come to the mass on Holy Thursday when we commemorate the Last Supper. Afterwards, sit with Jesus for a while contemplating the garden of Gethsemane. Have you known such fear and uncertainty? Be there to find comfort in the silence. On Good Friday afternoon, grieve with us over the cross and venerate the sacrifice Jesus gave that day long ago. Then on Holy Saturday gather with us at dusk and see the kindling of the new fire, and rejoice in the light of Christ. It can be moving; it can be exhilarating; it can be our chance to share deeply in the "supreme goodness of knowing Jesus and the power of his resurrection."

4th Sunday of Easter, Apr. 21, 2013:

TRUSTING IN GOD

(Acts 13:14,43–52; Rev 7:9,14–17; Jn 10:27–30)

It has been quite a week, hasn't it? When we hear about senseless violence like the bombing in Boston, or the terrible explosion in the factory in Texas, or the earthquake in China, it can be very scary and upsetting. It all seems so random and irrational. And when you add to that all the things we face personally, like the loss of a job or a bad diagnosis or the death of a loved one, we can be knocked off our feet for a time, unable to respond adequately to the challenges we face. We might wonder, what do we have that we can set against such terrible difficulties? What resources can we bring to that kind of time of testing? Our readings today offer us three good resources: faith, hope and love. By 'faith' here, I mean the theological virtue of faith, which we might define as an abiding trust in God. Faith together with love and hope make a self-reinforcing package of virtues that can help us in times of difficulty. Much more than bullet-proof glass or armor plating or guns, these three virtues will help us to pull through difficult times like these.

Our readings show us how these three virtues reinforce each other. In the gospel, Jesus tells the disciples that God the Father is holding them in his hands, and no one and nothing can remove them from that loving care. He is using their love of God to reinforce their trust. Now, we don't know exactly when Jesus spoke these words, but it was probably just a few months before he died. It says in the gospel that after he said these words an angry crowd picked up stones and almost stoned him to death right then and there. So maybe the Apostles were already becoming worried that that things were not going to turn out well, but they could not have guessed how soon Jesus would be taken from them, and how devastated they would be by the experience. By using the image of God holding them in his hands, Jesus is trying to give his disciples the trust in God they would need to survive that awful experience.

When I think about that image of God holding us in his loving hands, I can't help but think about the time when I was first learning to swim. I was about 6 years old, and my parents enrolled me for beginners' lessons. I did pretty well, except for one thing: floating on my back. Fear told me that that was never going to work, and seeing people doing it did not help. Finally, my sister Mary, who was 7 years older than I, came to my rescue. She took me into the shallow water and said to lie back and rest on her hands, and she would slowly lower her hands, and I was to notice carefully what happened. When I felt the pressure of her hands on my back become less, that was not because she was dropping me, but rather it was because I was beginning to float. She promised that her hands would stay right there ready to catch me. Well it took a couple of tries, but eventually I trusted her enough to do as she asked, and lo and behold, she was right. I learned how to float.

To me, learning to trust God is a lot like learning to float. When we don't feel his loving hands on us, we should rejoice, because that means we are learning to manage on our own, and we can still trust that his hands are right there ready to catch us if things go wrong.

So our gospel reading today shows us love turning into trust. Our reading from the book of Revelation shows us trust turning into hope. The book begins with the author telling us that he was on the island of Patmos because he proclaimed God's word and witnessed to Jesus. Patmos was a prison colony of the Romans on a remote island in the Aegean Sea—think of Alcatraz, but without so many buildings. In that difficult environment, John kept his trust in God's promise, and there he had his visions of God's throne room in heaven that gave him hope for the future, a hope that he shared with the community he had left behind. The content of his visions sounds somewhat strange to our modern ears, but that shouldn't stop us from cherishing our own visions of what heaven and the coming Kingdom of God will be like.

When I was a child and first learned about heaven, my visions of what that might be like were full of piles of candy and green beans that taste like French fries, and other comforting ideas. Then, when I got to be a teenager, I rejected all such notions as childish. I guess I must have learned in religion class that really heaven was going to be like one long liturgy of the Mass. A Mass … that would go on … for eternity. I think that this was based on the ideas of Thomas Aquinas, maybe, and far be it from me to contradict good Saint Thomas. I think, that on a good day as a teen, I could imagine that being something desirable. At least, I wanted to want that kind of heaven, even if I never quite could desire it as much as I had desired heaven when I was a child.

Well, now that I have passed out of my teenage years and lost some of that teenage self-assurance of being right in every particular, I am thinking that really I was on a better track as far as imagining heaven when I was a child. I think we should feel free to fill our visions of heaven with any good thing that we really love. So, if in this endlessly delayed spring season, you are really looking forward to the roses of June, feel free to imagine that heaven is going to be an infinite succession of rose gardens in all their splendorous colors and scents.

Of course, when we get there, it might not turn out to be exactly that way. But when we do get to heaven, if we find that heaven isn't all full of rose gardens, that will only be because it is full of something even better. And when we see what *is* there we will say to ourselves "Everything I ever loved about rose gardens is right here, even more real and beautiful than any rose garden I saw on earth. Everything I loved about the Mass is right here more joyous and more fulfilling, than any Mass I every celebrated on earth. Even everything I ever loved about French fries is right here." On that day, we will say to ourselves in wonder "To think I could have wanted any of those things when I could have this!" That is what heaven is going to be like. John imagined it one way because of the situation he was in, and we will imagine it a different way, because of our particular situation. And there is nothing wrong with that. The important thing is that our contemplation of heaven should nurture the virtue of hope in our lives.

Finally, in our reading from the Acts of the Apostles, we find hope and trust creating more love. We see Barnabas and Paul out on their first missionary journey. Barnabas came to the faith before Paul did, but both of them had been believers for many years before they found that their hope and trust was overflowing in love for people they had never even met. Their trust in God let them answer that call. In to-day's reading we see them arrive at Antioch in Pisidia, which is in present-day Turkey, more than a hundred miles from where Paul grew up. When they got there, they had such great success in sharing their message of hope with the people that they fell afoul of certain power-ful people in the town and ended up being persecuted and run out of town. We don't know exactly what is meant here by "persecuted" but it was unlikely to be something pleasant.

The thing for us to notice especially today is how they reacted to this seeming setback on their mission. Our reading says they were filled with joy and the Holy Spirit. Now, I don't know about you, but that is not usually how I respond to being persecuted and run out of town. We can admire the trust and hope that Paul and Barnabas had which overflowed in love and joy even in the midst of their difficulties. That is something we might want for ourselves. This week we could thank God in our prayer and meditation for the faith, hope, and love we already have, and try to get a virtuous upward spiral going in which the virtues of faith, hope and love reinforce each other and give us the strength we need for these trying times we live in.

Pentecost, May 19, 2013:

A HOLY LONGING FOR THE LORD

(Acts 2:1-11; 1 Cor 12:3,7,12-13; Jn 20:19-23)

On special feast days like today, our lectionary offers us a different set of readings for the vigil mass than those used for the masses celebrated on the day itself. Often the readings for the vigil focus on the time leading up to the event that is commemorated by the feast. That is certainly what we have in our readings this evening; they speak very eloquently of a longing for the Holy Spirit. This evening, we are invited to stand on the very threshold of the feast of Pentecost and experience a strong desire for the Holy Spirit to come to us with his aid.

Focusing our attention on a state of unfulfilled desire in this way is not a thing we are very comfortable with in our culture today, but it is spiritually beneficial for us to pause in this moment and do so, because being aware of what that desire feels like will help us to know when we have a special need to call on the help of the Holy Spirit and also it will help us to recognize his answering gifts when they come to us. In his letter to the Galatians, Saint Paul lists nine fruits of a life in the Spirit: love, joy, peace, patience, kindness, generosity, faithfulness, gentleness and self-control (5:22). If, like me, you have ever longed for more of one of these in your life, this is your feast day.

Our first reading records a vision of the prophet Ezekiel. He was sent by God to the Jewish people in a time of terrible trauma, after the destruction of Jerusalem by the Babylonians. Prior to that event, there had been a feeling among the leaders of the people that they were secure in God's good will and they were untouchable by any mere human army. The wholesale destruction of Jerusalem and the humiliation of their king and his army brought them down off their high horse and gave them a lot to think about. The memory of battlefields littered with unburied soldiers must have haunted them as they were led off into captivity, but the vision of Ezekiel that we hear today was not really about those who had died in the attacks of the Babylonians, it was about those who had survived physically, but were in spiritual shock from those terrible events. There is love and sadness in God's voice when he tells Ezekiel "these dry bones are the whole house of Israel." That is, that was the demoralized state of the people to whom Ezekiel was being sent to bring a word of comfort and renewal. God asks Ezekiel "can these bones come to life?" and Ezekiel responds "Lord God, you alone know that."

God then shows him that it is possible—a fact which Jesus affirms in the gospel. This can be a comfort to us when we live through our own traumatic events and wonder how we can possibly move on from there. The context of Jesus' words is that he had come to Jerusalem for the feast of Tabernacles. This was the fall harvest celebration of the Jewish people, in which the priests of the temple would gather water from the pool of Siloam, and carry it in procession around the altar of sacrifice at the temple. The people would walk with them carrying leafy branches in one hand and a lemon or lime in the other to symbolize the harvest. It was a happy occasion, and water played a central part in the celebration in part because Jerusalem was nearly unique among the capitals of the ancient world in not being located on a river. It was on a mountain top at the edge of a desert. Its water supply came from a large natural underground reservoir that fed the pool of Siloam and other wells. The residents saw this water as God's special gift to "his" city. John's gospel often shows a spiritual dimension of the events of Jesus' life. In this case, just as God blessed high and dry Jerusalem with a source of life-giving water, Jesus blesses all who come to him with the life-giving Spirit of God.

Saint Paul's offering today comes from a time well after the feast of Pentecost, and it reminds us that even after that initial influx of the Holy Spirit's power, we can still find ourselves in a place of need for the Spirit's aid. Saint Paul says that all creation is groaning with labor pains. This is a difficult but hopeful image, which can focus our attention on the new life that can come out of a time of trials and uncertainty. In Saint Paul's description, the aid of the Holy Spirit does not change our situation so much as it gives us the hope we need to work out the puzzles that life presents us with.

Would that such puzzles were as easy to solve as the ones we used to do as children! When I was growing up, I used to love to do jigsaw puzzles. Not the ones that you sometimes see today, in which the picture is just a pile of coffee beans or something crazy like that, but normal pictures, like sailboats on a lake, or something else nice to look at. Then when I got married, I was pleased to discover that my wife's family's custom was to do a big jigsaw puzzle together as part of their Christmas celebration. After Christmas dinner, the dining room table was cleared off and a big jigsaw puzzle had pride of place on the table for the rest of the visit. However, they took puzzle-solving to a new level for me, because they considered it unsporting to look at the picture on the box lid. You had to work the puzzle without being quite sure what it was supposed to be a picture of.

As I think about it now, that seems to me a lot like life. By and large, we are trying to put together the puzzle of our lives without really knowing what it supposed to look like when it's done. That can be a bit scary at times, but it is also worth pointing out that there is a freedom in it and it is not necessarily a distressing situation to be in. I sometimes counsel engaged couples, and given their time in life, they usually have only fitted together a few of the more important pieces of their life's puzzle—sometimes it is just this one: "I love this person and I want to be together with him or her forever." But where they are going to live, how they will pay the bills, when children come into the picture, all those pieces have yet to be put into any kind of a firm place in their lives. Yet, they are, for the most part, happy in the midst of all of life's uncertainty. They are ready, even eager, to start putting the other pieces of their lives together around this fixed point, and for the unknowable part, they trust that when the time comes, all the pieces will click together just as they ought to. God bless them and may he make it so!

We would do well to take a lesson from the attitude of such young couples. If we can just get a few of the big pieces of our life's puzzle into place, we can be happy while working on the rest. Maybe, in fact, the real source of joy for the disciples on that first Christian Pentecost was that the Holy Spirit helped them to see how a few of the big pieces of the puzzle fit together in their lives. We don't need to imagine that in that moment of inspiration, when the flames settled on their heads, that all the disciples' questions about the future were answered, only a few critical ones: this is where God goes in the picture, this is where Jesus fits in, and this is where I belong. The invitation of today's celebration is that the Holy Spirit offers us that same kind of inspiration.

That doesn't mean that the puzzle will be finished, far from it. We won't get the last piece in place until we are ready for heaven, and even then God may have to fix a few pieces that we've mashed up along the way. But the Holy Spirit offers us counsel and comfort in our ongoing discovery of God's will in our lives. The joy and love and peace that flow from that are something to desire with our whole heart and to celebrate and accept gratefully on this holy day.

11th Sunday in Ordinary Time, Jun. 16, 2013:
TRUSTS BROKEN AND RESTORED

(2 Sam 12:7-10,13; Gal 2:16,19-21; Lk 7:36-8:3)

Today is Father's Day, and so I would like begin by extending to all the fathers here with us today our best wishes for the day. The role of a father in the modern world has gotten very complicated and multi-faceted, and anyone who is willing to step into this role, whether as a natural father or a volunteer, deserves our great respect and admiration. On this day we also remember those of our fathers and grandfathers who have gone home to God. It is a day to pause in thanksgiving for all the good things they have done for us, and also a day to forgive any faults and failures there may have been along the way. Lastly, we might ask forgiveness of them, either in prayer or in person, for our own failings as sons and daughters. Today is a day to say the words I never said enough to my father: "Sorry for all the drama, Dad." and "I love you."

In fact, today's readings are all about seeking out and finding forgiveness, and to help us appreciate them better, I'd like to share with you a true tale of forgiveness that involved some friends who used to belong to this parish, but have since moved away. They were quite open about this story, so I sure it's OK to share it with you, but just to be careful, I will call the two people "Mary" and "John"—common names because this story could happen to any of us.

Soon after John and Mary got married, John took a new job that was going to require his intense involvement for a few years. They agreed that Mary, who was between jobs at the time, would run the household, including the family finances. Money was tight, but they made a sensible budget, which included putting some money away every month in a "rainy day" fund. As time went by, John was pleased to see how well Mary was coping with the finances. He was proud of her and marveled that there always seemed to be money to go out for a night on the town or to a concert, just like they did before they got married. Now, what John did not know was that Mary was using the money from the rainy day fund to pay for these little adventures. He seemed so happy, she did not have the heart to tell him.

Mary was able to keep up this pretense until the time came for them to move to a new house and they needed to make a large down payment to make the deal work. John said "No problem! We can use the rainy day fund." Well, at that point Mary did not have the courage to tell him that the rainy day fund was as dry as the Sahara desert. Instead, she concocted a wild plan which involved taking out a short-term loan, which meant forging John's signature on the loan papers. She was getting in deeper and deeper, but in the end, with intense effort on her part, she made it all work. She even made enough of a profit on the house deals to repay the loan and replenish the rainy day fund, so John never needed to know about any of it. But, of course, Mary knew, and it bothered her more and more and she knew she had to tell John what she had done.

When she finally screwed up her courage and told him, John met her with love and forgiveness, saying "Why did you put yourself through all of that? Why didn't you just come and tell me? We could have worked it out together." It is easy to imagine the emotions that Mary felt as she received John's love and forgiveness. There was relief and gratefulness and a matching outpouring of love for him. The love that Mary felt for John in that moment is a good image to take with us as we examine today's readings. So many times, God says the same thing to us. "Why did you put yourself through all of that? Why didn't you just come and tell me? We could have worked it out together."

Three ideas stand out to me as I consider Mary and John's story in the light of the readings we have today. The first idea is that even though John forgave Mary, their relationship was not quite the same as before. The broken trust needed to be restored. This required a process in which Mary demonstrated her trustworthiness in practical ways, and John needed to give her that opportunity, which he did in a loving way.

The natural consequences of our failings are also on display for us in our first reading. Notice what God says to King David through the prophet Nathan: "because of what you've done, the sword will never leave your house." This was not a punishment on God's part, nor a curse on him from Nathan. It is simply a statement of the natural consequences of the way King David had ruled his kingdom. He had messed up his relationship with his family and with his nation, and those relationships would not be easily repaired. If we listen, we can hear God's great sadness in those words.

And for the woman whom Jesus forgave in the Gospel, there was still society to be dealt with. Jesus' forgiveness would not have repaired her relationship to her community. Notice that right after this story, Saint Luke tells us about the group of women disciples whom Jesus had helped, and who accompanied him on his journeys and supported him out of their own pocket. There is room to hope that the woman we hear of today was welcomed into that fellowship and was able in this way to begin a new life. This is something to watch out for in our own lives. Often it happens that one of the graces that comes with asking forgiveness from God is an insight into a way forward, a way to make a new beginning.

The second thing that strikes me about John and Mary's story is how easily Mary slipped into her very awkward situation. At the beginning, she acted unwisely, but with good intentions. Whether it was sinful at the beginning would be hard to say. That is something she had to work out with her friendly neighborhood confessor. She wanted to please John and maintain the singles life-style that they had enjoyed before they got married. I am sure that the first time she delayed putting money into the rainy day fund, it was with a sincere intention to make it up the next month. But when the next month came it wasn't any easier to stretch the paycheck to cover all the things they felt they needed. And before long, the problems snowballed. She didn't mean for it to end up as it did, but then neither did the woman in the gospel. Perhaps you can remember the possibility of such a thing in your own past; I know I can. The possibility of sliding down a slippery slope into seriously immoral behavior is very real and we need to be prudently on guard against it.

The final idea that is worth considering is the hints that our readings contain about how we can avoid getting into such problems, and that has to do with maintaining an attitude of gratefulness in our lives. Notice that Nathan rehearses all the wonderful things that God did for David, turning him from a shepherd into a king. I can't help but think that if David had just been able to concentrate more on being thankful for the things he had already, he would have been less likely to make a sinful grab for more. The same goes for all of us. Being grateful for what we have leads to peace, always focusing on what we don't have may lead to sin. I know when I was sick a while back, I would get despondent sometimes about the five percent of my body that was not working right. One of the things that sometimes helped was to meditate thankfully on the 95 percent of my body that was working just fine. An attitude of gratefulness can get us through very tough times.

One of the things we can surely be grateful for this day is the many times God has already forgiven us and helped us to make a new beginning. Our tradition teaches us that if we fail again, despite our resolve today not to do so, and we come again to Jesus with remorse in our hearts, we will be privileged to hear him say lovingly once more "Your faith has saved you. Go in peace."

TRUE SECURITY, TRUE OPENNESS AND TRUE JOY

(Eccl 1:2,2:21-23; Col 3:1-5,9-11; Lk 12:13-21)

The story that begins today's gospel takes an interesting twist. Notice that the man who comes to Jesus with a complaint about his brother believes that justice is clearly on his side. He is convinced that he deserves a part of the family inheritance, and he wants Jesus, in his authority as a teacher of the law, to make that happen for him. But Jesus sees a deeper problem in this conflict between brothers. He understands from the beginning that there is no Solomon-like legal division of the property that is going to fix the real problem that exists between the two of them. That is going to require a change of heart, not a change of finances.

In this regard little has changed between Jesus' time and our own. As I think about the situation of those two brothers, I am reminded of the advertisements that were on TV earlier this summer from a certain magazine distributor who was running a raffle that offered a lucky winner a prize of 5,000 dollars per week for life. And then, to top it off, the winner could name a second person who, upon the death of the first winner, would continue to receive 5,000 dollars per week for the rest of his or her life. The ads were full of joyous scenes of earlier winners being informed of the bounty they were to receive. This grand prize was presented as an unalloyed good, but would it really be a good thing to receive such a prize? What do you think it would do to your relationships to other people if you were to win? No matter if you were generous with the winnings or stingy, I think it would do much to distort and harm your relationships with family and friends. Now, suppose a relative won the prize and named you as successor. What would that do to your relationship to others in the family? Or, even worse, suppose a relative won the prize but didn't name you. How would that feel?

This prize, which from a materialistic point of view seems a great goodness, would, I'm convinced, end up being a disaster for any of us. May God keep such 'prizes' away from our door!

In this obvious way, and in many more subtle ways besides, the strong emphasis of our popular culture on the importance of money and the acquisition of whatever is new and cool and in style does much to distort our personal relationships and our choices in life. All of our readings today ask us to turn away from such greediness in all its forms. Our first reading calls the striving for more and more stuff to be the "vanity of vanities." The phrase refers to something that is completely empty and fruitless. Today we might say that the mindless pursuit of material gain is "emptiness squared". In a similar way Saint Paul tells the Colossians to turn away from all such worldly concerns. This is not a comfortable message to hear, especially if we feel that we are working as hard as we can and just barely keeping our heads above water. To be told to just turn away from all striving to get ahead in life seems un-American and completely out of touch with reality.

In part, I think that this impression comes from the fact that these readings only talk about the negative side of the equation. They tell us clearly what to turn away from, but not so much about what we should turn toward instead. Lest you think that this is all the gospel and the Church have to offer us in this regard, I would like to share with you three points that Pope Francis brought up in one of his homilies to the World Youth Day crowd. These points come from his homily at the shrine of our Lady at Aparecido. This homily was reproduced in full on the last page of last week's bulletin, but the points are so important and speak so directly to the problems in today's readings that I want to go over them again. He presents them as three attitudes of a Christian. To me they stand in direct contrast to our culture's attitude toward money. They speak to the way we try to attain security in this life, and the way we try to control our lives, and the way we place a value on the things that come our way.

First, to the matter of our natural desire for security. All of us want to be secure against the uncertainties of the future. We might have bottled water and batteries on hand, and even a portable generator in the garage waiting for the next natural disaster. This is not a bad thing, unless it gives us the illusion that we can be prepared in this way for every eventuality. We can't of course, and for some of the things that might befall us, like the death of a loved one, or divorce, or a health emergency, the practical and financial parts of the situation are only a small part of the problem.

Pope Francis urges us to find our sense of security in a very different place. He says that an important attitude of a Christian is hopefulness born out of our understanding that no matter what sort of disaster may come our way, God will be right there beside us, helping us through. He will not let us be overwhelmed. Accepting this truth of our faith naturally leads to a hopeful attitude about the future. If God is involved, how could everything not come out well in the end? With this thought in our hearts we can prepare sensibly for the future, without getting all bent out of shape about worst-case scenarios and pessimistic assessments.

The second area is how we seek a sense of control over our lives. We have the feeling that with the correct application of money and effort we can control all the important aspects of life. When that control fails, as it almost certainly will, it can leave us with a sense of helplessness. Pope Francis calls us to something different. He says that an important attitude of a Christian is openness to being surprised by God. Even in the midst of our difficulties, God acts, and sometimes in surprising ways.

I recently had a situation like this. I went to the doctor with a complaint, and his prescription was two weeks of rest; no going to work. My first reaction was "That's impossible. I have too much to do, too many responsibilities." But, after a time, I came to see God's hand in this giving me a surprise vacation that was just what I needed. God continually provides us with surprises big and small, but we will not recognize them as such unless we are willing to let go of some of our attempts at control over our lives and allow God to surprise us by his love.

The third item to be considered is how we place a value on the things of this world, and how we find joy. If we follow the world's way of looking at things we will value the car in our driveway not for how it gets us where we need to go, but for how much it cost. We may find joy in some new gizmo, but that joy will fade as soon as there is a newer, more fancy model on offer.

Pope Francis wants us to live joyfully, but to find our life's joy in a much more sturdy place: here at this table. Every Christian can tap into a deep sense of joy from being a companion of Jesus and Mary and all the saints. That knowledge of God's abiding love is something that no natural disaster or changing fad can ever take away from us.

Pope Francis offers us these three attitudes: Hopefulness, openness to God's many surprises, and a deep sense of joy, all arising from the core of our Christian faith. Those three are the change of heart that are an antidote to the false promises of wealth. They are three things that we can depend on as we face a constantly changing world.

20th Sunday in Ordinary Time, Aug. 18, 2013:

LONG-TERM PEACE

(Jer 38:4-6,8-10; Heb 12:1-4; Lk 12:49-53)

In chapter one of Luke's gospel, Zechariah, the father of John the Baptist, says this about Jesus: "In the tender compassion of our God, the dawn from on high will break upon us, to shine on those who dwell in darkness and the shadow of death, and to guide our feet into the way of peace." In chapter two, the angels announce Jesus' birth by singing "Glory to God in the highest, and on earth, peace on those on whom his favor rests." Then, in almost every chapter that follows those first two, Jesus shows through his gentleness and his compassion and his healing touch exactly what that peaceful kingdom will be like. That is, until we get to chapter twelve, which we read from today. In the verses we just heard, Jesus says that he has come to light a fire on the earth, and he explicitly denies that he has come to establish peace. He says instead that soon many households will be divided in response to his message.

Our challenge as people who take every verse of the Bible seriously is to somehow fit together today's verses with the broad sweep of the gospels which clearly show the peaceful nature of Jesus. Our goal is to integrate both images of Jesus so that we can create a fuller picture of Jesus' mission on earth than either one alone provides. This is not an easy task, but I would like to share with you three ideas that have helped me as I try to do this for myself.

The first idea turns on the meaning we give to Jesus' words that he has come to light a fire on the earth. Today, we might hear that word 'fire' in the context of what has been happening in the western states over this spring and summer. Whether they started by accident or by someone acting with a sick or evil intention, the fires that have blazed across the west have often raged completely out of control and created no end of misery and destruction. Brave people have worked tirelessly to minimize the damage, but still many innocent lives have been undone by these disasters.

Uncontrolled wildfire is *not* the notion of 'fire' that Saint Luke had in mind when he preserved these words of Jesus for us. We should think instead of the refiner's fire. This is a fire so hot that it can take a lump of unrefined ore and burn away all of the useless bits, leaving behind a flowing stream of pure gold or copper or iron. It is a fire which has a good purpose and is under the careful control of the one doing the smelting. In the gospel context, we are to think of ourselves as the ore that is submitted to the fire, and in our desire to be more pure and holy, that we welcome its cleansing heat. This kind of fire has a strong connection to the tongues of flame that descended on the disciples on Pentecost, and also to the sacrament of confirmation. In the sequence for Pentecost we invite the fire of the Holy Spirit to enter our lives to "Bend the stubborn heart and will./Melt the frozen, warm the chill". *That* is the kind of fire that Jesus was so eager to set alight on the earth.

Refocusing the poetical image of fire in today's verses is the first thought that can help to integrate these verses with the rest of the gospel. A second idea concerns Jesus' statement that he has not come to establish peace, but rather division, particularly divisions within families. We may find this image unsettling, but it is important to note that it would have been even more so to the first recipients of the gospel. In the time of Jesus, the extended family was a much more cohesive unit than it is today. One lived together with close relatives, and it was expected that the family would think and act as one. In that time, people did not aspire to think out moral and ethical issues for themselves. In this part of the gospel Jesus is actually quoting from the prophet Micah. Micah was painting a vivid warning for the king of Judah of the breakdown in the social order that would come about when the Assyrian army finished dismembering the kingdom of Israel and turned its attentions on Judah. So this is really startling rhetoric on Jesus' part; what he is saying is undoubtedly to be taken very seriously.

Here I think we need to say that Jesus is speaking from the anguish of his heart about an unavoidable consequence of his message of peace and reconciliation. It is only an apparent contradiction to say that the Good News of Jesus brings us peace in the long term, but may cause divisions in the short term. This is because the message of Jesus calls us to a change of heart, and change is always difficult. This is especially true when change is happening (or not happening) in those with whom we are in a loving relationship. Any change to an important relationship can become a source of anxiety.

The word of comfort to be found here is that this division within families is an unintended consequence and is going to be temporary. Eventually, the fire of the Holy Spirit will warm the chill of everyone whose heart is well disposed toward it, and what temporarily divided us will begin to unite us.

The third thought to keep in mind as we read today's gospel in the context of the rest of the Good News of Jesus is something that our reading does *not* say. That is, the reading does not say that disagreements that arise over the Good News must necessarily turn rancorous and lead to heated arguments and to the break up of the family. There is room to hope that if we approach these disagreements in the way that the rest of the gospel would counsel us to do, that we may preserve some level of peace within the family, and in society generally.

For example, many young people today are inspired by the social justice message that is part and parcel of the Good News of Jesus. They look at the world and rightly wonder why one hundred generations of Christians that came before them have not been able to do more to banish poverty and injustice from the world. They are naturally impatient with those of us old fogies who have made our compromises with life and are content to just write a check to Catholic Charities each year and say we have done our duty by the poor.

If we approach such a disagreement with a sincere belief in the good intentions of the other person, and with the love of God in our hearts, we will be able to find the patience to really listen to what the other person is saying and the disagreement will be disarmed of its potential for pulling the family apart. The key word here is patience: patience with the impetuous ideas of youth and patience with the lumbering thoughts of the older generation, and patience with the slowly evolving plan of God. So, I would like to end today with some sage advice about patience from Pierre Tielhard de Chardin, a thinker who certainly took the long view on life:

> *Above all, trust in the slow work of God. We are*
> *all quite naturally impatient in everything to*
> *reach the end without delay. We should like to*
> *skip the intermediate stages. We are impatient of*
> *being on the way to something unknown, some-*
> *thing new. And yet it is the law of all progress*
> *that it is made by passing through some stages of*
> *instability—and that it may take a very long time.*
> *And so I think it is with you; your ideas mature*
> *gradually—let them grow; let them shape them-*
> *selves, without undo haste ... Only God could say*
> *what this new spirit gradually forming within you*
> *will be. Give our Lord the benefit of believing that*
> *his hand is leading you, and accept the anxiety of*
> *feeling yourself in suspense and incomplete.*

Jesus came to guide our feet into the way of peace, and learning to accept the anxiety of feeling ourselves in suspense and incomplete will sure help us to avoid the rancorous divisions that so worry Jesus in today's gospel.

BECOMING A SAINT

(Amos 8:4-7; 1 Tim 2:1-8; Lk 16:1-13)

Thomas Merton, the Trappist monk and celebrated author, wrote a powerful autobiography of his early life, which he called "The Seven Storey Mountain", a reference to Dante's vision of climbing up through the seven circles of purgatory. In the book, Thomas shares with us a hard look at his life growing up. In one very moving part he describes the time when he first went away to college. He was living in England and had just graduated from an all-male boarding school with strict rules. At the advanced age of eighteen he thought himself an adult and the master of his own fate for the first time. His uncle was bank-rolling his education at Cambridge University, and was steering him toward a nice job in government. The world was at his feet.

Thomas made use of his new-found funds and his new-found freedoms to indulge himself in all the pleasures that were available to a Cambridge undergrad in the roaring twenties, and there were many. After a few months of this, however, he began to notice a curious thing: he was not happy. Indulging himself in every pleasure that came his way was making him feel more and more empty and isolated and depressed—worse than when he was at boarding school. He recognized this as a paradox, but had no clue how to change the situation. If doing what he *liked to do* did not make him happy, surely not doing those things could only make matters worse. He began to think that there was something wrong with him. But, knowing nothing else, he continued to go around with his gang of buddies running up bar bills for his uncle to pay, and he continued to get in trouble with the college authorities for his crazier escapades. Thomas knew something was wrong, but he didn't know how to make it right.

This experience of the young Thomas Merton illustrates very well what Jesus is talking about at the end of today's gospel, when he talks about "dishonest wealth". Money and the things that it can buy make promises to us that they cannot keep. They promise us instant happiness or a fix for our problems or popularity with the opposite sex, but that is all smoke and mirrors, with nothing real behind it. If we fall for such promises, all too soon we find ourselves a little poorer and with all the same problems we had when we started.

What Thomas Merton did not know about, at that point in his life, is the alternative that Jesus points out today: the "true wealth" of the love of God brought to us in the gospel. That true wealth can bring us happiness, though we may end up in the process doing lots of things we might not have chosen to do otherwise, like serving meals at a soup kitchen, or marching for the rights of immigrants or the unborn.

Keeping in mind the distinction between dishonest and true wealth can help to make sense of today's parable about the crafty steward. Admittedly, this is a very difficult parable to interpret. Exactly what is the steward being praised for? Scholars disagree. Maybe there are some things we don't know about how stewardship worked in Jesus' part of the world that would help us sort this out. Personally, I like to think that the steward used his own money to make up for the bills he discounted from his master's accounts, but that is pure speculation.

What we do know is that the master praises the man for his prudence. The steward knew true value and how to use it well. It is significant that we heard Jesus praise that same virtue in our Sunday gospel about a month ago. Then Jesus said that his followers should give away their possessions to the poor and receive treasure in heaven. He followed this up with a parable about stewardship, saying to be on guard and ready all the times for the Master's return. Later Peter asked Jesus whether this message was meant for the Apostles alone or all disciples. Jesus answered with a question "Who is the prudent steward?" Then he answered his own question by explaining that the prudent steward is the one who cares well for the treasures of the Master.

We are all called by God to that kind of stewardship. The things we have in this life are given to us as stewards, not owners. We need to use the things that come to us to do the Master's bidding, not our own. This is not always an easy task to accomplish. Dishonest wealth is a tool that can turn in our hand and end up doing what we did not mean it to do. But we will surely be on safe ground if we use our worldly wealth to lighten the burden of the needy as Jesus directed us to do.

We also have a certain amount of true wealth that has come our way: our faith, that is to say, our understanding of God's love and his place in our lives. Looking back, this was something that Thomas Merton felt was sorely lacking in his early life. We need to be good stewards of that wealth as well. This means receiving faith with joy, and cherishing and preserving it, and passing it on to others who would benefit from it.

Today we have a special opportunity to show our appreciation for some members of our parish who have answered the call to this kind of stewardship. I am referring to the teachers and helpers in our religious education program. They have stepped forward, not because they think they are more holy than the average person, but rather because they understand the value of our faith and want to make sure that this true wealth is passed on to the next generation. We should take time to thank them for this contribution to our parish and pray for them. May God grant success to the work of their hands!

All of the demands of good stewardship might sound like a heavy burden to carry, and it is true that it requires our careful attention, but it is not all that hard. Here again, the life of Thomas Merton has a lesson for us. This story comes from about six years after his experiences in Cambridge. Cast off by his uncle and living in New York, he was working on a graduate degree in literature. He had found the Catholic faith, but for him it was still something purely intellectual, and not yet down in the heart.

One time, he was walking with an older and wiser friend who asked him "what do you want to be?" Thomas replied that he wanted to be an author whose books were read and appreciated by many people. His friend shook his head and said "wrong answer, what you *should* want to be is a saint!" Thomas protested that he could never be a saint. That was much too hard and he wasn't cut out for it. Perhaps he answered in much the same way as we might. Just as we might be telling ourselves we could never be a truly prudent steward of all God's gifts. But Thomas' friend replied that it was the easiest thing in the world to be a saint. The only thing you have to do, is to want it. God will do the rest. How could God not lend his help to fulfill such a desire? I think there is some real truth there. If we make the act of will to be a good steward, God will show us the way. Opportunities to exercise prudent stewardship will fall in our laps, and because we want it so much, we will recognize them and act accordingly.

The necessary thing for us to do is to keep the desire to be a good steward burning brightly in our hearts. Perhaps this week we might pray about this, telling God that we *DO* want to be his prudent stewards and asking him to show us the way. This is a prayer that God will surely be quick to answer.

In today's parable we have one of those wonderfully strong female images that Luke's gospel is so famous for. I can just see that plucky little widow catching up with the unjust judge out on the street somewhere and going after him with her umbrella. "Hey you! When will you render my judgment?" poke, poke, poke. "Give me justice!" Whack, whack, whack.

This image is so entertaining that we might miss the fact that it is being offered to us today in service of a deep mystery: How does God answer the prayers of those in need?" Remember that the gospel begins by saying that we will receive a lesson about the necessity of persistence in prayer. Then, at the end of the gospel, Jesus tells us that God will not be like the unjust judge. He will answer our prayers quickly. There is a certain tension between these two statements, and I think probably that this is a tension that many of us may have experienced in our own lives. Not that we have been oppressed by a corrupt judge necessarily, but there may be more than a few of us here who feel we have been the victims of a more cosmic kind of injustice. I am referring to the random injustice of a serious illness, either our own or that of a loved one. I know I felt that way when my father was dying of Alzheimer's disease.

It seemed incredibly unfair how that disease robbed my parents of their retirement dreams, and me and my sisters of our father's care and guidance. I was living too far away to be of much practical assistance during the ten years that he lived with Alzheimer's, but I prayed about the problem a lot. I prayed that he might be miraculously cured. I prayed that some scientist might find a drug that would arrest his symptoms. I prayed that he might at least regain the ability to recognize my mother who was beside him every step of the way. But none of those prayers were answered in any way that I could perceive. So what went wrong? Where was God's promise of a speedy response?

It is true that today's gospel talks specifically about prayers for justice, but elsewhere the discussion is more general. Near the end of Mark's gospel, for example, Jesus talks about moving mountains with prayer. What he says is difficult to translate precisely into English, but the intent seems to be that if you truly believe that what you are praying for has already happened, then it will be so (Mk 11:23). This is an important promise, but also a difficult one. I am imperfect. My belief is imperfect and my prayers are imperfect. If I have to wait until my belief is perfect before God will answer my prayers, I may as well give up now.

I take more comfort from an earlier place in Mark's gospel in which a distraught father brings his son to the Apostles for healing, but they can't do it. They bring the pair to Jesus, and the man asks Jesus "Please heal my son, if you can." "If you can?", Jesus responds "All things are possible for those who have faith!" The man answers "I do believe. Help my unbelief" (Mk 9:24), and his son is cured. That is a prayer I can say with all sincerity: "Lord, I do believe. Help my unbelief".

I also take comfort from the way Saint Paul talks about prayer in his letter to the Romans. He says flat out that we do not know how to pray as we ought, but the Holy Spirit takes the "inexpressible groanings of our souls" and turns them into prayers acceptable to God (Rom 8:26). What I hear in these two selections is that our prayers of petition are a part of our greater relationship with God. Jesus is there to help our unbelief. The Holy Spirit is there to interpret our confused desires. God the Father knows our needs and responds.

Exactly how this applies to the situation with my father is unclear, but perhaps it would have been better if I had not always been telling God what to do in my prayers, and instead sometimes *asked* him what to do. If I had been able to pray "Lord, what do you want me to do with this pain and frustration that I feel?" I might have been in a better position to hear what God had to say to me during those difficult years.

This is one of the great mysteries of prayer: God accepts our imperfect prayers and in his great kindness, he gives us the thing we should have been praying for in the first place. There is another great mystery in prayer that I want to also consider today and that is that God often invites us to be the answer to someone else's prayer. God does not always answer prayers with miracles; more commonly he sends one good person to help another.

If we keep our eyes and ears open we will find many such opportunities. When we notice someone in need, we need not respond with grand words of philosophy or deep theological insights. More likely what will be needed is a hug, or a wet washcloth, or ten games of gin rummy, or a chapter of "Winnie the Pooh," or a phone message that says "I haven't seen you around for a while. How are you?" There are a million different ways that God is calling on each of us to be his answer to someone's fervent prayer, and we should try to master as many of those techniques as possible. We should all be on the lookout for opportunities to deliver God's loving assistance to others, for in doing so we prove true the words of today's gospel—the Good News that God will not delay in answering the prayers of those who call upon his name.

We have a special opportunity to act on this message at today's mass since this is World Mission Sunday. By making a donation today we can help to answer the prayer of someone living far away, someone we will probably never meet this side of heaven. It might be a mother who has no food to give her children, or a frustrated father who cannot find work, or perhaps a teenager who does not know how to pray, but who has an empty space inside him that only God can fill. All these things are being accomplished every day by the Pontifical Mission Society which will receive the money we give today.

Now it may seem like we get this same appeal every year and nothing seems to change. But this is where persistence is a great virtue. I have seen for myself what just a small part of this money has done in the lives of some beautiful little orphans living in Bolivia, and I am constantly amazed at how a small amount of money here can do great things in the lives of people living in the third world. So, I ask you to think about how you want to respond to the World Mission Sunday appeal today.

The wonderful thing about these two great mysteries of prayer we have been talking about this morning is that they reinforce one another. The more we respond to God's invitation to be his answer to the prayers of others, the deeper our relationship with him becomes. And the deeper our relationship with God becomes, the better our prayers of petition become, as they become ever more closely aligned with God's will. This is something we might meditate about this week, seeking to understand better our own place within these great mysteries.

And when times get tough and our prayer seems to be going nowhere, as it will surely do for all of us at some point, may we all remember the example of persistence in that plucky little widow with her umbrella, and may we make good use of the prayer of the distraught father who cried out to Jesus "Lord, I do believe. Help my unbelief."

4th Sunday of Advent, Dec. 22, 2013:
THE VIRTUES OF SAINT JOSEPH

(Is 7, 10-14; Rom 1, 1-7; Mt 1, 18-24)

Our gospels provide us with two different accounts of the events leading up to the birth of Jesus. One comes from Luke's gospel, which we have read from often in the preceding year. This gospel tells the story of Jesus' birth from the perspective of Mary. For example, in this gospel we have the story of the Angel Gabriel visiting Mary, and the story of Mary vising her kinswoman Elizabeth.

The other account that has come down to us is in Matthew's gospel, which we will be hearing from often in the coming year. Matthew's gospel does not recount for us either of those two stories featuring Mary. Rather, Matthew's gospel tells stories featuring Joseph. The story we hear today is about Joseph receiving his own visitation from an angel in a dream, and there are other stories in which Joseph is guided in dreams to take his family into Egypt for safety, and then later to lead the family back to settle in Nazareth in the Galilee.

Since I take Saint Joseph as my patron saint, I am happy to have him step out of the shadows just a bit this Advent, so that he can be an example to all of us about how to live a virtuous life. I would like to share with you three important virtues that Saint Joseph displays in the gospel, so that we can all follow his example.

The first virtue that I would like to consider this morning is Saint Joseph's great trust in God. As our gospel says, he listened to the words of the angel in his dream and did as the angel commanded. This required him to set aside the sensible decision he had already made, and follow God's path instead.

It is important to keep the dream visit by the angel in perspective. We might think to ourselves that we would easily be able to trust in God's word if only it were delivered to us by an angel. But there is more to it than that. First of all, Joseph had to be open to hearing the words of the angel. Undoubtedly he felt torn and undecided about the delicate problem that was before him. He must have prayed to God often as he considered his alternatives, asking for guidance. These prayers were part of his trusting relationship with God built up over the years, and they prepared him to receive the angel's words. When he woke up, they also helped him to discern that the message truly came from God and was not just a wish-fulfilling dream on his part.

The second thing to think about concerning the angel's words is that the angel's explanation of why he was to accept Mary into his home would have been hard for Joseph to understand. It is only through our many hearings of these stories in the context of what followed that we can become comfortable with the idea of God's spirit overshadowing Mary and producing a child. Furthermore, the command to take Mary into his house was certainly understandable, but was also a bit short on the details. Exactly what was he supposed to tell his neighbors? How would he deal with the skepticism of his close relatives about this wonderful event? He had to trust that God would provide good answers to all of those questions when the need arose. At the moment of decision, he had to make his choice in great uncertainty about the future, trusting in God's loving kindness.

We too often face times when we feel uncertain about the way ahead, and we can learn from Saint Joseph to approach such situations with meditation and prayer and openness to God's guidance, however that may come to us. We will probably not be in possession of all the facts when the moment for decision comes, and we need to trust that God has our best interest at heart and will lead us in the way we need to go. A prayer to Saint Joseph when we find ourselves in that sort of a situation will surely help.

A second important virtue that Saint Joseph displays in Matthew's gospel is courage. His trust in God did not lead him to passivity, assuming that God would take care of all contingencies without his lifting a finger for himself. Think about what it must have been like when the angel told him to flee with his wife and young child into Egypt.

It is most likely that, prior to that time, Joseph had never been more than fifty miles from his birthplace. Egypt was probably little more than an exotic name to him, laden with ideas taken from the story of Moses and the Exodus. Those impressions would be of little help in the real Egypt of his own day. The language was strange; the customs were strange. Undoubtedly the responsibility of being husband, father and protector of his family weighed heavily on his mind. It required great courage to pull up stakes and head for the horizon under those circumstances.

Often the circumstances of our lives require courage on our part. Even if we get through the phase of meditation and prayer and feel we know what God wants us to do in a difficult situation, we still have to do it. We might be called to act to protect one of our loved ones, or we might be called to strike out on a new path in our lives, which could feel as strange as moving to Egypt on short notice. Here too, we can pray to Saint Joseph for help. He can lend us some of his great courage, and go with us on our journey, wherever it may take us.

The third virtue of Saint Joseph that would be good for us to meditate on this Advent is his great love. His trusting in the word of God and his courage in carrying out all that the angel's instructions were in the service of his love for Mary and for Jesus. Those other virtues fed into this greatest of virtues.

Next week, on the feast of the Holy Family, we will be hearing a beautiful reading from Saint Paul's letter to the Colossians. In it he provides a whole litany of virtues that serve to build up our relationships with others. It is a list we would all do well to study. And then he adds this: "and over all these virtues put on love, that is, the bond of perfection." This is an important insight. The virtue of love perfects the rest and keeps them on the right track. Here too we can pray to Saint Joseph for help.

In all these things, our prayers to Saint Joseph can be simple and direct. But in this day of celebration, I would like to finish with a beautiful prayer to Saint Joseph written by Kathy Sherman, a member of the Sisters of Saint Joseph. This prayer invites Saint Joseph to teach us as he taught Jesus.

Baptism of the Lord, Jan. 12, 2014:

LIVING WATERS

(Is 42, 1-4. 6-7; Acts 10, 34-38; Mt 3, 13-17)

Some years ago, I had a discussion with the Saint Paul's Youth Group about Baptism, and I asked them what practical difference it made in their lives that they had were baptized Christians. After some reflection, they came up with some really good ideas. Here is one. Princeton High requires a service project for graduation, and some kids treat it as a joke. But the kids in the youth group, based on their faith grounded in Baptism, found they couldn't do that. They respected the call to service and felt the need to make their service projects be of real help to others.

I think this is a great example of the influence that our baptism continues to have on us throughout our lives. In order to understand this powerful sacrament better, I would like to explore with you the origins of the sacrament in John's baptism.

John's baptism was a symbolic action. That is, it involved physical things and particular actions, but it had a meaning that extended beyond the physical. Submersion in the waters of the Jordan represented a washing away of sin and inextricably it also represented a submission to God's will. That is what John's words about repentance were all about. The Greek word used in the gospels for repentance means a fundamental reorientation of heart and mind. All of that deep meaning could be packed into the simple action of John's baptism because of the revered place that water held in the life of the Jewish people.

The Jewish people understood water as a gift sent by God to do his will, namely to bring life to the land. They had a special reverence for water which appeared to be moving of its own accord. They called it "living water". That might refer to rain, or a rolling river, or a spring welling up from the ground. They believed such water to be specially endowed with God's life-giving power.

Their catechism for this belief was the land itself. The northern part of the land of Israel, the Galilee, was well supplied with rain. It was a good place for farming, and produced an abundance of grains and grapes and olives. However the further south you went the sparser the rains became, until by the time you reached Jerusalem, almost all of the rain fell on the western plains. To the east and south of Jerusalem lay the Judean desert. This was not a desert of sand dunes, but rather it was a hard-scrabble place consisting mostly of rocks, rocks and more rocks. What a potent sign this was of what happened when God's life-giving gift was absent.

A similar lesson could be learned from observing the river Jordan. Arising in a series of springs and waterfalls in the foothills of Mount Hermon in the north, the river refreshed the Sea of Galilee, and then rushed south to its endpoint, which we, with good reason, call the Dead Sea. At that terminus nothing grew, but until the river got that far south and stopped, it supported trees and greenery along its banks.

As we look at the river Jordan today, it does not seem very impressive, but that is because much of its waters are being siphoned off for agriculture. In ancient times it was apparently a strong river. There is a story from the Exodus about the time when the tribes were finally ready to cross the Jordan into the Promised Land, but they arrived in the springtime and the river was in flood stage and overflowing its banks. Once they got to the river and saw what they were up against, Joshua gave the people three days to prepare to cross over, so they must have been quite concerned about the strong currents. In the end, God intervened and told Joshua to have some of the Levites carry the Ark of the Covenant into the midst of the river, and miraculously as soon as their feet touched the water, the river Jordan turned back on itself and allowed the people to cross on dry land. What a wonderful sign that was. Even the powerful waters of the Jordan acted in accord with God's will.

Now at this point we might begin to think that the beliefs of that long ago time were very quaint, while we have knowledge of physics, hydrology and meteorology. Our scientists can tell us a lot about the behavior of water without any reference to God. They might even explain the Joshua story by supposing that there was a landslide upstream that blocked the river for a time. Such things did happen. But it is a mistake to contrast scientific explanations and religious ones. Our science does not tell us anything about the meaning people find in water, and how it impacts their emotional and spiritual lives. It is that deeper level of meaning that our religion hopes to provide.

So, with that understanding of the place of water in the faith and culture of the Jewish people, let's try to imagine what it would have been like to go out from Jerusalem to see John at the Jordan. The first step would have been to take the road that went from Jerusalem down to Jericho through the northern reaches of the Judean desert. This 12-mile trip would take the better part of a day. The way went steeply down, but it was an important trade route and the road was probably kept in fairly good repair. Even so, there would have been many places where you would have had to watch your step carefully to avoid turning an ankle. As you finally reached bottom, at the oasis of Jericho, the scenery would change dramatically. There would be trees and bushes and birds and the smell of life all around you. We don't know exactly where John did his baptizing, but our best guess is that you would still have had a hot 6-mile walk from there to the tree-lined river bank where John preached.

As the people listened and thought about their lives, many might have recognized that their current life was as dry and lifeless as the wasteland they had just crossed, and they would have wanted deeply to have God transform their lives.

There is a famous renaissance painting of John baptizing Jesus. In it, John and Jesus stand ankle deep in a pool of water so crystal clear that you have to look carefully to see that there is any water there at all. This a beautiful devotional meditation on the sacrament of baptism, but probably not a realistic portrayal of what John's baptism was actually like. Rather we should think of him standing up to his waist in a strong current, ready to immerse repentant people in that powerful flowing water. After all, the word baptism originally meant to wash by immersion.

Imagine yourself standing on the riverbank. You know that to step out into that living water is to make a commitment to repent, that is, to submit your will to God's will. The power of the river shows that this is not a trivial commitment. After baptism, you are no longer in complete control of your life, any more than you can control the river. When John helps you go down under the water you feel God's power swirling around your whole body, tugging and pulling at every part. When you go in, you know who you are, but who exactly will you be when you come out? It is exciting and a bit scary to imagine what God might lead you to. Imagine your joy if you could trust God well enough to overcome your natural reservations and take that plunge.

Now how about Jesus? Would he want to participate in such a powerful symbolic action? I think he would be happy for the opportunity. His whole life was in grand submission to God's will, beginning even with his birth. Truly this symbolic action at the beginning of his public ministry "fulfilled all righteousness". It was a public proclamation of who he was, and it was given a seal of approval by God the Father through the appearance of the Holy Spirit.

Finally, how about us? Our baptismal ceremony is very different from John's, but our baptism does still involve a rejection of sin and a commitment to allow ourselves to be guided by God's will. This week we might follow the lead of our teenage prophets and recommit ourselves to that calling, so that the blessings promised by the prophet Jeremiah might also apply to us:

> *Blessed is the man who trusts in the Lord,*
> *Whose hope is in the Lord.*
> *He is like a tree planted beside the waters*
> *That stretches out its roots to the stream.*
> *It fears not the heat when it comes,*
> *Its leaves stay green;*
> *In the year of drought it shows no distress*
> *But still bears fruit. (Jer 17:7-8)*

Part B: HOMILIES DELIVERED *in* SPANISH

Many thanks to my daughters, Beth and Anna, for their many corrections of their Father's Spanish, and indeed for translating whole-sale for him when schedules were tight.

.

La Solemnidad de Santa María, Madre de Dios, 1 Enero 2008

(Núm: 6:22-27; Gál 4:4-7; Le 2:16-21)

Celebramos hoy el tercero de cuatro días que conmemoran el nacimiento de Jesús. Empezamos con la Natividad del Señor. Ayer, celebramos la fiesta de la Sagrada Familia. Hoy celebramos la fiesta de María, Madre de Dios, y el siguiente domingo celebraremos la fiesta de la Epifanía del Señor, cuando Jesús se dio a conocer a los reyes magos y también a todos nosotros. Este tiempo de navidad esta lleno de alegría porque hay cuatro días de fiesta durante solo doce días. Cada uno de estos días nos da una perspectiva ligeramente diferente del misterio maravilloso en el cual Dios vino a vivir con nosotros como bebe.

Es algo muy especial que Dios escogió estar con nosotros, como un niño de una familia de la clase trabajadora, no como un rey entre la gente rica y poderosa, ni como un general a la cabeza de un ejercito. La sagrada familia nos da un ejemplo para nuestra vida, y para nuestra familia. Por ejemplo, hoy en la lectura del evangelio, oímos que María guardaba los recuerdos de su familia en su corazón. Esto nos hace recordar que las historias de nuestra vida son también importantes. Debemos valorarlas y compartirlas con nuestra familia. Pienso que es muy importante que los nietos conozcan los cuentos de sus abuelos. Deben conocer todo sobre como vivían sus abuelos, los problemas que tenían, y como ellos pudieron resolverlos. Entonces, estarán orgullosos de su herencia, y sabrán resolver mejor sus propias dificultades.

Estos días de celebración son mas que una fuente de buenos ejemplos. San Pablo nos dice que hay mucho que conmemorar aquí. El nos dice hoy que nosotros somos niños adoptivos de Dios—somos también parte de la familia de Dios. Cuando yo pienso en eso, inmediatamente digo "no es posible—no soy digno de esto," y tal vez tu piensas lo mismo. Es verdad que no merecemos este regalo tan grande. Nadie lo merece. Pero Dios nos ama tanto que nos invita a una relación especial con Él mismo. Es parte de la alegría de la navidad que Él nos llame hijos. Es buena idea reflexionar sobre Jesús como nuestro hermano y María, Madre de Dios, como nuestra madre. Cuando estamos lejos de nuestra mamá, o después de su muerte, todavía nos queda una madre que puede hablar con nosotros en la oración y consolarnos en nuestra vida.

En la lectura de san Pablo hay aun mas regocijo. Nos dice que porque somos sus hijos de Dios recibiremos una herencia de el. Es una idea maravillosa considerar que todo valores de Dios algún día serán nuestros.

Hace unas semanas buscaba algo en una caja vieja en mi casa y encontré una moneda que mi abuelo me dio cuando yo era niño. Es un dólar en moneda de plata, y es del ano mil-novecientos veintitrés. Es bastante grande, y recuerdo que pesaba mucho en mi mano pequeña. Aunque era muy joven, sabia que era mas importante que las monedas pequeñas con que compraba leche y pan para mi familia. Mi madre me dijo que lo guardara bien, y estoy muy feliz de haberlo hecho, porque ahora cuando lo tomo, me lleno de recuerdos de mi abuelo, y siento que el esta mas cerca de mi.

La herencia de Dios, nuestro Padre, es algo así. Es mas preciosa que las cosas ordinarias. La promesa que somos herederos por la voluntad de Dios significa que tendremos una vida en el cielo con Él, después de la muerte. Esto es muy importante, pero pienso yo que no es solo algo que recibiremos en el futuro, sino también lo que obtenemos de Dios hoy.

Hay muchas maneras en que podemos disfrutar de nuestra herencia aquí en la tierra, y les contare tres. Oímos que María mantenía las historias de su familia en su corazón. La familia de Dios ha estado guardando sus historias durante muchas generaciones, y hoy las tenemos en la Biblia. Esta colección de historias es nuestro recuerdo precioso de todo lo que Dios ha hecho por nosotros. Debemos leer mucho las historias de la Biblia para consolarnos. Cuando lo hacemos, Dios pareciera mas cerca de nosotros, como lo esta mi abuelo cuando tomo la moneda que me dio hace muchos anos.

La segunda parte de nuestra herencia de Dios son los doce frutos del Espíritu Santo. Cuando nuestra vida esta llena del Espíritu Santo, estos frutos mejoran nuestra vida. Los tres primeros frutos son: el amor, el gozo, y la paz; luego están paciencia, bondad y generosidad. Después viene la fidelidad, la gentileza y la disciplina. Y por ultimo, la modestia, la moderación y la castidad. Cada uno de estos frutos maravillosos es como una pequeña parte del cielo que podemos disfrutar aquí y ahora. Mejoran nuestra vida en todas las situaciones. Piensa solo en uno de estos, por ejemplo, la gentileza. La vida puede ser bastante difícil, pero cuando alguien que amamos nos trata con gentileza es tan bueno como un toque del cielo. Cuando escogemos tratar con gentileza a los que encontramos, somos mas parecidos al bebe manso que vemos en el pesebre.

La tercera parte de nuestra herencia de Dios es los sacramentos que tenemos aquí en la comunidad de fe. En la Eucaristía, Dios nos da el pan para nuestro camino. Recibimos la fuerza que necesitamos para la semana. El sacramento de la confesión nos ayuda a vencer los obstáculos en la vida que nos separan de Dios, y que nos dificulta sentir el amor y la paz y la alegría que dios quiere que engamos. Recibimos estos sacramentos dentro de una comunidad de gente que también quiere tener una vida llena del Espíritu Santo, y que también nos da fuerza. Cuando conocemos sus historias de fe, nos ayuda a seguir adelante.

Continuemos con la misa, recordando con alegría que somos hijos de Dios, y que tenemos una herencia valiosa que puede aquí y ahora mejorar nuestra vida. Que resolvamos tener una vida llena de la presencia de Dios, para que podamos disfrutar los frutos del Espíritu Santo, incluyendo la paz, el amor y el gozo.

Que tengan un ano nuevo lleno de salud, prosperidad y felicidad, y que esté lleno de las bendiciones de Dios.

La Solemnidad de Santa María, Madre de Dios, 1 Enero 2009

(Núm: 6:22-27; Gál 4:4-7; Le 2:16-21)

Hoy Celebramos una fiesta muy importante. Honramos a la virgen María y le damos el titulo de "Madre de Dios". Este nombre señala un gran misterio. María era una creatura de Dios, entonces ¿Cómo es posible que ella dio a luz al mismo Dios? No lo entendemos, pero creemos que eso fue lo que exactamente pasó. Es bueno para nosotros que pensemos en lo que estamos celebrando hoy y que meditemos lo que este misterio nos muestra. Hay dos razones para hacer esto: la primera es que nos conduce más cerca de conocer el misterio de quien es Jesús, y la segunda, nos conduce más cerca del mundo que tanto ama Jesús.

Primero, consideremos quien es Jesús. Creemos que Jesús es el Dios verdadero. Es una parte de la Santísima Trinidad. Porque es Dios, es una parte importante en la creación del Universo. Igualmente, creemos que Jesús fue un hombre verdadero. Nació y murió. Era una persona como nosotros en todas las cosas, excepto en los pecados. No entendemos como es posible que las dos naturalezas puedan coexistir en una persona, pero estamos seguros que es la verdad. Esta seguridad se confirma cuando leemos la biblia, y en nuestras propias experiencias de Dios y Jesús en la vida.

La contribución más importante de la fiesta de hoy es para entender mas bien un aspecto de este gran misterio. Nunca ha existido un tiempo en que Jesús fuera hombre y no fuera Dios. Hace muchos años, unas personas pensaban que Jesús nació hombre, y que llegó a ser Dios por su gran bondad y por los designios de Dios. La Iglesia ni cree, ni enseña eso. Durante toda su vida en la tierra, Jesús era Dios y también hombre. Era Dios y hombre cuando nos enseñaba a llamar a Dios, nuestro Padre. Era Dios y hombre cuando curaba a los enfermos. Era Dios y hombre cuando murió en la cruz. Aprendemos por la fiesta de hoy que era Dios y hombre aun cuando estaba en el seno materno de su madre, la Virgen. Apreciamos la fiesta que celebramos hoy, porque ésta nos ayuda a entender más profundamente el misterio de la naturaleza de Jesús.

Hay otro aspecto de la fiesta muy importante. Esta fiesta nos puede llevar más cerca del mundo que Jesús ama tanto. Jesús nació solo una vez, por el poder del Espíritu Santo en la vida de la virgen María. Pero cuando nos comportamos como Jesús, podemos sentir la presencia de Jesús en el mundo casi como si hubiera nacido otra vez. Decimos que una madre "da a luz" a su hijo. Me gusta mucho esta frase. ¿ De qué manera podemos "dar a luz" hoy a Jesús en el mundo?

Una oportunidad la encontramos en nuestras familias. Jesús siempre aceptaba a las personas como eran. El amaba a todos: a los santos y a los pecadores, a los enfermos y a los sanos. Cuando aceptamos a nuestros parientes y los amamos con todas sus virtudes y defectos, nos comportamos como Jesús.

También, podemos dar a luz a Jesús en nuestro campo de trabajo o escuela. Cuando las cosas se hacen difíciles en nuestro trabajo, hay enfado, temor o envidia, podemos tratar de recordar la paz que encontramos aquí en este templo. Es posible que podamos compartir un poco de esto con nuestros compañeros, de la misma manera que Jesús lo haría.

Así como Jesús estaba presente hace muchos años, Jesús quiere estar presente en el mundo hoy. Somos privilegiados en ayudarlo a hacer esto, como fue privilegiada su madre.

Por el Monseñor Nolan, y el Padre René, y mis hermanos diáconos aquí en la parroquia, espero que ustedes tengan un año nuevo lleno de paz y alegría. Espero que tengan un año en que entiendan más y mejor los grandes misterios de Dios, y en el cual Jesús sea realmente dado a luz en nuestras vidas.

(Is 60: 1–6; Ef 3: 2–3. 5–6; Mt 2: 1–12)

Hoy celebramos la cuarta y última fiesta de las Navidades. Empezamos con el Nacimiento de Jesús, luego celebramos la fiesta de la Sagrada Familia y la fiesta de María, la Madre de Dios. Hoy terminamos este tiempo con la Epifanía del Señor.

En el Evangelio, escuchamos la historia de los Reyes Magos de Oriente, que visitaron al Niño Jesús. El titulo "mago" indica una persona llena de sabiduría. Estas personas usaban su sabiduría en astronomía para encontrar al Señor. Caminaron desde muy lejos para verlo y le llevaron al Niño regalos de oro, incienso y mirra.

Tenemos dos magos aquí ahora. El otro se queda atrás. Pienso que este en el aeropuerto de Newark, pero no estoy seguro.

Para la Iglesia, los regalos de los magos representan tres papeles que hace Jesús en nuestra vida. El regalo de oro representa a Jesús como rey. El incienso representa a Jesús como sacerdote. Y la mirra representa a Jesús como profeta. Cuando reconocemos que Jesús es el rey en nuestra vida, también nosotros le damos un regalo de oro. Igualmente, le damos regalos de incienso y mirra, cuando reconocemos que Jesús es nuestro sacerdote y profeta.

¿De que manera podemos reconocer que Jesús es nuestro rey? El rey da la ley y enseña a la gente como debe comportarse. Nuestro rey, Jesús, hace lo mismo. Por ejemplo, el rey Jesús nos dice que necesitamos vivir en paz con nuestros hermanos. Un aspecto muy difícil de esto es que necesitamos perdonar a los que nos ofenden. Y no solo una vez, sino muchas veces. El Señor dijo a San Pedro que debemos estar dispuestos a perdonar a nuestros hermanos setenta veces siete, si es necesario.

Esto no es fácil para mí. En particular, si alguien hiere a un miembro de mi familia, me será difícil perdonarle. Recuerdo una vez en que mi madre me contó sobre una situación hace muchos años en que otra persona que conocía bien le hizo algo que la hirió a mi madre. Mi madre le perdonó, pero yo no pude hacerlo por un largo tiempo. Poco a poco trataba de imitar el buen ejemplo de mi madre. El perdón es muy precioso—mas que mucho oro. Cuando perdonamos a nuestros hermanos, le damos a Jesús un regalo apropiado para un rey.

Y ¿de que manera podemos reconocer que Jesús es nuestro sacerdote? En la carta a los Hebreos, se dice que Jesús es el sumo sacerdote, que intercederá ante Dios por nosotros. Pero un sacerdote necesita un templo, y el templo que Jesús desea sobre todo es nuestro corazón. Amamos a Jesús y queremos darle nuestro corazón por templo, pero esto también es un regalo muy caro. Jesús no puede quedarse en un sitio lleno de ídolos. Por ejemplo, a veces el dinero llega a ser como un ídolo en nuestra vida. Pensamos solo en ello. Claro, tenemos necesidades, y necesitamos un poco de dinero para comprar lo que nos hace falta. Pero, queremos hacer de nuestro corazón un templo bonito para Jesús. Por eso, necesitamos quitar de nuestro corazón el ídolo del dinero.

También, queremos darle a Jesús un sitio que es limpio y ordenado. San Pablo nos dijo que nuestro cuerpo es un templo del Dios vivo, y por eso, necesitamos purificarnos de toda mancha del cuerpo y del espíritu. Cuando tratamos de purificar nuestras vidas de todos los males para preparar un sitio para Jesús, le damos a Jesús un regalo de incienso de olor muy agradable.

El tercero regalo de los magos es el de mirra. Mirra es una mezcla de especias de rico olor, y se usan para preparar el cuerpo para el entierro. ¡No es un regalo usual para un niño recién nacido! Pero, para un profeta, es apropiado y necesario. El sacerdote habla a Dios por nosotros. El profeta habla a nosotros por Dios. A veces, sus palabras nos dan consuelo y alegría. Otras veces, sus palabras nos da una crítica, y nos muestran que necesitamos cambiar la vida. No hay mucha gente que les guste esto. Muchos de los profetas fueron eliminados por la gente que no querían escuchar sus palabras duras. Cuando Jesús expulsó a los vendedores del templo, hizo el papel del profeta, y mucha gente se enojó.

Cuando escuchamos todas las palabras de Jesús, no solamente las palabras dulces y suaves, le aceptamos como profeta. Este también es un regalo muy caro, porque cambiar es siempre difícil. No nos gusta la crítica. Pero, es posible oír el amor de Dios en las palabras del profeta, aunque parecen duras al principio. Si Dios no nos amaba, no nos corregiría.

Hace unos pocos años, mi hija tenía un trabajo temporal en el que necesitaba ingresar información a un archivo de datos que tenia muchas reglas muy complicadas y específicas. Un día, se dio cuenta que su jefe estaba corrigiendo los datos que ella entraba, sin explicarle qué faltaba en su trabajo. A mi hija no le gustó esta situación. Le parecía que su jefe no confiaba en ella. Quería mejorar su trabajo, pero sin las críticas de su jefe, era imposible. Nosotros queremos ser Cristianos mejores, pero sin las críticas del Señor, no sabemos qué es lo que necesitamos hacer. Jesús espera que nosotros aceptemos su crítica de esta manera. Cuando hacemos esto, le damos un regalo de muy grato olor.

El evangelio nos invita hoy a darle a Jesús regalos muy preciosos. ¿Cuál es el más difícil para usted? Podemos tratar en la próxima semana de pensar en esta pregunta. Y también pensamos cuál regalo queremos darle a Jesús en el año nuevo. Jesús entiende que los regalos que le damos son muy caros para nosotros, y Él los recibirá con mucha alegría.

El Sexto Domingo de Pascua, 13 Mayo 2012

(He 10: 25-26,34-35,44-48; 1 Jn 4: 7-10; Jn 15: 9-17)

Hay una canción de Mercedes Sosa que es muy bonita y también un poco triste. Se llama "Todo Cambia". En esta canción, la cantante enumera numerosas cosas de este mundo que cambian: el follaje de las arboles, el clima, un caminante en su camino. Cosas superficiales cambian, y cosas profundas. Nosotros cambiamos también. Crecemos y poco después nos envejecemos.

Al final de la canción, la cantante cuenta una sola cosa que no cambia. Dice

> *"No cambia mi amor*
> *Por más lejos que me encuentre*
> *Ni el recuerdo ni el dolor*
> *De mi pueblo y de mi gente."*

Su amor para la familia, el pueblo y la patria no cambia jamás. Sus palabras son bonitas y llenas de fuerza.

Pienso en esta canción cuando escucho el Evangelio de hoy. Durante algunas semanas hemos escuchado las palabras de Jesús de la noche antes de su pasión y muerte. El Señor sabía que el mundo de los Apóstoles pronto iba a cambiar, y de manera profunda. Por eso, les enseñaba la importancia de agarrarse bien de la única cosa que no cambia: el Amor de Dios, diciéndoles: "Como el Padre me ama, así los amo yo. Permanezcan en mi amor."

El ejemplo de Jesús y de sus Apóstoles nos muestra la manera en que debemos responder a los cambios difíciles en nuestra vida. A pesar de sus sentimientos de miedo o de enojo, ellos siempre respondían con amor, y nosotros debemos hacer lo mismo. Si nuestra salud se debilita, o si hay problemas en nuestra familia, o si nuestro trabajo se pone difícil, debemos imitar a Jesús y a los santos, y responder con amor. De esta manera podemos permanecer en el amor de Dios. Pero esto no es muy fácil, y podríamos decir que Jesús y sus discípulos, y muchos de los santos, vivían en tiempos lejanos que no se comparan con nuestros tiempos y, además, ni los conocemos personalmente.

Afortunadamente, tenemos otros ejemplos más cerca, personas que sí hemos visto y con quienes compartimos nuestra vida cotidiana. Hoy celebramos el Día de la Madre, y las madres de todo el mundo son famosas por su amor que supera toda dificultad y se mantiene fiel a pesar de todo. Cuando nos encontramos con una persona difícil en nuestro diario caminar, antes de responderles, debemos hacer una pausa y preguntarnos: "¿Qué quisiera la madre de esta persona que haga yo por ella?" Posiblemente la persona necesita corrección, pero una buena madre le corregiría con amor. Posiblemente la persona necesita ayuda, y una buena madre le ayudaría con amor. Si podemos imitar este tipo de amor maternal, estaremos seguros de que amamos a los demás como Dios nos ama, porque Dios nos ama como una buena madre.

Jesús nos dice en el Evangelio que ya no somos sus siervos, sino sus amigos, porque todo lo que su Padre le ha dado a conocer nos ha revelado a nosotros. Esto nos permite entender lo que Dios quiere para cada uno de nosotros: que lleguemos un día a estar con Él en el cielo. Quizá somos conscientes de esto en los acontecimientos grandes de nuestras vidas, en los cuales podemos palpar fácilmente el Amor del Padre y su plan para nuestra vida. Pero hay muchas otras situaciones en nuestra vida en las que no sabemos el pensamiento de Dios, o a dónde nos está llevando. Como Jesús y los Apóstoles, necesitamos confiar en el Amor de Dios. Necesitamos tener fe de que Dios puede sacar el bien de cualquier cosa que pasa en nuestra vida. Por eso, tratamos de escuchar, en las palabras de la Misa de hoy, la voz de Dios diciéndonos:

"No cambia mi amor
Por más lejos que me encuentre
Ni el recuerdo ni el dolor
De mi pueblo y de mi gente."

El Trigésimo Tercero Domingo en Tiempo Ordinario, 18 Noviembre 2012

(Dn 12:1-3; Heb 10:11-14,18; Mc 13:24-32)

Al leer las lecturas de hoy, es importante recordar que los santos escritores no escribían estas palabras porque querían asustar a los que las leían. Al contrario, escribían a un pueblo que ya estaba asustado. Escribían en tiempos de muchas dificultades, tiempos de guerra y persecuciones. Por ejemplo, la primera lectura es del libro de Daniel. Fue escrito para fortalecer y consolar a los judíos durante el tiempo en que fueron gobernados por un rey griego muy malvado. El libro cuenta la vida de Daniel y sus compañeros, hombres sabios y valientes, que vivían muchos años antes del tiempo en que el libro fue escrito. El libro incluye algunas de las visiones que tuvo Daniel que prometen una liberación futura para el pueblo. La Iglesia cree que Jesús es el cumplimiento de estas visiones.

Las intenciones de los escritores de las lecturas de hoy son dos. Primero, querían advertir a la gente que su situación posiblemente iba a empeorar antes de mejorar. Segundo, querían asegurarles que, a pesar de todo, Dios permanecería con ellos y que aún los amaba y protegía.

A veces, nosotros también nos asustamos, por muchas razones diferentes. En este año, tuve problemas de salud. La salud debilitada es un problema frecuente para muchas personas. Otras tienen problemas en sus familias o en la escuela o el trabajo. El dinero también es un problema para mucha gente. En este mundo hay muchas causas de preocupación y miedo y, para nosotros, los dos mensajes de las lecturas de hoy son los mismos que eran para el pueblo de Dios: es posible que nuestros problemas vayan a empeorar antes de mejorar, y Dios aún nos ama y nos protege.

Hoy tenemos la oportunidad de reflexionar sobre nuestras reacciones en situaciones de preocupación y miedo. Cuando están asustados, hay personas que responden como el tigre. El tigre tiene dientes puntiagudos y garras afiladas. Cuando un tigre se siente atrapado, muerde y araña a cualquier persona que se le acerca. Es difícil ayudar a un tigre atrapado.

Otras personas ante el miedo responden como la tortuga. La tortuga tiene un caparazón duro. Cuando una tortuga se sienta amenazada, se retira dentro de su caparazón y no habla con nadie ni participa en la vida. Es difícil ayudar a una tortuga que está escondida en su caparazón.

Hoy Dios nos invita a responder, ante las dificultades de esta vida, no como el tigre ni como la tortuga, sino como la oveja. ¿Qué protección incorporada tiene la oveja? Parece que ninguna. No tiene dientes puntiagudos, ni garras afiladas, ni un caparazón duro. Pero sí tiene defensas importantes. Tiene paciencia y un deseo a estar junto con sus amigos en tiempos de dificultad. Por eso, es fácil para la oveja recibir ayuda. Pero la defensa más importante que tiene la oveja es su confianza en el pastor del rebaño. Como dicen las lecturas de hoy, en esta vida tenemos un pastor muy digno de confianza. Debemos depositar nuestra confianza en Él.

¿Cómo podemos demostrar nuestra confianza en el buen pastor? Como los profetas nos explican, debemos cumplir sus órdenes. El profeta Miqueas vivía en un tiempo de prosperidad para los ricos y dificultad para los pobres. Al el norte de su país llegó un ejército extranjero, muy fuerte y peligroso. La gente no sabía cómo responder a estos problemas. Miqueas dijo que Dios quería protegerles y sólo exigía tres cosas de su pueblo: que practique la justicia, que sea amigo de la bondad, y que camine humildemente con su Dios. Cuando hacemos estas tres cosas en momentos de dificultad, estamos reaccionando como la oveja: con nuestra confianza puesta en nuestro Dios.

Cuando estamos preocupados, es difícil hacer estas tres cosas. Tampoco era fácil para la gente en el tiempo del profeta Miqueas. Si pensamos que no hemos recibido lo justo en nuestra vida, nos es difícil dar lo justo a los demás. Cuando sentimos que nos está costando compartir con nuestros hermanos, debemos recordar los regalos gratuitos que hemos recibido en el pasado, como los buenos consejos de parte de nuestros padres y profesores. Debemos recordar toda la ayuda de nuestros amigos y parientes y ofrecer lo mismo a otras personas.

¿Y cómo podremos ser amigos de la bondad? Buscando cada oportunidad para ayudar a los que hacen el bien y tratando de animar a los demás a hacer lo que es justo. Cuando alguien nos pide un consejo, debemos pensar cuidadosamente antes de responder. Debemos pensar: ¿qué es el consejo que Jesús quiere que demos a esta persona? Así esperaremos lo mejor de nosotros mismos y de todos con quienes nos encontramos.

Finalmente, Miqueas nos dice que necesitamos portarnos humildemente con Dios. Muchas veces, creemos que entendemos bien cada parte de nuestra propia vida y que sabemos exactamente qué es lo que Dios debe hacer por nosotros y por nuestros seres queridos. Pero, cuando pensamos humildemente, reconocemos que no sabemos todo lo que vaya a pasar si recibimos lo que deseamos, y por eso le rogamos, junto con Jesús: "hágase tu voluntad, Pastor Bueno."

Al fin del evangelio de hoy, Jesús nos dice que el cielo y la tierra podrán pasar, pero sus palabras no pasarán. Y aunque nuestro mundo corre peligro, actualmente, de llegar a la ruina por muchas causas distintas, esta promesa permanece. En momentos de peligro, Jesús no estará lejos de nosotros. Sin duda estará muy cerca. Nos dará su consejo y sentiremos su presencia, como Señor y hermano nuestro.

La Solemnidad del Rey del Universo, 25 Noviembre 2012

(Dn 7:13-14; Ap 1:5-8; Jn 18:33-37)

Hoy celebramos una fiesta muy especial. Este es el último domingo del año en la Iglesia, y con mucha alegría reconocemos a Jesús como el rey del universo y el rey de nuestros corazones. ¡Que viva Cristo! ¡Viva el Rey! ¡Viva el Señor Jesús! ¡Un fuerte aplauso para Jesús!

En el evangelio de hoy, encontramos a Jesús hablando con Pilato, un hombre muy diferente de él. En esta conversación, parece que un hombre está preso y el otro está libre, pero, a veces las apariencias engañan. Pilato era el altísimo representante del gobierno romano en una gran parte de la patria de los judíos, incluyendo Jerusalén. En todas partes en su país, la palabra de Pilato era la ley. Pareciera como si él fuera el hombre más libre en todo el país, pero el evangelio de Juan nos muestra que, en verdad, Pilato no estuvo libre para hacer un juicio.

San Juan nos cuenta que los jefes en Jerusalén llevaron a Jesús a Pilato, pero no quisieron entrar en su palacio porque quisieron permanecer puros para la fiesta de la Pascua de los judíos, que era muy próxima, y la ley de Moisés no permitía entrar a los judíos a un edificio de los paganos. Por lo tanto, se quedaron afuera con una multitud de gente de Jerusalén. Pero Pilato necesitaba interrogar a Jesús en el sitio de su trono, dentro el palacio. Y cuanto más le preguntaba a Jesús, más preguntas tenía para los jefes que se encontraban afuera. Entonces, tuvo que hacer muchas idas y vueltas, primero para preguntarle algo a Jesús, y luego para preguntar lo mismo a los jefes. De esta manera, San Juan hace la burla de Pilato y nos muestra que todo el poder de Pilato era inútil. Pilato tuvo miedo de la muchedumbre enojada, y por eso era preso él mismo de la opinión de ellos.

La situación de Jesús era muy diferente. Claro, había sido detenido por los soldados de Roma. Estuvo atado de manos y de pie delante del trono de Pilato. Pero San Juan nos muestra que Pilato sólo tuvo preguntas en su alma, pero Jesús tuvo la verdad. Pilato no entendía nada de lo que pasaba, pero Jesús, por su propia cuenta, había decidido estar allí, y supo muy bien lo que iba a pasar. Jesús era libre, porque tenía mucha fuerza interior y pudo caminar por el camino que su Padre había escogido para él.

San Juan nos invita a reflexionar: ¿qué es la libertad verdadera? Y también: ¿qué cosas en mi vida me hacen más libre, y cuales cosas me atan? La voluntad de Dios es que tengamos libertad verdadera. Esta es nuestra herencia como sus hijos, pero nuestra cooperación es necesaria para acceder a esta herencia.

En primer lugar, es importante recordar que, aunque tenemos muchas responsabilidades en esta vida, ellas no deberían hacernos presos. Los padres son responsables por sus hijos, las esposas son responsables por sus esposas y vice versa, los amigos son responsables por sus amigos. Y, yo sé que la palabra "esposas" se refiere la parte femenina de un matrimonio y, a la vez, algo que se utiliza para atar las manos, pero no es más que una coincidencia del idioma (y también un poco chistoso). Pero el matrimonio no nos debería atar sino liberar en el amor.

Recuerdo bien un tiempo hace muchos años, cuando mi hija menor era bebé. Al principio, mi esposa se quedaba en casa con nuestra hija. Pero después de seis meses, mi esposa tenía que volver a su trabajo, y, por eso, quisimos ponerla en una guardería. Buscábamos una que atendía muy bien a los niños y finalmente encontramos una que nos parecía bien, pero, desde que la empezamos a llevar, ella se enfermaba con frecuencia.

Después de visitar muchas veces el medico, decidimos que la guardaría era demasiado peligrosa para su salud, y tuvimos que encontrar una situación diferente. ¿Pero, que pudimos hacer? Yo trabajaba, y mi esposa también. Durante tres meses yo trabajaba una parte del día, y mi esposa la otra, y la niña se quedaba en casa. En muchos sentidos era un tiempo difícil para nuestra familia y parecía que no tuviéramos tiempo para nada; a veces, incluso, nos sentíamos un poco atrapados.

Pero, al otro lado, era un tiempo bueno para nosotros, porque aunque muchas veces mi jefe no era contento, yo tengo muchos recuerdos bellos de esos días en casa con mi hija pequeña. Al final, encontramos una vecina que podía ayudarnos a cuidar a nuestra niña durante el día, y nuestros horarios de trabajo volvieron a la normalidad.

Muchas familias tienen dificultades como esta, y algunas tienen mucho más grandes. Cuando afrontamos nuestras dificultades con amor, no nos imponen restricciones a nuestra libertad. Al contrario, ellas son el modo por el cual demostramos nuestra libertad. Este es el ejemplo de Jesús delante de Pilato.

Pero hay cosas en este mundo que sí imponen restricciones a nuestra libertad. Cualquier cosa que no nos deja cumplir nuestras obligaciones o realizar nuestras promesas importantes, son cosas que nos encarcelan. Sin omitir las cosas obvias que nos quitan la libertad, como el abuso del alcohol y las drogas, hay también otros problemas más sutiles que debemos considerar. Por ejemplo, podríamos preguntarnos si estamos pasando demasiado tiempo mirando la televisión o surfeando el internet.

A veces, somos un poquito como Pilato, preocupándonos demasiado por la opinión de la muchedumbre. Escuchamos las voces de la gente en nuestro trabajo o nuestra escuela e ignoramos el conocimiento de lo justo que ya tenemos en nuestros corazones.

Otras veces, nos sentimos tan preocupados o estamos tan cansados, que pensamos que no es posible cumplir lo que hemos prometido. En este caso, podemos pedirle al Espíritu Santo que nos llene de su fuerza; podemos orar el salmo de hoy, salmo número noventa y tres, y reconocer a Jesús como único rey de nuestras vidas. También podemos orar el salmo número noventa y uno, un salmo muy bonito que, sin duda Jesús conocía y oraba con frecuencia. El salmo empieza:

> *Tú que habitas al amparo del Altísimo,*
> *Y resides a la sombra del Omnipotente,*
> *Dile al Señor: Mi amparo, mi refugio,*
> *Mi Dios, en quien yo pongo mi confianza.*

Este salmo es un fuente de la paz y esperanza en tiempos de dificultades.

El domingo que viene es el primer domingo de Adviento. El Adviento es un tiempo de preparación. Hoy, si miramos para atrás y examinamos el año que ya termina, y sentimos que no hemos abrazado la libertad de los hijos de Dios, debemos pasar una parte del Adviento buscando la manera de quitar de nuestras vidas todas las cosas que no nos permiten ser verdaderamente libres. Así podremos vivir todas nuestras responsabilidades con amor en el corazón, y también podremos cumplir todas las promesas que hemos hecho a los que nos rodean. De esta manera, demostraremos que somos verdaderos ciudadanos del Reino de nuestro Señor y Rey, Jesús.

¡Que viva Cristo! ¡Viva el Rey! ¡Viva el Señor Jesús! ¡Un fuerte aplauso para Jesús!

La Fiesta de la Conversión de San Pablo, 27 Enero 2013

(Es-Ne 8:2-4,5-6,8-10; 1 Co 12:12-30; Lc 1:1-4,14-21)

Posiblemente algunos de ustedes saben que, desde hace unos años, he tenido problemas de salud. Durante muchas conversaciones con los médicos, he aprendido mucho mas de lo que antes sabia, sobre las diferentes partes del cuerpo; por ejemplo, sobre las funciones diversas del hígado y las actividades de otras partes mas pequeños del cuerpo, como el bazo y otras, que tienen nombres que no se encuentran en mi pequeño diccionario de español. Realmente, en la salud y en la enfermedad, el cuerpo humano es maravilloso, compuesto por muchas partes complicadas. Pero normalmente, cada parte hace su propio trabajo discreto y tranquilamente, sin nuestra conocimiento o ayuda.

Hoy entendemos mucho mas sobre las funciones de las partes del cuerpo de lo que entendía San Pablo, pero nuestro conocimiento solo aumenta nuestro aprecio por el milagro del cuerpo humano.

Con un gran aprecio en su corazón, San Pablo compara la comunidad cristiana con un cuerpo que funciona bien. Y no solo dice que somos como un solo cuerpo; él dice que somos el mismo cuerpo de Cristo. Tan grande es nuestro honor y tan grande es nuestra responsabilidad. Los diferentes ministerios dentro de la Iglesia se complementan y juntos hacen muchas cosas mas grandes de lo que una persona podría hacer sola.

Mucha gente siente por primera vez este tipo de cooperación en sus familias de nacimiento. En el plan de Dios, los padres de la familia son una sola carne. El padre y la madre trabajan juntos por el bien de la familia, y los hijos ayudan mas y mas a medida que van creciendo. Posiblemente, los abuelos y los tíos y primos también ayudan. Cada uno hace lo que puede, y cada uno recibe lo que necesita. Por lo menos, este es la idea, pero sabemos que algunas veces, las cosas no van de acuerdo al plan, por varias causas. Aunque una persona no encuentre cooperación y amor en su familia de nacimiento, aun puede encontrar estos elementos en la familia cristiana.

La Iglesia debe ser como una gran familia. Muchas veces, San Pablo llamaba a la gente a la que escribía "hermanos" y "hermanas". Esto es mas que una manera de hablar. Esto es, o puede ser, una realidad. Aquí en la Iglesia encontramos aceptación y comprensión. Como hemos oído en las lecturas de la semana pasada, en la Iglesia hay muchos ministerios diversos, pero un solo Espíritu. Si, se lo pedimos, el Espíritu nos enseñará como podemos cooperar los unos con los otros.

He visto en Bolivia unos templos grandes que me han demostrado las obras grandes que son posibles cuando el Pueblo de Dios trabaja en comunidad. Estos templos fueron construidos en el campo en el este de Bolivia, muy lejos de las grandes ciudades. Fueron construidos en el siglo diecisiete. Cuando fueron construidos, mucho del país era todavía selva. En este tiempo llegaron los jesuitas, enseñaron a la gente sobre Jesucristo y la fe cristiana y, juntos con la gente que vivían allí, ellos construyeron templos muy grandes y bonitos. El mas grande está en un pueblo que se llama Concepción. Ahora es una catedral grande y hermosa. Para la construcción de este templo se utilizo la madera de dos mil arboles. Y ahora tres mil personas pueden venir al templo y participar de la santa Misa. Posiblemente no es tan alto como las catedrales famosas de Europa, pero seguramente les iguala en belleza.

Podemos estar seguros de que los jesuitas no podían haber construido templos en la selva sin ayuda, porque fueron muy pocos y los modos de construcción que llevaron de seco España no servían en la mojada selva. De la misma manera, antes de la llegada de los jesuitas, la gente no podría haber construido edificios grandes como esos. Pero, juntos, ellos han descubierto nuevos modos de construcción, y han construido templos bonitos y escuelas grandes para la gloria de Dios. De esta manera, ellos actuaban como verdadero Cuerpo de Cristo. Los templos que hoy podemos encontrar allí, construidos hace tres siglos, son un testimonio de lo que es posible hacer cuando todos creemos y sentimos que somos como un cuerpo, con diferentes miembros y todos igualmente importantes para desempeñar una función específica.

Y cuales son nuestras obras? Aquí, Princeton, ya tenemos un templo grande y bonito. Ya tenemos una escuela católica. Pero nuestras obras aun son muchas. En primer lugar, debemos llenar este templo con alabanza. Debemos aprender los himnos y cantarlos con gusto. Dios quiera un templo vivo y no mudo.

Y hay mas. Si deseamos ser el Cuerpo de Cristo en realidad, necesitamos hacer lo que Cristo haría si estuviera aquí en su cuerpo, que somos cada uno de nosotros. Ciertamente, esto incluye las palabras del profeta Isaías: llevar a los pobres la buena nueva, anunciar la liberación a los cautivos y la curación a los ciegos, y dar libertad a los oprimidos. En el evangelio de hoy Cristo nos mandó que llevemos este mensaje a todo el mundo. Cada persona que encuentra a uno de nosotros debe sentir que ha encontrado el amor de Cristo. Debemos acoger al desconocido calurosamente. Tan grande es nuestro honor, y así de grande es nuestra responsabilidad.

Algunos días, siento el honor muy fuerte en mi corazón. Otros días la responsabilidad es como una pesa fuerte de llevar. Pero, por el honor o por la responsabilidad, necesitamos continuar. He visto algunos de las buenas obras de ustedes, y yo se que ya hacen muchos de las cosas de que hablo. Pero nuestra ejemplo de servicio es Cristo, y el amor de Dios constantemente nos invita hacer mas. Me gusta mucho las bonitas palabras de Santa Teresa de Ávila:

> *"Cristo no tiene otro cuerpo que el tuyo*
> *y no tiene manos sino las tuyas.*
> *Sus únicos pies son los tuyos*
> *y tuyos los ojos con que la compasión de Cristo*
> *mira al mundo.*
> *Tuyos son los pies con los que camina para ir*
> *haciendo el bien,*
> *tuyas son las manos con las que ahora tiene que*
> *bendecirnos"*

Sigamos, pues, adelante construyendo la comunidad que Jesús quiere, a través de los carismas que el mismo nos ha regalado, a fin de que como dice Santa Teresa, nuestros ojos, manos y corazón, sean las manos, los ojos y el corazón de Jesús. Amen.

El Segundo Domingo de Cuaresma, 24 Febrero 2013

(Gén 15:5-12.17-18; Fil 3:17-4:1; Lc 9:28-36)

Nuestra tiempo en este templo sagrado es, aunque de menor grado, como la visitación de los Apóstoles a la cima del Monte Tabor con Jesús en el evangelio de hoy. Por ejemplo, no es fácil venir a la misa en la noche. Algunas veces, ¡es más difícil que subir una montaña! Cada uno de nosotros tiene muchas cosas para preparar para la semana que viene. Y recuerdo bien las dificultades que los padres encuentran al preparar y llevar a los niños a la misa. Esta es una obra laudable. Dios les page por sus esfuerzas. Con todas estas dificultades, es aun más difícil venir al templo preparados para oración. Cuando entramos en el templo, necesitamos dejar a un lado cualquier dificultad que hemos encontrado, y pensar únicamente en la idea que hemos venido para orar con Jesús. Él nos ha prometido que donde estén dos o tres de sus discípulos, él estará allí también. Jesús quiere que nosotros seamos sus compañeros en su viaje espiritual.

En la montaña, los Apóstoles oyeron la palabra de Dios, y en la Misa oímos también la palabra de Dios en las lecturas de la Biblia. Debemos escuchar atentamente, con el mismo respeto con que los Apóstoles la escuchaban. Debemos escuchar para poder sacar un mensaje que aplique a nuestra vida. ¿Qué querrá Dios decirme esta noche? Una palabra de consolación, una palabra de corrección, ciertamente una palabra de amor.

En la transfiguración en montaña, los Apóstoles vieron una realidad que normalmente era escondido. Nosotros también participamos en una transfiguración en la misa, cuando el sacerdote, actuando en la persona de Cristo, transforma el pan y el vino en el cuerpo y la sangre del Señor. Este es un milagro para nuestra tiempo.

San Pedro, San Juan and Santiago tuvieron una experiencia maravillosa en la montaña, pero no pudieron quedarse allí. Tuvieron que bajar de la montaña y volver otra vez a sus vidas. Pero, al bajar, ellos no eran que antes de subir. Lo que habían visto y oído transformó sus corazones. Nuestros corazones también son transformados por nuestra participación en la santa misa. Y al fin de la liturgia, cuando nos vamos de aquí, podemos volver a nuestras vidas con un poco más de la paz de Cristo en nuestros corazones. De allí sacaremos la fuerza de tener un poco más paciencia con nuestras familias y nuestra compañeros. Y si compartamos en la compasión de Cristo, también compartiremos en su gloria. Amen.

El Sexto Domingo de la Pascua, 12 Mayo 2013

(He 15: 1–2, 22–29; Ap 21: 10–14, 22–23; Jn 14: 23–29)

Hoy celebramos el Día de las Madres. En esta fiesta muy especial, celebramos el amor muy grande que las madres tienen para sus hijos, que ellas demuestran en las cosas humildes y pequeñas de cada día. Me gusta mucho la historia que mi abuelo contaba sobre el amor de su madre: cuando era joven, mi abuelo salió de su tierra natal de Bohemia y se fue a los Estados Unidos en un barco grande de pasajeros. Su madre tuvo miedo de que su hijo sufriera mareos durante su viaje y, por eso, le preparó una mezcla de hierbas con grasa de ganso y le dijo que debería tomar un poco de esta mezcla con agua caliente si se sentía mareado. Mi abuelo no me dijo si probó lo que le preparó su madre, pero estoy seguro de que, para él, fue un gran consuelo durante el largo viaje el solo hecho de tener ese frasco consigo, preparado con cariño por su madre. Él siempre recordaba ese signo de amor de su madre.

Esto es típico de los regalos de una madre. Son prácticos, por ejemplo comida buena o ropa limpia, y algunos veces, cuando los recibamos, nos no demos cuenta de ellos. Pero en la memoria, las dones de nuestra madre son más preciosos que el oro. Al mismo tiempo, sabemos que nuestras madres son personas humanas con sus propios problemas. Tal vez había momentos en los que no podían ser las madres que necesitábamos o deseábamos en ese momento. Igualmente, tal vez había momentos en los que no fuimos los hijos que ellas necesitaban. Por eso, hoy es un día de pedir perdón a nuestras madres y también, de perdonarles.

Para muchos de nosotros, hay también otras personas que hacen las veces de madre en nuestras vidas. Por ejemplo, una abuela, una vecina, o una amiga que tiene un poco más años y mucha más sabiduría que nosotros. Hoy celebramos todas las que son, para nosotros, como nuestra madre. Damos gracias a Dios por cada mamá que Él nos ha regalado, y les agradecemos a ellas por su amor.

Hoy reconocemos también que la Iglesia Católica quiere ser como una madre para nosotros. Así, nuestro obispo David pide que hoy, en todas las parroquias, reflexionemos sobre los regalos más grandes que recibimos de la Madre Iglesia. Uno de estos regalos es la Biblia. En los años de los Apósteles, muchas personas escribieron lo que habían vivido junto a Jesús, o lo que habían escuchado de Él. La Iglesia examinó todas esas historias cuidosamente y conservó las que en vedad fueron inspirado por el Espirito Santo, y las juntó con las sagradas escrituras de los Judíos en la Santa Biblia para todos los cristianos de todos los siglos.

Recuerdo bien el día en que fui ordenado diácono por el obispo John Smith; él me dio el libro de los Evangelios y me dijo: "Recibe el libro de los Evangelios, de los cuales serás un heraldo. Cree lo que lees, proclama lo que crees, y vive lo que proclamas." Fue una muy buena advertencia para todos de nosotros. Hemos recibido la Biblia de la Iglesia y debemos creer lo que leemos, proclamar lo que creemos, y vivir lo que proclamamos. Porque cada uno de nosotros es un mensajero de la Buena Nueva.

Hay dos cosas importantes que debemos recordar cuando pensamos en la Biblia. La primera cosa es que la Biblia es un regalo con un único objetivo: nuestra salvación. San Juan nos explica la intención de su Evangelio así: "Muchas otras señales milagrosas hizo Jesús en presencia de sus discípulos que no están escritas en este libro. Estas han sido escritas para que crean que Jesús es el Cristo, el Hijo de Dios. Crean, y tendrán vida por su nombre."

Este objetivo importante explica lo que encontramos en la Biblia y lo que no encontramos. Por ejemplo, en la Biblia no encontramos ninguna descripción física de Jesús. ¿Era alto o bajo? ¿Tuvo una barba o no? ¿Tuvo el pelo rubio o negro? ¿Cuál era el color de sus ojos? Si uno de nosotros quisiera escribir la biografía de alguien, sería natural comenzar con una descripción de su aspecto físico. Pero, los Apósteles no incluyeron esta información sobre Jesús en ninguna parte de sus libros. ¿Por qué no? Porque el aspecto físico de Jesús no es importante para nuestra salvación. Los evangelios no son biografías de Jesús. Son la parte más importante de la larga historia del amor de Dios, que nos salve.

La segunda cosa que es importante recordar, cuando reflexionamos sobre la Biblia, es que la Iglesia también nos da otros regalos preciosos y prácticos. Estos otros regalos son llamados "la tradición de la Iglesia" e incluyen la Santa Misa, las diferentes oraciones y las obras de los santos. La tradición complementa la Biblia y nos ayuda a entender el mensaje de salvación. Junto con la Biblia, la tradición nos guía en el camino cristiano. La Biblia no es suficiente por sí sola. Es un libro muy complicado, escrito en varios tiempos muy diferentes que el nuestro y necesitamos la tradición para explicar e interpretar sus verdades.

La oración del "Ave María" es típica de la tradición de la Iglesia. La primera parte de esta oración familiar nos viene directamente de la Biblia: "Dios te salve María" es la frase que el ángel dice a María en el Evangelio de San Lucas cuando le anuncia que será madre de Jesús; "Bendita tu eres, y bendito es el fruto de tu vientre" es casi palabra por palabra lo que Isabel, la prima de María, le dice cuando se encuentran en el momento de la Visitación. La segunda parte de esta oración "Santa María, madre de Dios…" es la respuesta de la Iglesia a la primera parte y es el fruto de muchos años de meditación por parte de muchas personas santas y sabias. Nos alegra y nos consuela unirnos de esta manera, por medio de esta oración, a los que han caminado delante de nosotros en el sendero de la fe. Esta oración tan sencilla y tan bonita nos muestra el poder de la Biblia en conjunto con la tradición de la Iglesia.

De la misma manera, la Misa es una rica mezcla de versículos de la Biblia y reflexiones de la Iglesia. Es una mezcla muy poderosa, preparada con el mismo amor con el que la madre de mi abuelo preparó su mezcla de hierbas.

Hoy tenemos muchas cosas por los cuales podemos dar gracias. Mientras continuamos con la Misa, pensemos en todos los dones que hemos recibido, de nuestra madre natural y también de las otras mamás que Dios nos ha regalado, y prometamos usar estos regalos preciosos en una manera digno de la memoria de las que nos han dado tanto. Amen.

Appendix I:
GO ASK *the* DEACON

Most of the questions you find here were asked at a confirmation retread held at Saint Paul church, when the participants were divided into small groups and were encouraged to "ask the deacon" about anything in their faith that they had questions about. The remaining questions were offered in the back of church after a mass or came to me by email. The answers you find here are mostly what I wished I had said, if only I had thought of it at the time.

What can I say when we're in history class and they talk about evil popes, or the inquisition?

Our Church has been around for 2,000 years, and has spread all over the world. That means a lot of people have been out there acting in the name of the Church for a long time. Many of them have been very good people doing very good work, but not all. Some have done stupid things with the best of intentions. Others have done evil, and some spectacularly so, at least according to our standards today. And there are special dangers for those in positions of power within the Church, because power in the wrong hands can be a corrupting influence. It is one of the mysteries of life that God does not generally stop us from doing evil, even if we do it in the name of his Church.

The Church is and always has been composed of imperfect people. Many overcome their imperfections and act honorably and are ignored by the press; a few act badly and these make front-page headlines. It is a true sign of the presence of the Holy Spirit that despite the bad things that some people have done, the Church has survived for so long and still accomplishes so much good in the world.

Because of these considerations, we should not feel that it is necessary to defend every action of everyone in church leadership, but what we should always feel proud of and ready to defend is the principles that our Church teaches, such as respect for life, reverence for God, compassion for the suffering, and concern for the poor. Our Church tries to live by many virtues: honesty, humility and prudence, among others. Those are all wonderful things that we stand for as a Church. They are very high standards. It is not surprising that some people through the ages have failed to live up to them. 500 years from now, people may look back at us and wonder how the people of Princeton could sleep at night when there are so many people who go to bed hungry or are without hope. But here we are, mostly trying to do the best we can in the situation in which we find ourselves. We shouldn't be judged by the standards of the future, and we should not try to judge those who lived 500 years ago by today's standards. We can leave it to God to be the just judge for us and for those who came before us.

What does it mean when it says in the Apostles' Creed that Jesus descended into hell?

In ancient times, it was believed that there were just three places that one could be: (1) up in heaven with God, where everything must be perfect, because God is perfect. (2) on earth among the living, or (3) in the abode of the dead, called Sheol in Hebrew, Hades in Greek, Inferno in Latin and Hell in Old English. Generally Sheol was thought to be underground someplace, as heaven was thought to be "above the sky" someplace. When the lines "he descended into hell" were added to the creed, it seems to have been to emphasize that Jesus did not hide in the tomb for 3 days, nor did he go to heaven for 3 days, he did what all the dead naturally do, which is to go to Sheol, a place where nothing much happens, and everything is grey and dull, dull, dull. The point being that Jesus really truly died—it was not pretend or play-acting in any way.

However, there does seem to be a little more to the story than that. In the first letter of Peter it says that after Jesus died and before the resurrection, "he preached to those in prison". What exactly is meant by that has been discussed by scholars and mystics for millennia. Here is one common explanation that comes out of that discussion. Before Jesus came into the world, there were good people and there were bad people. But the good people couldn't be really, really good, because it was just too hard to do that with all the evil around, which was "left-over" from the sin of Adam and Eve. So, when those people died they could not go straight to heaven, because they were not perfect, even though that's where God wanted them to be. They were all in Sheol waiting for Jesus to set things right and make it possible for good people to get to heaven. After Jesus died, the first place he went was to those good people and "opened the gates of heaven" for them.

This idea of hell as the abode of the dead is slightly different from hell as a place of judgment. That is more of an end-of-the-world notion. In the final judgment, those who have rejected being with God will get their wish and be locked out of God's presence and the happiness of heaven. The Hebrew word Jesus sometimes uses for their place of exclusion is "Gehenna" which was the name of the valley south of the city of Jerusalem that was used as a garbage dump—a pretty stinky place. That is where such people will end up.

The ideas of Sheol and Gehenna got further elaborated over time, but the Church has never completely embraced any exact formulation of where different classes of people are put after death but before the final judgment happens. We say that people who die who love God, but are not quite perfect enough for heaven, spend time in "purgatory" but we think of that as a state of being rather than a physical place. We don't know how long it takes, or even if "time" is the right concept to describe it. These days, the tendency is be quite humble about our lack of understanding of such matters and to leave all that in God's hands, knowing that somehow the demands of justice and mercy will both be met on the last day, if not before.

That being said, there are two things the Church is very definite about in her teaching concerning those who have died. These are: (1) it is appropriate and very beneficial for us to pray for those who have died and (2) those who have gone before us can be of assistance to us when we pray to them to intercede for us with God.

Wasn't Jesus a poor person; why do we have all those gold and silver dishes and cathedrals and stuff?

One of the beautiful things about our Church is that it is accepting of many different ways to live a holy life. There are many holy people in our Church who follow the way of radical simplicity and poverty, and they are witnesses to a value we hold dear. But that is not the only way there is of being "Catholic". In many of our churches we try to assemble many beautiful things, like gold dishes and stained-glass windows, and those things can give us a different, but equally valid, experience of holiness and Godliness. The Church invites us to use whichever mode of expressing holiness makes us feel most close to Jesus.

Another thought to keep in mind is that we reverence Jesus as our king. We celebrate this with a special feast day at the end of the church year. One way of expressing our belief that Jesus truly is our king, is by using only the best and most beautiful things we have when we invite him to be with us in our house of worship. That is what we would do with any honored guest.

Why do we have statues of Jesus and Mary in the church? Aren't those idols?

In many churches in Latin America in the back of the church there is a glass case holding what appears to be a dead body. It is an image of Jesus (often life-sized) as he was just after being taken down from the cross. These statues tend to be pretty bloody and gruesome to look at, except that Jesus always has a very peaceful face.

It is a powerful emotional experience to look at such images. We know in our heads that Jesus died on the cross, and that that was a very painful experience, but we are more than just our heads. We also have bodies, and those images give us a gut-wrenching and heart-felt understanding of just how big a sacrifice that was for Jesus.

Here in the US, we tend to have much statuary that is easier on the eyes, but they serve somewhat the same purpose. They involve us at more than a thinking level; they appeal to our senses and to our emotions. One of the great strengths of the Catholic Church is the way that it uses physical things to be signs of deeper spiritual realities. The statues in our churches are not idols, because we do not worship them. We use them as a springboard, so to speak, to help us to better worship the invisible God. We use the word "veneration" to describe the way we treat such objects, to make it clear that we treat them as special, but we do not worship them.

It may be that there are some people who are so holy that they do not need such physical reminders to be able to love God "with all your heart and with all your soul and with all your mind", as Jesus tells us to do, but for the rest of us, we should take any help we can get to bring us more completely into a loving and worshipful experience. So bring on the statues and the incense and the bells and the sacred music and the standing and the kneeling and all the other worship aids.

Is it a sin if you're very angry at someone (like a teacher) and you talk behind their back about how bad they are?

The answer to this question depends on the circumstances. When we think about what makes a sin, we want to keep in mind the great commandments to love God with our whole heart, and to love our neighbor as ourselves. When it comes to what we say about other people this might make us ask two questions: (1) is the thing we are saying true? And (2) is it kind? Perhaps a good practical guide is to not say anything about other people that we would not be willing to say in front of them. Following that simple rule will tend to make our life a lot more simple.

On the other hand, it is also very useful to have a trusted person with whom we can "vent" our anger about things that happen to us, and to whom we can say in complete privacy anything that is on our mind. This should be a person who is not involved in the situation in any way, and who has the spiritual maturity to help us sort through our feelings and help us distinguish the reality that is behind our perceptions. Examples of people that we might trust in this way are parents, aunts and uncles, god-parents, grandparents, and older brothers or sisters. We should keep searching until we find a person like that, whom we can trust with our deepest thoughts and emotions. To be trusted in this way is a great honor and a grave responsibility.

Why do so many teenagers go away from the church?

Generally speaking, people want to go where they feel welcomed and nourished and find answers to their questions. For teens, such questions might include "What should I do with my life?" "How can I be happier than I am now?" "What's wrong with me; why don't more people like me?" "How can I make a difference in the world?" "How can I get my parents off my case?" "When will I find a soul mate, someone who knows me and loves me?"

These are questions that all of us ask ourselves at times, but they are particularly on the minds of many teenagers. Until we can help teenagers understand that our faith does have useful things to say about such important questions, we will have trouble getting them to make the effort to come to church.

What will we do all day in heaven? Won't it get boring after a while?

When I was a child, I often went fishing and crabbing with my parents. They have been dead for some years now, but still I occasionally have dreams in which I am there with them again and we are out fishing. And when I wake up, I feel that if I could just go fishing with them again, that would be heavenly. So, will there be fishing in heaven? I don't know the answer to that, but I firmly believe that if there is not any fishing in heaven, it will only be because there is something there that is much better. So much better that when I get there I will say to myself, "who would want fishing, when I can have this?" Of course I will be much more perfect before I ever get to heaven, so right now I have trouble imagining what that other thing might be. As Saint Paul tells us "Eye has not seen and ear has not heard, nor has it so much as entered the mind what God has ready for those who love him."

"Doing things" is something we worry a lot about here on earth, but I think that in heaven it will not be so much about "doing" as it is about "being". I have been married for 35 years now, and sometimes in the evening my wife and I are just sitting on the sofa, not doing much of anything, maybe I'm just looking at my wife as she reads or does a crossword puzzle, but still I am very much content and at peace with the world. I think that heaven might be a little bit like that: being surrounded by our loved ones, especially God, and feeling very happy and content and at rest.

Why do we need to come to church? Can't we just be good spiritual people on our own?

There are people who do go it alone in their spiritual life, like the monks who go off and live alone in the desert. But that is not an easy way to live. And It is even harder to live a holy life on our own and stay in the rough and tumble of our normal daily life. That is why the monks go off in the desert —to get away from all the confusions and temptations of the world. Being part of a community of people who are all trying to live out the same ideals as we are, is generally much easier way to maintain a healthy faith life. Our situation is somewhat like logs in a fire. If you have ever tried to make a fire in a fireplace with only one log, you know how hard it is to keep the flame going.

But if you put in lots of sticks and logs of different sizes, all pointing in different directions, then each burning stick heats up the others, and keeps the flame going. When I come to church on Sunday feeling a little bit shaky in my faith, and I stand with everyone and recite the creed, the voices of those who are feeling strong in their faith today give me comfort and support in my weakness.

Being a part of a faith community also has another advantage, and that is that it can give us a needed "reality check". When we listen to the words of Scripture, and explore those readings together in the homily, we might find ourselves being challenged out of our cozy assumption, that really, we are doing plenty to be good followers of Jesus. Being shaken out of that dreamy state and being woken up to hear the voice of the poor and neglected and to go out and do something for someone, is a precious advantage of being a part of a faith community. It is very hard to get that if we are trying to just be a good spiritual person on our own.

Finally, hearing the stories of people we know in the community about how they have gotten through difficult crises in their lives can help us to have courage when we face difficult times. And we will find that we have a ready supply of friends to help us when we are in trouble.

Why doesn't God make any new revelations?

In one sense, God reveals himself to us all the time through our prayer and life experiences, but these revelations are meant just for the one receiving them. In addition to private revelations, God has graciously revealed himself to the community at large. This revelation came to a pinnacle in the life of Jesus, and that kind of direct revelation came to an end with the death of the apostles who knew Jesus personally, because God's self-revelation was complete at that time. Once you know Jesus, you know all there is to know about God. All the rest of the teachings of the wise and holy people who have come later are commentaries on this revelation and those teachings need to be judged for their consistency with that earlier body of revealed teaching.

And yet, there definitely seem to be some holes in God's revelation. There are questions we are curious about, but we can't really answer, like "How far away is heaven?" or "What are angels really like?" Most of these unanswered (and maybe unanswerable) questions seem to be about the details of the spiritual realm. In thinking about such questions we might be in a situation a little bit like caterpillars thinking about what it will be like when they become butterflies. (Saint Teresa of Avila has a similar meditation about silk worms and moths, but thinking about caterpillars and butterflies seems a little nicer somehow.)

If we try to imagine what it might be like to be intelligent caterpillars who know that we will someday turn into butterflies, we might imagine all the questions we would have. For example, a caterpillar would probably see how useful his many feet are for climbing up grass stems, and would worry how one could possibly get along with only six legs and four wings.

As intriguing as such questions are, they are probably a distraction, both for the caterpillar and for us. The caterpillar needs to be thinking about how to be a good caterpillar, and not how to be a good butterfly. It is by being the best caterpillar he can be that he will end up making a good start at being a butterfly. The situation is somewhat the same for us. Revelation teaches us all that we need to know about being good human beings and good followers of Jesus, everything we need for salvation. By concentrating on those things, we will be preparing ourselves as well as possible to be a living part of the realm of the spirit.

What happens when we die?

The short answer here is that nobody knows. As Saint John says "What love God shows us in letting us be called children of God! Yet, that is what we are. What we will someday be has not been revealed, but we know that we will be like him, for we shall see him as he is." So we can know no more about this question than we can know what it like to be God.

Piecing together hints from Scripture, here are the highlights of the Church's traditional answer to this question. When we die, we face our own particular judgment. Those of us who at that point are not quite perfect enough to endure the perfection of God, are, by the grace of God, given a last chance at purification (purgatory). What that is like we *really* have no idea, despite the many "revelations" to saints and mystics that paint horrifying pictures. The Church has always taught that those dreams and revelations are personal ones, not meant for the Church at large. Purgatory may be as simple as the sickening instantaneous realization of all we have done wrong in life, and a heart-felt rejection of that. We just don't know. Those who accept the gift of purgatory, and those who have no need of it (like the martyrs) are admitted to the beatific vision: the unfiltered presence of God. That is what we mean by heaven.

When the end of the world comes, there will be a general judgment, and at that time those who have chosen not to be with God will get their wish and be sent to live in the only place apart from God: hell. Here the ideas get complicated, because we do believe in a physical resurrection. We will have bodies of some kind, but that will be like is hard to imagine.

The Church also teaches that between now and then, we have some connection with those who have died. As the wake service liturgy says "we believe that the ties of love and kinship that knit us together in life do not come unraveled at death." In some mystical way, we can help them and they can help us. It seems unlikely to me that the dead perceive time in the same way we do, so what that is like for them is completely beyond me.

Regarding the two great commandments: 1. Love God and 2. Love your neighbor as yourself. Does fulfilling directly #1 indirectly fulfill #2? Does fulfilling directly #2 fulfill #1 indirectly?

First I think we need to be clear about what we mean by "love" here. It is not the emotion of love, which we cannot control, but an active commitment and concern for the beloved, which naturally is expressed in concrete actions which are meant to benefit or please the beloved. Such actions are not only done when it is convenient, but whenever the opportunity presents itself, often acted out at great personal expense to the one who has made the commitment to love.

I have known people who are agnostic or atheist who, in the sense above, love their fellow humans at least as well as I do. So, if I want to grant myself any measure of following #2, I feel I must grant the same to them.

In addition, I have known people who seem to be fulfilling #1, in the sense of attending liturgies with reverence and praying frequently, who do not seem to me to be fulfilling #2 at all. They seem to love God at least as well as I do, but have an ill-disguised contempt for the people around them. Some of these were members of the clergy who have such a low opinion of their fellow man that they hardly notice how little they care for them. They may have had a slightly warped view of who God is, but then all of us have an imperfect understanding of who God is, so I can't say they don't love God.

I find the first of these two sorts of people sad but noble in a way, as if a person has made a commitment to do something nearly impossible. I find the second sort of person sad but revolting. One must fool oneself badly about what it means to love God if one can not also love man who is made in his image, and not just Man in the abstract, but the individual imperfect people we interact with on a daily basis.

So I would say #2 is possible but very difficult without #1, but #1 is necessarily woefully deficient without #2.

Appendix II:
WOBBLING OFF *to* INFINITY:
a Personal Reflection on Life with Cancer

12/1/11

Every cancer story is different Mine began eleven years ago when a sharp-eyed radiologist noticed a lump on my left adrenal gland peeking in at the edge of a chest x-ray taken for a different problem. Ignorant of physiology, I had no clue what that meant. I remember vividly sitting in my primary-care doctor's office with him on the phone to the radiologist, and his summary to me when he hung up: "She thinks you have cancer." Fittingly, my education began with picture books in the doctor's office. Where is the adrenal gland? (awkwardly placed for direct examination) What does it do? (keep you alive, but don't worry, you have two of them)

More than a year of observation and testing lulled us all into complacency about that little lump, and for the past four years we have been paying the price of that time lost. When the tumor finally came out, it weighed almost four pounds. Two major surgeries, and a few minor ones have now brought the cancer to a point that it seems a manageable problem. The offending adrenal gland is long gone, along with my spleen and gallbladder, and about three quarters of my liver (since grown back). I am getting low on optional and back-up equipment down there, but the remaining spots in the lung and liver seem for the moment to be under control. Good news for now, but the matter remains unsettled.

So far, mine is a relatively gentle, slow-growing cancer, unlike the more ferocious ones so many good friends have been faced with. This has given me the gift of time to consider how this event, which has loomed large in my life for a number of years now fits in with my faith in a loving God. Hard questions come to mind: Why me? Why did mine go like this when theirs went like that? Where is God in all this? I don't pretend to have complete answers for any of these questions, but here are some premises that have been guiding my thoughts about my life with cancer. I call them "premises" because I can't deduce their truth from any simpler statements, and accepting them helps me make sense of my situation. These premises are mostly cobbled together out of the Catholic tradition, but that tradition is rich and varied and I have not found all parts of it equally helpful.

- God is almighty, but God has chosen not to micro-manage the currents of creation. I don't know if this is the reason, but it seems clear that if God did micro-manage everything, that would make human free will irrelevant. God apparently values our free will very highly, and wants us to get much practice at using it well.

- The world is developing according to God's will at a macro level, but on the micro level things are more chaotic and sometimes move in contrary directions. The discovery of simple behavioral rules that overcome randomness and a lack of coordination to create wonderful structures in nature (like how termites build nests) indicates to me that it is logically possible for the "macro" world to move forward even while the "micro" seems to dither around. God's simple rule is "love one another" and the structure going up in fits and starts is the kingdom of God.

- While "good" and "bad" are serviceable words with objective meanings, events in the human sphere are anything but simple, and we are often reduced to using qualifiers like good-when and bad-how. To do so is not "relativism." In the face of the complexity of human events, humility requires us to be slow to label events one way or another.

- Despite my belief that God does not try to micromanage the world, I also do not believe that we live in a world in which bad things do not matter. They do matter, and when bad things happen, love rushes in to ease the pain and fill the void. God is the source and guide of this response.

- My getting cancer was a bad event that has had some good consequences. C. S. Lewis likens God to a dentist who sometimes causes us momentary pain, but only when that is necessary to fix an underlying problem. This may be so, and it is true that we who cannot see inside our own mouths so well may not perceive the severity of the problems that the good dentist is attacking with such vigor, but I cannot believe that this analogy explains all the pain there is in the world. An analogy that seems better is that God is like a parent trying to teach a child to ride a bike, who knows that when he lets go of the bike, disaster might ensue, but until he does let go, the child will not learn to control the bike. Nor would it serve the goal to have the path ahead be perfectly smooth, because learning to deal with bumps in the road is part of learning to ride.

- My cancer may have been caused by something I did, or by some ill-tuned 1950's x-ray machine, or maybe it was a truly random event. I can learn to forgive whoever or whatever is responsible—even myself.

- My cancer is not God's judgment on me or anyone else, nor is it the work of some evil power trying to shake my faith or destroy me. This is not a test. Here I am thinking mostly about the book of Job, which I understand as a story stretched to cartoon-like extremes in order to make a point. I get the point, but do not find the book to be a good model for my own experience.

- My tumor is a part of me, not something foreign. It is probably the worst of the numerous imperfections of my natural bodily form. It is more like an annoying unwelcome guest than an enemy.

My encounter with cancer has so far been very light. I noted above the gift of time to reflect that has come to me. Other gifts that I have noticed in my life are listed below. These are things I may have known partially before this all began, but the experience of them in illness has been something else entirely. I don't doubt that there are other gifts that I fail to notice, or react to in a timely fashion.

• The gift of loving care. First and foremost from my wife, my constant companion in all this, but I have also learned to lean upon my suddenly-grown-up children and my sisters, my clerical brothers, as well as my parish family, friends from work, and far-flung family and friends. My wife and I have benefited from all kinds of help: practical, emotional and spiritual. I find that whenever I have been able to overcome my manly distain for asking help from others, it has been a good experience.

• The gift of heroes to admire and emulate. Being too cheap to pay for a single room in the hospital, I have met numerous people in various stages in their cancer. One man in particular that I roomed with, whose cancer was far advanced, impressed me as incredibly gentle and good-spirited in his difficult situation. May I someday react so well! I am further humbled to recall that this truly virtuous man was not a believer in God.

• The gift of clarity so well described by Samuel Johnson: "Depend upon it, Sir, when a man knows he is to be hanged in a fortnight, it concentrates his mind wonderfully" How precious today the colors of autumn, the warmth of flannel, the pungency of onion cooking, the tartness of grapes, the soft breathing on the pillow next to mine.

• The gift of living with limitations. I am repeatedly reminded that I am not Superman, nor even the Lone Ranger. As the Shaker hymn has it "'tis a gift to come down where we ought to be." I have come to understand that life is at once incredibly fragile and incredibly resilient. It is easily damaged, but difficult to destroy.

• The gift of a large scar on my belly like a crooked peace-sign, or maybe a cross drawn by a 2-year old, which reminds me every day "You are dust and to dust you shall return." "Don't delay in doing good," the angel whispers.

In his book *A Grief Observed*, C. S. Lewis had this to report about his and his wife's experience of cancer:

> *Yet H. herself, dying of it, and well knowing the fact, said that she had lost a lot of her old horror at it. When the reality came, the name and the idea were in some degree disarmed. And up to a point I very nearly understood. This is important. One never meets just Cancer, or War, or Unhappiness (or Happiness). One only meets each hour or moment that comes. All manner of ups and downs. Many bad spots in our best times, many good ones in our worst. One never gets the total impact of what we call "the thing itself". But we call it wrongly. The thing itself is simply all the ups and downs: the rest is a name or an idea.*

This quote speaks to my experience, though those two pioneers have gone much further along this road than I ever have. Seen from a distance, Cancer with a capital C might seem incompatible with Faith with a capital F, but up close, the lived experience of cancer has not been incompatible with the lived experience of faith.

I find I cannot write a proper ending for this essay, for the event is ongoing. For the moment, I am wobbling along on the bicycle of faith and hope. So far I have kept my seat on the bumpy ride, but if it should happen that I someday fall off of the bike, I am sure that love will be there to pick up the pieces.

POSTSCRIPT

4/27/14

Although I still recognize myself in the words above, I see my life a bit differently now. I have been in an in-home hospice program for a month now, and due to some painful hernias, my physical world has shrunk to a few rooms on the first floor of the house. It is as if my bike is now in the bike rack, and I am in God's waiting room, waiting for the train that will finally take me home. Sometimes I am disappointed by the announcement of "not today" and at other times I am relieved, but mostly I am at rest in a state of contented waiting.

It has not been a lonely wait. Many friends and relatives have dropped in (by arrangement) to reminisce and allow each of us to expresses thanksgiving for the other's presence in our life. This has been a great joy.

There are other joys too. For example, a few days ago a friend visited and brought some flag lilies to brighten the room. The next morning, as the sun was rising, I watched the sunlight play across the intense purples and yellows of those flowers, and I was completely enthralled by how the colors changed as the angle of the light changed. That quiet experience of beauty made up for all the pain of the night before, and some time before that too.

So, still no ending for the story, only an ongoing revelation of God's love.

Made in the USA
San Bernardino, CA
07 June 2014